HOW TO PRODUCE A WEST END SHOW

Julius Green

HOW TO PRODUCE
A WEST END SHOW

OBERON BOOKS
LONDON

WWW.OBERONBOOKS.COM

First published in 2012 by Oberon Books Ltd

521 Caledonian Road, London N7 9RH

Tel: +44 (0) 20 7607 3637 / Fax: +44 (0) 20 7607 3629

e-mail: info@oberonbooks.com

www.oberonbooks.com

Reprinted with revisions in 2014

A catalogue record for this book is available from the British Library.

PB ISBN: 978-1-84943-025-8

E ISBN: 978-1-84943-523-9

Printed, bound and converted by CPI Group (UK) Ltd, Croydon, CR0 4YY.

To Dianne

Acknowledgements

I would like to thank the following for their patience, advice and support during the writing of this book:

James Hogan, Andrew Walby, Melina Theocharidou, James Illman and all the team at Oberon Books; Andrew McKinnon and the staff and students of Birkbeck College; Pat Penson and Lucinda Harvey at the Society of London Theatre; Steve Potts, Alan Sharp, Robert Brown, Hannah Wills, Sarah Loader, Rebecca Cutting and all my colleagues at BKL; Sean Egan, Roy Marsden, Philippe Carden and Deborah de Moll.

Special thanks to my friend Mark Shenton for suggesting that this book should be written and for encouraging me to get on with it.

And I will always be grateful to Bill Kenwright, Ian Lenagan and Dick McCaw for making my journey in theatre possible and for teaching me to keep a sense of perspective about it all.

Contents

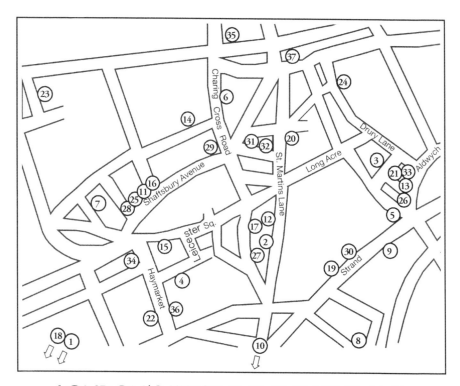

LONDON'S WEST END THEATRELAND

AMBASSADOR THEATRE GROUP
1. APOLLO VICTORIA
2. DUKE OF YORK'S
3. FORTUNE
4. HAROLD PINTER
5. LYCEUM
6. PHOENIX
7. PICCADILLY
8. PLAYHOUSE
9. SAVOY
10. TRAFALGAR STUDIOS

DELFONT MACKINTOSH THEATRES
11. GIELGUD
12. NOËL COWARD
13. NOVELLO
14. PRINCE EDWARD
15. PRINCE OF WALES
16. QUEEN'S
17. WYNDHAM'S
18. VICTORIA PALACE

REALLY USEFUL GROUP THEATRES
19. ADELPHI
20. CAMBRIDGE
21. THEATRE ROYAL DRURY LANE
22. HER MAJESTY'S
23. LONDON PALLADIUM
24. NEW LONDON

NIMAX THEATRES
25. APOLLO
26. DUCHESS
27. GARRICK
28. LYRIC
29. PALACE
30. VAUDEVILLE

INDEPENDENTLY OWNED AND OTHER THEATRES
31. AMBASSADORS
32. ST MARTIN'S
33. ALDWYCH
34. CRITERION
35. DOMINION
36. THEATRE ROYAL HAYMARKET
37. SHAFTESBURY

Theatre ownership details are subject to change.

Map shows main streets of Theatreland.

TRUST ME, I'M A PRODUCER

London is the undisputed theatrical capital of the world, boasting an extraordinary variety of performance spaces from the subsidised monoliths of the National Theatre and the Barbican via the unabashed grandeur of the Palladium and Theatre Royal Drury Lane to a multitude of claustrophobic pub back rooms. If you are a theatre producer then there is no better place to ply your trade, and although the streets may not be paved with gold and Shaftesbury Avenue is a boulevard of broken dreams, it offers an unparalleled theatrical melting pot with a heritage stretching back to Shakespeare and Burbage and beyond. Within London's plethora of theatrical endeavour, the gaudy glamour of 'The West End' retains a special cachet despite the increasing challenges of maintaining the crumbling theatre building 'stock' and creating the work which it houses.

Theatre producers present their work in a huge variety of buildings and locations, and much of the knowledge that you need and many of the skills are the same wherever you are staging your production. But this book is specifically about producing shows in London's West End Theatreland, and the considerable challenges and unexpected delights which are unique to this particularly unpredictable environment.

When someone 'pitches' a show to me which I believe has West End potential but which for one reason or another I can't help them with, I will suggest to them that they hire a West End theatre and produce it themselves. This suggestion, which is a perfectly genuine one, is sometimes met with a look of blank incomprehension or even fear, and more often with a nervous 'you must be joking' laugh. But I'm serious. If you have an idea for a West End show then why not do it yourself? If you would like to take up the challenge then I hope that this book will prepare you for the experience of being a producer and give you some indication of the extraordinary journey that you are about to undertake.

This is an adventure yarn not an academic textbook. It does not include lots of useful appendices, an index, a glossary of terms, contractual and financial templates or a reading list. It may not even be entirely factually accurate, although if I have made any errors then I have been getting away with them for twenty-five years so the chances are that you will as well. Neither is this a book of scandalous anecdotes; it doesn't 'lift the lid', name names or tell you where the bodies are buried (I could tell you, but then I would have to kill you). It is, however, full of my personal opinions regarding the custom and practice of the West End theatre industry, a subject which I am very passionate about. I must stress that these opinions are entirely my own, and that there are of course many other points of view about all the matters that I discuss.

It is very odd that so few people, even those who work in theatre, seem to have a proper understanding of the role of the producer. I recently saw a magician on television lamenting the fact that so many of his colleagues were now giving away their tricks that it was becoming increasingly difficult to fool the audience. But no one can ever accuse producers of deliberately keeping their 'tricks' to themselves. If there's one thing we enjoy doing it's talking about what we do; and one of the great things about what we do is that the learning process is continuous. Every day brings a new set of unexpected circumstances and a new discovery. When I was starting out I was extremely grateful for all the advice, encouragement and support I received from the 'old guard'. These days opinion is divided as to whether it is more beneficial to undertake some sort of training in the subject or just to get on with it, grab what advice you can along the way and learn by your mistakes. If you want to follow the training route then the Society of London Theatre (SOLT) is a useful starting point. SOLT is the professional organisation that represents London theatre producers and owners and negotiates their collective agreements with the entertainment unions. It also operates a number of marketing initiatives on behalf of the industry and supports Stage One, a charity which encourages and assists the work of new producers via short courses, work placements and professional mentoring. It's a sign of old age when you get invited to one of their 'networking' events as a dispenser rather than a seeker of advice.

Even the academic community is starting to cotton on, with MA degrees in theatre producing now being offered by at least one university and two drama schools; although the continued use of the phrase 'creative producer' in academic circles is discouragingly indicative that there is still some confusion about the role. To my way of thinking, being a producer is by definition about as 'creative' as it gets; you are quite literally 'creating' every aspect of a production from scratch. The phrase 'creative producer' is a tautology and seems to imply that there is such a thing as a *non*-creative producer. If these do indeed exist then I have never met one. And for those who still seek clarification on the difference between a producer and a director, I can only point out that the clue is in the titles. To produce is to '*create* by physical or mental effort'. To direct is to 'indicate the way'. Dictionary definitions, not mine; but in any event it sounds like these two characters should be able to get the job done between them.

There is a misconception that theatre producing is a male-dominated profession and that it's a game for city types who smoke big cigars and drive flashy cars. Nothing could be further from the truth. Many of the most successful and powerful West End theatre producers are women, and the most adept producing students are more likely to have experience in stage management than stocks and shares. Stage managers tend to be calm and well-organised and to have a basic knowledge of how a show is actually put together. If you fit this profile then training as a producer could be quite a savvy move. There certainly seems to be a gap in the market. I know plenty of theatre people who are unemployed but I don't know a single producer who isn't overworked.

Whether you take a course, become an apprentice in an established producer's office or just rely on expert advice, one of the most important things that you'll learn is that it's all done to a certain extent with smoke and mirrors. This is showbiz after all, so nothing is quite what it seems and everyone involved is playing some sort of a role both on and off stage. There are very few hard facts to grasp hold of and many unfathomable shades of grey to sink into. Indeed, I once heard the producer's art described as 'management by astonishment'. So, with this all this in mind, I'm going to attempt to explain to you how to produce a West End show from a standing start. All you need is a good idea for a project, a mobile phone with internet access and a copy of the indispensable industry directory *Contacts*. Oh, and this book.

Trust me, I'm a producer.

1. HOW TO SET UP A WEST END PRODUCTION COMPANY

'I think only people in the theatre know what a producer is. The public does not know. It knows a writer writes, and an actor acts, and a director tells them what to do. A producer raises money. Well, he does, and in some cases that's all he does. But the workers in the theatre know that this is not the real thing. A producer is a rare, paradoxical genius – hard-headed, soft-hearted, cautious, reckless, a hopeful innocent in fair weather, a stern pilot in stormy weather, a mathematician who prefers to ignore the laws of mathematics and trust intuition, an idealist, a realist, a practical dreamer, a sophisticated gambler, a stage-struck child. That's a producer.'

– Oscar Hammerstein II

British theatre is divided into two great sectors; the commercial and the subsidised. In no other country is the balance between the two so successfully achieved, and the creative sparks that fly when the two rub together have given rise to some truly excellent work. The defining characteristics of each sector are that subsidised practitioners budget their activities for a deficit in order to attract government funding and commercial ones budget for a profit in order to attract investment. The only certainties are that between them they lose a vast amount of other peoples' money and in the process create a vast amount of extremely good theatre.

The idea that the government should provide substantial financial support to theatre is a post-war phenomenon and has given rise to the role of the 'administrator' or, in a big organisation, 'chief executive'. This is the salaried senior manager of the operation, responsible for co-ordinating the logistical infrastructure that facilitates the creative process and for ticking enough boxes to ensure a continuous drip-feed of money from the Arts Council, who distribute it on behalf of the government. Their counterpart in the world of commercial theatre is the 'producer'; a self-employed entrepreneur who has somehow got it into their head that if you put on a good show then enough people will buy tickets for it to cover its costs and even generate a profit. Or at least who believes that they can convince a number of investors that this is the case.

It is no coincidence that the enduring paradigm of commercial theatre production and legendary *éminence grise* of the West End, Hugh 'Binkie' Beaumont (1908-1973), was a pioneer of the interface between the commercial and 'not for profit' theatre (albeit along with a bit of fancy footwork when it came to his interpretation of the laws regarding the taxation of ticket sales). Or that the most successful theatre producer of all time, Cameron Mackintosh, built his vast commercial empire to a large extent on the global success of *Les Misérables*, a show that was originally created by the subsidised Royal Shakespeare Company. But although the two sectors can work very productively together, and although there is a certain level at which the theatre administrator and the commercial producer share a skills base, the two are really very different animals. Both are key players in the collaborative process of making theatre, but the detail of how they achieve it and what it is that makes them tick as individuals tends to be quite different. Of the two, only the producer is an entrepreneur, only the producer's living is dependent on the outcome of their work, and only the producer cannot claim a 'right to fail'.

For all this talk of vast theatrical empires, the unpredictable nature of a producer's income means that one of the most important rules is to keep your overhead as low as possible. Many thriving commercial production companies in reality consist of little more than the producer and an assistant. Once the production process on a show actually starts the core team is augmented by an army of specialists and consultants, but the ability to downsize quickly when a show closes is strategically essential. There is often a temptation to take on additional permanent staff when things are busy, but it is all too easy to get trapped into a cycle of employing extra people to cope with the workload and then having to generate yet more work simply in order to pay for them. Even an assistant is a luxury item until the point where you are actually in production with your first show. Similarly, whilst it is a good idea to have an office to get up and go to in the morning rather than working from your kitchen table, it's not necessary to rent a swanky establishment on Shaftesbury Avenue just because you are a West End theatre producer. A desk, a phone and a couple of chairs in a shared space are all you need, as well as access to a meeting room relatively close to the centre of town. Negotiating all of these for free will be amongst the first deals that you do as a producer.

Right from the start you are going to need to define clearly the entity on behalf of which you are raising money and entering into legally binding contracts. This is most likely to be a company limited by shares, of which you are the salaried managing director. You may have other directors and shareholders in the company, but in any event they probably won't be the same people who end up investing in your actual productions. This structure means that if you run into trouble, and provided you have not been completely irresponsible, you will enjoy a certain degree of protection for your personal assets (if indeed you have any). There are alternative ways of operating, of course, including registering as a 'sole trader' (which links your own fortunes more directly to that of your business operation) and 'company limited by guarantee', which is more suitable if you are raising the funding for your shows on a not-for-profit basis.

Having set up your production company, each show you produce is then individually financed by investors in that specific project, via a dedicated bank account or sometimes even a dedicated satellite company. Each project generates income in the form of management fees and expenses to the benefit of the production company, irrespective of the individual project's own overall profitability. Provided that this income exceeds the company's overheads then there should be enough money left over to pay you a salary. Every so often one of the projects themselves may become profitable, in which case the production company will effectively receive a bonus that can either be used to invest in infrastructure (another assistant, maybe) or paid out as a dividend to shareholders.

It's easy enough to register a company with Companies House on the internet these days, but if you are doing this for the first time then it's worth involving a solicitor to ensure that you are following all the correct procedures and indeed that you have chosen the appropriate company structure for the operation that you intend to run. A solicitor won't charge you much to do this, and it is also an opportunity to strike up a working relationship with one should you require any legal advice in the course of your work. It's important from the outset to use a specialist in commercial theatre production, and it's advisable to seek a recommendation from someone who is already working in the business.

New producers often make the mistake of asking lawyers to negotiate and draw up key agreements such as investment documents, play licences and contracts of engagement. If you do this then you are simply paying out good money for the wheel to be reinvented. All of this paperwork follows a pretty standard format and there are numerous readily available templates and examples that you can base your own documents on. If it is the first time you have drafted one of these documents then do get a solicitor to dot the i's and cross the t's before you issue it, but that should be the extent of their involvement. And if you can't negotiate the actual terms of these agreements yourself then you really are in the wrong business. In America, just about everything is handled by 'attorneys', which is one of the many reasons why putting on shows there is so much more complicated and expensive. The most you will probably ever use your solicitor for is to discuss an unexpected legal development down the phone for ten minutes (although don't forget that they may even charge you for this).

Litigation is almost unheard of in the West End Theatre industry and in reality many of the contractual documents that are exchanged are not worth the paper they are written on. If you have engaged someone to work on a show, and they then decide that they don't want to after all, it is impossible to force them to do so or to quantify the compensation due to you if they do not. Similarly, if you run into financial difficulty then people will usually rally round and come to the table to renegotiate their terms. Commercial theatre production is a small industry where long-term reputation is always more important than short-term financial gain. It is good faith, good sense and persuasive argument that holds it all together rather than the threat of legal action. Having said that, it is always reassuring to know that you have a good lawyer at the end of the phone when you need one.

As soon as you register a company you will need to consider the matter of accounts. As with your choice of solicitor, it is important to engage a firm, or preferably an individual, with a specialised knowledge of your area of work. Theatrical accounting has some unusual quirks which can be counter-intuitive to even the most qualified of practitioners, and things can get very muddled very quickly if your accountant is not conversant with the very particular methodologies applicable to commercial theatre production.

Filing your annual accounts should be a fairly straightforward process, and something you pay a one-off fee for. But once your project is up and running someone needs to be in charge of the weekly cycle of processing the payroll and other expenditure, obtaining the box office receipts from the theatre via a process of invoicing and counter-invoicing, and correctly accruing for employer's National Insurance contributions (where applicable), holiday pay and VAT. This all requires detailed, prompt and accurate record-keeping, and you may well find that a freelance bookkeeper who visits your office a few times a week is the most practical and cost-effective solution, with the accountant themselves keeping track of the overview and producing the final audited accounts both of the individual productions and of the company. The fact that each show is financed as a separate entity through third party investment means that you have to be meticulous about the 'paper trail', with a proper system of purchase orders and invoicing applied at all times; and it is particularly important that the financial operation of each show is clearly separated from that of the production company itself.

Whilst it may be up to others to carry out the detailed work involved, it is entirely your responsibility to be fully aware of the state of the finances of both your show and your company at any given moment, both in terms of profitability and of cashflow. Only if you are armed with this information at all times will you be in a position to take the critical decisions that you will have to make as a producer on an almost daily basis and often at very short notice. In delegating the workload you are not delegating the responsibility, and in any case it is almost impossible to get either lawyers or accountants to take the blame for any errors in their work. Any accounting and legal costs that are incurred as a result of the operation of a production, as opposed to the operation of your company, are rechargeable to that production's separately-financed budget.

One person you won't be needing on your team is a general manager. A general manager is effectively a 'producer for hire' and is engaged by a producer (in return for a weekly fee) to manage all aspects of a production on their behalf. This is a key appointment if the producer concerned is based overseas and needs to have a representative looking after their interests 'on the ground', or is simply a newcomer with insufficient knowledge of the production process to do it themselves. Using your skills as a producer to general manage a show for someone else can be a good gig if you need to replenish your own production company's coffers, or indeed just cover its outgoings for a while; but lines of communication with overseas bosses can often be frustrating, and being seen to implement the sometimes naïve decisions of a novice producer can have a negative effect on your own professional credibility. The one piece of advice you won't hear from a general manager, of course, is 'don't do it', as they have the ultimate vested interest in just about any project that they are offered going ahead. It is notable that some of the more legendary West End flops have been 'general managed' on behalf of third parties, which is not so much an indication of any lack of skill on behalf of the general managers concerned as of the fact that the projects themselves were stinkers in the first place.

The West End theatre production machine is often seen at its shabbiest when a fully financed, pretty-well-guaranteed-flop musical hoves into view; more often than not general managed by a professional team on behalf of some wealthy but ill-informed dreamer whose lifelong passion the project is. Theatre owners, marketing agencies, artiste agents, equipment hire companies, production staff and 'essential' expert consultants on all things theatrical scramble over each other to slap their rate cards on the table and make a quick buck in the short-lived feeding frenzy before the ship goes down with all hands. On the other hand, the operation of some of the most successful productions currently running in the West End is entrusted by overseas producers to London-based general managers (sometimes styled 'associate producers'), so at its best the system can work very successfully. However, the whole point of this book is that you are the producer and are responsible for every aspect of both your production company and your production. So if you are planning to engage a general manager to do all your work for you then you might as well stop reading now.

By contrast, the most essential member of your core team is the production manager. They will receive a one-off fee (plus expenses) during the production period (i.e. while the show is being set up) and are one of the very few experts to whom it is actually worth paying a weekly retainer once it is up and running. Again, all of the costs incurred in engaging a production manager can be recharged directly to the project concerned. The production manager is effectively your head of logistics, and needs to come on board in the early stages of a production's development. They will supervise all technical and staffing aspects of the operation and are responsible for the transition from drawing board to reality in all the design departments, ensuring that everything is delivered on time and on budget. They will book everything from the rehearsal rooms to the lorries delivering the set to the theatre, arrange for the hire of all the lighting and sound equipment and engage all of the technical staff and stage management team for the show. They will draw up and oversee the production schedule so that everything and everyone involved in the process is in the right place at the right time and directly supervise the installation of the show into the theatre and all technical aspects of the rehearsal process. Most importantly, they will provide costing estimates for your budget for all of the areas that they supervise and take responsibility for cost control once the production process is up and running. I've actually used the words 'responsible for' a couple of times here although, of course, if the production manager does get something wrong then the buck, as ever, stops with you.

However good your production manager is it is important to engage fully with every aspect of what they are doing rather than just leaving them to it. It can sometimes be tempting to let them get on with all the 'boring bits' while you rub shoulders with your writer, your director and your stars. But, as a producer, correct scheduling and costing are absolutely central to everything that you do and to be honest the challenges faced by the production manager, particularly those involving the logistics of the design process, are often far more interesting than anything that's going on in the rehearsal room. If the production manager mumbles something about 'we're getting behind schedule' then the producer had better sit up and listen, as it will be the producer standing in the auditorium three days later explaining to the director and cast that they don't have time for a dress rehearsal due to 'technical issues'.

Here is a favourite story of mine about the working relationship between producers and production managers:

> A man in a hot air balloon drifts off course. He reduces altitude and spots a man below. He descends further and shouts, 'Can you help me? I promised someone I would meet them an hour ago, but now I'm lost. Can you tell me where I am?' The man below replies 'You are in a hot air balloon hovering 30 feet above the ground. You are between 50 and 51 degrees north latitude and 3 and 4 degrees west longitude.' 'You must be a production manager' comments the balloonist. 'Indeed I am' replies the man below, 'but how did you know?' 'Well' answers the balloonist, 'everything you told me was technically correct, but I have no idea what to make of the information you've given me and the fact is that I am still lost. Frankly you have not been of much assistance so far.' The man on

the ground responds 'you must be a producer'. 'Indeed I am' replies the balloonist, 'but how did you know that?' 'Well' says the man, 'you don't know where you are or where you are going. You have risen to where you are due to a large quantity of hot air. You have made a promise to someone which you have no idea how to keep, and you expect me to solve your problem for you. The fact is, you are still in exactly the same position that you were in before we met but now, somehow, it's my fault.'

Your production manager will help you to draw up a timeline for the rehearsal process and for the physical realisation of the show; but whilst the schedule for steering the artistic aspects of the production from page to stage is very similar to that for the same process in a subsidised production company, you are starting from the distinct disadvantage that you have no finance, no theatre and no administrative infrastructure. You are probably already sensing that this is all beginning to cost a bit of money irrespective of whether you actually have a project on the runway and ready to go. You've already registered a company, taken some advice from lawyers and accountants and picked the brains of a production manager so that you have an idea of how much finance you might need to raise. Added to which you have no way of supporting yourself while you put the whole thing together, so you may also have to be holding down a day job in the early stages of the process. SOLT's Stage One scheme offers a number of bursaries and grants designed to assist first-time producers in the early stages of setting up a project, and we will take a look at how to raise 'seed money' from investors, but if you have to take a job to keep a roof over your head while your project is in its early stages then at least make sure it's one in a theatrical environment. Working behind a theatre bar is more likely to put you in 'the right place at the right time' when it comes to networking with the great and the good of theatreland than working as a filing clerk for the Ministry of Defence.

Nerves of steel combined with an ability to focus on the big picture and not to sweat the small stuff (of which there is an extraordinary abundance in theatre) would undoubtedly be amongst the *clichés* at the top of the 'person specification' if the job 'West End Theatre Producer' was being advertised. Add to that a generally optimistic 'cup half full' approach, an unending ability to translate problems into opportunities and an extremely high tolerance level for people who in any other industry but theatre would be deemed as mad as a box of frogs. Theatre producing is, perhaps bizarrely, not a comfortable occupation for control freaks. You need to be able to delegate successfully whilst being aware of everything that's going on and taking ultimate responsibility for the results. Of all the people involved in a project it is you who has to be able to join the dots and see the wood for the trees. People will look to you to make the big decisions, and you've got to be relaxed about letting other people take the small ones so that you can keep a clear head for this.

A piece of theatre is a work of art, and as a producer that is what you are 'creating'. Assembling the multitude of inter-dependent artistic and financial elements that go into putting on a show is not a linear process. It is a seemingly endless vortex of Catch 22s, a veritable farmyard full of carts before horses and chickens before eggs, and an impressive three-ring circus featuring juggling, plate spinning and tightrope walking without a safety net. There is no single moment when you can sit back and say the project is 'green lit', although signing up your star actors, booking your theatre, or completing the raising of the finance (none of which is technically possible without the other two being in place) are all significant milestones. Financial decisions about a show may well have artistic implications, and artistic decisions may well have financial implications. If you see yourself primarily as a 'finance' person or as an 'artistic' person then it may well be that producing is not for you.

Unlike other art forms such as writing or painting, and unless you are presenting a one-man mime show in the street, the creation of theatre is an intrinsically expensive process. Far from being mutually exclusive, the art and the finance of theatre are thus two sides of the same creative coin, and only if you can grapple with the application of finance to the artistic process whilst simultaneously making artistic endeavour financially viable are you really fulfilling your role as a producer. Oddly, it is often the financial aspects of the equation that people find most daunting, whereas in reality that is the easy bit. Budgets are fairly straightforward, logical documents and investors tend to be fairly straightforward, logical people. But keeping control of the overall process in a manner that achieves your desired artistic outcome can be a real challenge, and a surprisingly physically and mentally draining experience. There is nothing at all straightforward or logical about the artistic realisation of a show, or indeed about most of the people who are entrusted with the job. Thank goodness. The extraordinary thing is that out of the seeming chaos of the process that you are refereeing emerges something as disciplined and sublimely well-crafted as a piece of theatre. Tom Stoppard summed it up famously in *Shakespeare in Love,* the best film ever made about putting on a show; 'Allow me to explain about the theatre business. The natural condition is one of insurmountable obstacles on the road to imminent disaster... Strangely enough, it all turns out well... It's a mystery.'

In the world of the producer the financial and the 'artistic' aspects of a production run parallel and are inextricably interlinked; you need to be equally well informed and at ease in a budgeting or marketing meeting as you are when discussing which translation of a Chekhov play to use or which lighting effect works best. Your financial acumen needs to be as finely tuned as your artistic judgement, and if either let you down then an ability to bluff (or, as some would have it, 'bullshit') convincingly comes in very handy as well. You need, in short, to be a jack of all trades and a master of at least some of them, or you will soon lose credibility and be rumbled as an imposter. It is your voice that ultimately has to be heard above the hubbub; but it has to be a quietly assured, credible and reassuring voice; not a didactic or strident one.

The producer's multi-faceted role in the creation of a production is not necessarily best understood by attempting to impose a chronology on it. You will see that my starting point is putting together a budget and raising the finance, but I want to reassure you that there is method in my madness. I am not suggesting for one moment that you should actually draw up your budget before deciding what project you are going to work on, or that VAT is more important than finding a good play. As we all know, 'the play's the thing'. But rather than following the timeline of the 'artistic' journey of putting on a show, which has been well documented in some excellent books by playwrights, actors and directors, I have structured things in a way that I hope will help to clarify the producer's perspective and thought processes. This chart, which is by no means definitive, may serve as a useful point of reference as the picture emerges. I call it the 'West End Whirlpool'. Let's dive in…

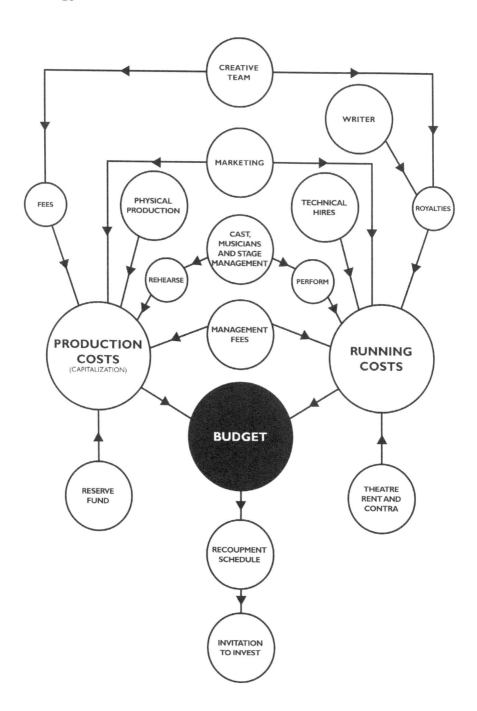

2. HOW TO BUDGET
A WEST END SHOW

'It's clearly a budget. It's got a lot of numbers in it.'

– George W. Bush

The budget is a summary of your show's anticipated
expenditure and is created and controlled by you, the
producer. Initially based on estimates, it will go through
several drafts as the details of the production are developed and
actual costs are obtained for them. Once the budget has been
sent out to potential investors it is considered as 'locked off'.
The producer has been trusted by the investors to spend their
money in the manner that has been described in the budget,
and any significant deviation from this plan may be challenged
by them. A good producer will create an accurate budget and
then ensure that the expenditure in each budget category does
not exceed the budgeted figure. It is important, though, not to
become identified by the production's creative team simply as
the person who stops them from spending money rather than
the person whose ceaseless endeavours have actually raised it in
the first place.

A good many 'artistic' people run a mile when they see a
spreadsheet full of figures, but the show's budget is absolutely
central to the entire production process and is a work of art in
itself. It is the framework upon which everything else hangs
and it informs just about every decision that you will make,
from the inception of the project to its conclusion. In the first
instance the budget will tell you whether your idea for a show is
viable at all, and throughout the life of your production it will

continue to be a crucial point of reference for monitoring and controlling the operation and for projecting outcomes.

Although the producer is the employer, a theatre production is a major work of creative collaboration and you are not going to get very far if you take the approach 'do as I say because I'm the boss.' In real terms it is the fact that the producer creates and controls the budget that vests in them the decision-making authority for every aspect of the project. The manner in which you choose to exercise this power is up to you, as is how much or how little budgetary information you choose to share with your creative collaborators. It is important that everyone involved knows the financial parameters within which they are operating so that they can tailor their contribution accordingly, and a degree of openness on monetary matters from the outset is important in order to establish a position of trust. However, disclosing too much information can undermine your authority and can limit your own ability subtly to manoeuvre the project's financial infrastructure in support of your own favoured creative outcomes. If you are going to wave the occasional magic wand and pull the occasional rabbit out of a hat when it comes to solving your project's financial and creative conundrums then, like any magician, you will need to keep a few tricks up your sleeve. Not to mention the fact that divulging too much financial data can also result in people jumping to misinformed conclusions about the perceived profitability of the production and in particular how much money you yourself are making out of it.

In any event, it is your complete and detailed understanding of every aspect of the budget that sets you apart from every other person working on the project, and it is thus the single most important tool that you have in achieving both your artistic and commercial objectives. Creating and managing it is at the very heart of your skills as a producer, so it is important that you don't rely on others to do this. Expert advisors like your production manager will obviously have plenty of input in obtaining accurate costings in the first instance and in controlling expenditure once the project is up and running, but you yourself should be responsible for the budget's overall construction and you should be absolutely familiar with its every detail. Don't worry if you don't have a 'head for figures'. What you need in order to draw up a budget is not a degree in maths but a good basic understanding of every aspect of the process of putting on a show; which is knowledge that you will need in any case if you are going to be a producer. The budget is no less than a detailed summary of the entire creative endeavour of your project, expressed in numerical shorthand.

Theatre budgets are divided into two main sections, which reflect a theatrical production's unique nature as an ongoing creative enterprise. The 'production budget' includes estimates of all of the costs incurred up to the opening of the show and the 'running budget' shows the anticipated weekly costs of actually operating it. The weekly costs are based on a standard eight show week, which is what the entertainment union contracts allow. Theatre is a hugely labour-intensive enterprise, and the weekly running costs of a West End show can be staggeringly high, from as much as £60,000 per week for a small play to four times that for a large-scale musical. The aim of the game is to take enough money at the box office every week to cover your weekly running costs, whilst slowly paying off your production costs out of any weekly surplus until you reach a point where the weekly surplus is actually profit.

There is no set format for a show budget and it is down to each producer to develop their own. When creating yours it is worth remembering that not everyone will be viewing it on a computer screen and it is important that it works as a document when printed out onto A4 paper. The fewer sheets of A4 it covers the better; the ideal format contains all of the relevant information (both production and running costs) on a single sheet so it can be seen at a glance. I know of only one production company that has succeeded in coming up with a single sheet format but, failing that, one sheet for production costs and one for running costs is almost as helpful. Actual budget headings and categories may vary slightly from producer to producer although ultimately the nature of the key information that is being conveyed is always the same. Once you become confident with the budgeting process you should literally be able to budget a West End musical in ten minutes on the back of an envelope. You will find, however, that investors and accountants prefer to receive the information on some sort of spreadsheet.

The 'production' section of the show's budget is typically divided into six main categories: Salaries, Fees, Physical Production, Theatre Costs, Marketing and Miscellaneous. Once you have estimated the costings for all of these elements you will have a clear picture of the nature of your project, and creating a budget thus also acts as a useful checklist to ensure that you have not overlooked any element of the production process.

Salaries in the 'production' section of the budget reflect the number of rehearsal weeks, and are usually expressed as a single sum broken down into number of actors and stage management x number of weeks (not forgetting to add accrued holiday pay over the period, employers' pension contributions and any employer's National Insurance contributions for which you may be liable). Salaries are paid weekly, and in rehearsal are paid at the minimum rate applicable to the size of theatre in question rather than the artiste's negotiated 'performance' salary. Those who live outside a certain radius of London will be entitled to a London Relocation Allowance. This is a weekly payment for a set number of weeks (currently thirteen) commencing with the first week of rehearsals. It is amazing how many performers appear to be based in London when they attend auditions but then turn out to live in Aberdeen when they provide their 'contractual address'.

Like minimum salaries, hours of work are dictated by a collective agreement between SOLT and the actors' union, Equity. This is renegotiated every four years by representatives of the two organisations and as a result is a ponderous tome that very much has the feeling of having been 'designed by a committee'. Contrary to popular belief, and although it is often referred to simply as the 'Equity Agreement', it is a two-sided document that is designed to protect the employer's position as much as the employee's. The Agreement allows sufficient hours for a fairly thorough Monday-Saturday working week during rehearsals, which you should take full advantage of; but be careful not to schedule in a way that incurs any overtime payments, particularly during technical rehearsals in the theatre. Also note that anyone who has been contracted with understudy responsibilities receives a weekly payment for this during rehearsals, and in respect of this you may reasonably expect that they are spending some of their time learning and observing their understudy roles. In some cases understudy duties are only allocated once the rehearsal process has started.

Most 'entertainers' (i.e. actors, musicians and stage management) are self-employed and sort out their own tax and National Insurance. However, your payroll may still include some people (such as technicians) from whom you need to deduct tax and National Insurance payments at source, and for whom you will need to make employer's National Insurance contributions. And anyone working for you who is paid by the week will be entitled to holiday pay on top of their agreed weekly rate, so this has to be accrued for. If for any reason someone does not actually take all or any of their holiday entitlement in the course of the contract (for instance in the case of a short season or engagement or a curtailed run), then any accrued but unused holiday pay is added to their final week's salary.

Calculating holiday pay used to be quite straightforward but when the statutory annual holiday entitlement increased from 24 to 28 days the maths suddenly got a lot more complicated.

In general, it has to be said that the law in respect of 'employee' holidays does not always sit comfortably with theatrical custom and practice, which is hardly surprising given that theatre generally offers short, consecutive, six-day week, fixed term contracts to people who are self-employed practitioners, and that these contracts often involve work on public holidays and are liable to be terminated at short notice. Not to mention the fact that the customer is often paying to see specific people actually carry out the work. If this stuff keeps you awake at night then there are plenty of good courses that will show you how to follow the letter of the law, but failing that then the relevant union agreements and a bit of good sense should suffice.

Despite being self-employed for tax and National Insurance purposes, entertainers have to be auto-enrolled for employee pension schemes along with the rest of your staff, which of course creates a financial liability for you which you need to accrue for in your budgets. The entertainment unions have established a methodology with SOLT for prioritising their own pension schemes and, tedious though this is, you need to be up to speed with the mechanics of it all. In reality, there are plenty of excellent older roles for those actors for whom working is more important than planning for retirement; I once employed a fellow who was quite happily treading the boards in the West End at the age of 88. And as a producer the best pension plan you can aspire to is of course a long-running hit show.

All of these bits and bobs add considerably to your weekly payroll costs, so don't forget to budget correctly for them. You'll need to know what the current rate for employer NI is (for those to whom it applies) and what the relevant annual holiday entitlements and employer pension contributions are. All of these areas are particularly prone to legislative interference, so make sure that you are always up to date with the latest thrilling developments.

If you are producing a musical you also need to budget for band rehearsals. Refer to the SOLT/Musicians' Union Agreement for the latest terms of employment and rates of pay for theatre musicians. Unless it is a new piece you shouldn't need many rehearsal sessions. The players are reading from the music, and if it is an established title then they are likely to be familiar with the material in any case. You will need the full band at the dress rehearsal, of course, and also to do a sound check with the actors so that the sound team can get everything balanced correctly. The band should not be called for the technical rehearsal sessions, although you will need a keyboard and probably a drummer to enable the songs and choreography to be delivered in some shape or form. As you are hiring an expensive theatre for a few days while you get everything set up it is worth seeing whether it is possible to schedule initial band rehearsals somewhere front of house in the theatre during this period. This also enables the music department to keep in touch with the rest of the team.

When you add the weekly cost of hiring a rehearsal room (usually under Miscellaneous) to the rehearsal salaries you will be surprised at what an expensive process rehearsing is. Some actors and directors seem to enjoy rehearsing so much, and get so absorbed in it, that they sometimes appear to forget that the actual purpose of rehearsals is to create something to put in front of an audience. It is also the case that an over-rehearsed play can be just as disastrous as an under-rehearsed one. Directors who have worked extensively in the larger subsidised theatres, where rehearsal periods seem to go on forever, can be particularly guilty of this. New musicals in the commercial sector can also have notoriously long rehearsal periods, particularly if the writers haven't completed their job before rehearsals start. The number of rehearsal weeks will be agreed with the director at the point where you draw up the budget, and as a general rule there should be a very good reason if rehearsals are scheduled to exceed three weeks for a previously performed play, four weeks for a new play or a previously performed musical or six weeks for a new musical. This schedule is more than achievable provided that everyone takes their responsibilities seriously, and that the director has prepared properly in advance, the actors have studied their roles and the designer has completed the set design by the first day of rehearsals. One way to encourage directors not to over-rehearse is to make it clear that you are paying their fee for the job and not by the week.

One-off fees and expenses are payable to the creative team (director, designer, choreographer etc.) for their work leading up to opening. These fees are negotiable, but minimum rates are set by SOLT and Equity for directors and members of the design team. Some of these rates are reduced if the production is being transferred from tour or another theatre, so it's worth checking that you are not over-paying. Creative personnel of calibre are likely to push for much higher fees than the minimum, but if you are being asked to pay more than 50% over the odds you should be taking a serious look at their CVs. There are detailed SOLT/Equity Agreements that cover directors and designers, but they are rarely used and provided you are not paying below the minimum rates it is fine to draw up individually tailored agreements for your team. As well as the director, set designer, costume designer, lighting designer and sound designer, if you are producing a musical then you will need to pay fees to a choreographer and a musical director. Creative team fees may seem a little low in comparison to other areas of the budget, but their real reward comes when their weekly royalties kick in. Most 'creatives' will insist that they need at least one assistant, but you should think twice before engaging an army of assistant directors, designers and choreographers and feel free to question what role they actually play or suggest that the person demanding an assistant engages and pays for them themselves.

The creative team will add expenses to their fees, which may include anything from train fares to hotel accommodation if they are living away from home, so it is important to establish parameters for these expenses (in the Miscellaneous section of the budget). The set designer will also charge additionally for preparing or sub-contracting the set model and technical drawings. When people start asking for per diems (a daily payment for living expenses, for food, etc.) on top of their fees and expenses then it is probably time to draw the line, unless of course you are engaging creatives from overseas, in which case your Miscellaneous budget will not only include their accommodation but also their flights (most people will settle for business class) and per diems.

If you are producing a new musical then the composer will probably expect their work to be completed by musical arrangers, orchestrators and copyists engaged by you. These folk can be shockingly expensive, so make sure the small print in your contract with the composer clarifies exactly what you are expected to provide. For most musicals you will also have to add a rehearsal pianist to the weekly payroll (this may be the person who eventually plays keyboards in the band). You should consider too whether your production will be needing input from specialists such as accent coaches, fight directors and the like, all of whom will charge daily rates to attend during the rehearsal period, and who will usually also be happy to turn up occasionally during the run of the production subject to their availability (and to payment of the appropriate fee, of course). If there's a fight sequence in the show then a good fight director is essential both from an artistic and a health and safety point of view, but make sure your rehearsal room (and indeed your budget) doesn't get too crowded with 'expert consultants' drafted in by the show's director.

If you are employing a production manager or a casting director then their initial fees appear in the 'Fees' category of the production budget. Your production manager will also introduce a number of staff who will require fees (as opposed to your stage management team who receive a weekly wage for attending rehearsals). These may include a wardrobe supervisor (responsible for ensuring that the costume designs become a reality), a moving lights programmer (most lighting designs include moving lights these days), an automation programmer (if required), a projection programmer (if required), a keyboard programmer (if it's a musical) and a props buyer, not to mention the heads of department responsible for the supervision of the installation of the set, automation (if any), projection (if any), lighting and sound equipment. A lot of these people are paid by the day, so for budgetary purposes their fee will be calculated according to the total number of days' work that is anticipated in each area.

Work that is paid by the hour will always expand to fill the time available, so keeping the time spent actually installing the show into the theatre (the 'get-in') to a minimum is very important. It is also worth making sure that the personnel supervising the operation are London-based, as there is no point in incurring hotel and travel costs on top of the substantial daily rates they charge. I often think the creative team would weep if they were to see the rates paid out to senior technical staff during the get-in period and compare them with their own fees. Having said that, it is important that this process is headed up by highly skilled people who know what they are doing, as time is literally at a premium and any mistakes or delays can be extremely costly.

The Physical Production budget heading covers the costs of creating or buying the set, costumes, wigs, furniture and props, as well as any up-front purchases by the lighting and sound departments. The production manager is responsible for obtaining costings for the set, which will be based on the designer's set model and technical drawings. He or she will obtain competitive quotes from rival workshops to undertake the 'build' and will identify the best one to go with. You also need to question at this stage how many crew this particular set design will require to operate it. The trend towards automated sets and projection will not only involve extra design fees and equipment hire costs but will result in yet more folk on your weekly payroll (and quite expensive, specialist ones in this instance). Even with old-fashioned sets, multiple flying cues and bits of scenery trucking on and off are indicators that you will be paying for a large number of backstage staff on a weekly basis. Similarly, in consultation with the costume designer and the wardrobe supervisor, the production manager will have identified the best place to get the costumes made or the best place to purchase them from.

It is worth remembering that the costuming for a period piece is likely to be considerably more expensive than for a production with a contemporary setting, particularly as this is also likely to involve the creation and maintenance of wigs. A cheap wig will always look like a cheap wig, and well-made ones are a major investment, not just in terms of their creation but also because of the number of staff required to maintain them properly. By committing to wigs you are committing to a considerable addition to your weekly payroll once the show is up and running. Also don't forget that every change of costume for an actor not only requires the purchase of a new outfit but is also an indicator as to how many 'dressers' you are going to need to engage on the show. Some or all of the costumes may be hired instead of made or purchased, in which case they become part of the weekly 'hires' budget instead of the production budget.

Budgeting the physical elements of the production is the most difficult part of the process. It is fairly straightforward to work out how many actors and stage management you are going to engage and for how many rehearsal weeks, and what your budget limits are for creative fees. But consider this. You can't contract set and costume designers until you know that you have the money to pay their fees. You don't have the money to pay their fees until you have raised it from investors. Investors won't put money into the production until they know what the budget is, including the costs of the set and costumes; and potential big investors may well want to see initial design concepts before signing up. Your production manager can't obtain costings until the designers have presented their designs. But the designers won't start work until they have been contracted…. This is absolutely typical of the plate spinning that a producer has to do. In reality, you should be able to persuade the set and costume designers to produce some initial concepts in the hope that the project will eventually go ahead. This will also involve some input from the director on the same basis, of course. The costings that go into the budget are thus not based on the final designs but on the production manager's estimates (probably with some advice from potential builders and makers). This is why the physical production (and onward costs in terms of staffing) is the area of budgeting that is most prone to error.

Ultimately, once the cost has been fixed in the budget, the production manager is responsible for delivering the designs to that figure. This can lead to some heated debates with the creative team, particularly if they experience a 'creative breakthrough' months after the budget has been locked off. It is notable, however, that creative breakthroughs always seem to involve increasing the cost of the designs rather than reducing them. The producer will be accused of being a Scrooge and stifling the creative process, but the fact of the matter is that a fixed amount of money is actually physically available (i.e. that which the producer has raised, based on the original budget) so creative compromises have to be achieved somehow or the show won't happen; perhaps the money can be found for a new flying piece in Scene Two that wasn't in the original budget provided that the back-cloth in Scene One is cut. Such compromises aren't always a bad thing, and working strictly to budget often helps the creative team to focus on what is really important to the successful delivery of the production. Don't ever be persuaded to go over budget by 'creative concerns'; the whole point of being 'creative' is that there is always an alternative solution to be found and necessity is always ultimately shown to be the mother of invention. Having said that, it is important to be sensitive to the fact that, although the designs should have been finalised before rehearsals start, the rehearsal process itself is likely to throw up a few new design ideas that are worth undertaking a bit of imaginative budget-juggling to achieve.

Another important thing to keep an eye on is that your production manager is succeeding in keeping the design and building process on schedule. As with all things, a rush job always costs more. And, of course, the sooner the set can get built the less time the creative team have for changing their minds. The most expensive bit of scenery is the one that is designed as an afterthought in the final week of rehearsals, built in a hurry, delivered to the theatre during the get-in and installed during the overnight break in technical rehearsals.

The get-in is a massively costly exercise, not only because of all the extra people who you will suddenly find yourself paying for, but because you are actually starting to hire the theatre from this point. You should be able to negotiate a deal with the theatre for the days before performances start, but they will still be calling in a lot of their staff during this period and incurring other costs such as utilities and rates, so they will at least want to recharge these costs in order to cover their own expenditure (such a recharge is known as a 'contra' because it is literally a charge 'against' the production). They will probably also want to start charging you rent after a few days. The ideal scenario is thus to restrict the get-in to as short a period as possible and commence preview performances towards the end of the first week of your occupancy of the theatre.

Although some West End production companies seem to specialise in legendarily long get-in and technical rehearsal periods for new musicals it is worth remembering that in most cases they probably also own the theatre, so the investors' money is finding its way into their pot one way or another. It really should take no longer than three days to install, technically rehearse and dress rehearse a play and a week at most for a musical. Of course the best way to keep the get-in and technical time to a minimum is to run the show in on tour or at an 'out of town' theatre so that it can arrive fully formed in the West End. This is particularly advisable if it is a new play or musical, especially the latter, as the last thing you want to be dealing with at this stage is changes to the script and direction.

The theatre will 'staff up' with temporary personnel to help with unloading and setting up the equipment during the get-in and will also have its own heads of department and staff on call. Creating a cost-effective interface between your own team and the theatre's in terms of scheduling, given the archaic and labyrinthine working practices of West End theatre technical staff, is a piece of alchemy that only a really skilled production manager can achieve. It is in these pressurised few days, with lorries delivering scenery, people rigging lights, automation programmers, lighting programmers and projection programmers all doing their thing, the band rehearsing in the bar and the director pacing up and down demanding that his actors get more time on stage, that the production manager really earns their fee. When skilfully orchestrated, this particular three-ring circus has a peculiar beauty of its own. All the producer can do is look on in awe, and as a general rule if there are not more than three people standing around drinking coffee at any one time then you are probably going to stay on schedule. After what seems like an eternity of chaos, a technical rehearsal and a dress rehearsal will eventually emerge and you will be ready to welcome your first audience.

Your production manager will be able to advise you of any additional crew costs for the get-in and you should also take account of the cost of the get-out in the production budget. A get-out will be more expensive if it is anticipated that the production is going to have a future life, as everything will be carefully dismantled and loaded to be taken to a store. If it is going to be driven to the dump and trashed then the process inevitably costs less. It is always tempting to think that a set will be used again, but it is worth considering this carefully before you commit to the costs of storage, particularly as you can't really expect your investors to pay for it. You can, however, include the cost of dumping the set in your production budget (though probably not directly described as such, as you don't want your investors to be imagining that particular scenario before the show has even opened).

Marketing, advertising and PR for a West End show account for a major part of the production budget, and your marketing agents will happily advise you on how to allocate as much money as you can throw at them. The expenditure in this category includes everything you commit up to the opening night plus the media advertising that takes place immediately after it (quoting all your wonderful reviews). You won't get much change out of £100,000 for even the smallest of productions, and the pre-opening spend for a big show can be several times that.

The Miscellaneous category forms the final section of this part of the budget. Along the way we have noted that any travel, accommodation and per diem costs for creative and production staff should be put in this section. Whilst most of your performers will simply receive the weekly relocation allowance on the payroll, if applicable, you may also have costs associated with looking after particular star performers during the rehearsal period. If you happen to be including a Hollywood star in your cast then although their actual performance wage may seem reasonable, and their rehearsal wage should not be more than the union rate, there can be considerable costs involved in flying them, their family and their entourage over, as well as accommodating them, feeding them and chauffeuring them around during the rehearsal period.

Also in this 'catch all' category will be the cost of rehearsal rooms and auditions. Auditions can be quite expensive, particularly for a musical, once you have hired a room and paid a rehearsal pianist the going rate. The director and choreographer should include attendance at auditions and any other meetings in their agreed fee. There will also need to be some money allocated to haulage; for transporting the set and costumes from the workshop to the theatre and then away again at the end of the run (not forgetting that you may have to pay to get parking meters suspended outside the theatre while everything is being unloaded). Everyone and everything will need to be insured from the first day of rehearsals, and the insurance premiums up to opening are expressed in the pre-production figure as a single sum; as are your pre-opening legal costs, payroll costs and accounting costs, plus the costs of preparing the final accounts after the show has closed. And don't forget that everyone will expect you to shower them with gifts and throw them a wonderful party on the first night.

Finally, remember to budget a little something for yourself. Custom and practice dictates that you can charge your weekly management fee and office costs from two weeks before rehearsals start up until two weeks after the end of the run. So for the purposes of the production budget you would show your management fee and office costs each as a single sum, calculated on the basis of weekly charge x (number of rehearsal weeks + 2 + 2). The management fee and office costs during the run are part of the weekly running costs.

Now draw a line under all of the above and add it up, plus a contingency to allow for any budgeting errors or for that absolutely essential additional piece of scenery. How big a contingency you put in is up to you. Investors like to see that you have put in something as it reduces the risk of additional funds being required at a later stage. On the other hand, if you are good at your job (and your production manager is good at theirs) then your budget projections should be pretty accurate. An additional 5% should be about right. We'll deal with the matter of 'reserve' funds when we take a look at investment structures, but a provision should also be made for these in the production budget. You have now completed your production budget and know how much your show is going to cost to get to opening night. Shocking, isn't it? However, the one thing you can be certain of is that it is about one third as shocking as if you were producing exactly the same show on Broadway.

The second part of the budget is the summary of 'Weekly Running Costs'. This is usually broken down into the categories Salaries, Technical Hires, Production Maintenance, Theatre Rent and Contra, Press and Marketing and, of course, the all-important Miscellaneous section.

The performers, stage managers, musicians and technicians on your payroll receive whatever you have agreed to pay them for an eight-show week, subject to the relevant union minimums (plus National Insurance for non-entertainers, holiday pay, pension contributions and any relocation allowances). People belonging to the technical union BECTU (the Broadcasting, Entertainment, Cinematograph and Theatre Union), many of whom work a five-day week unless you pay them extra, tend to be employed on the theatre's payroll and charged back to you on the weekly contra.

'Technical Hires' are the weekly payments you make to hire in lighting and sound equipment, plus any projection kit or other fancy stuff on the set. A West End theatre will have almost no technical kit, so you have to budget to bring in absolutely everything, including control desks and speakers for sound. Most theatres will have a lighting control desk of some sort but the lighting designer is likely to insist that one is brought in to their own specification. You will also need either to buy or hire the black drapes or masking flats to go at the side of the set, and these should be costed into the production or running budgets as appropriate. You'll also most likely have to buy or hire in washing machines, tumble driers and irons for your wardrobe department.

The weekly cost of major technical hires such as lighting and sound kit can be reduced if you pay for a fixed number of weeks up front, but this is difficult to express budgetarily and can leave you in 'negative equity' if the run of your show is curtailed. In any event, your production manager should source the best deals and present you with a range of options. Some sound designers are effectively 'in house' with certain kit hire companies, and will therefore insist that you use particular suppliers. This limits your ability to cut deals with the suppliers and you should make sure that any such relationships are made explicit at point of contract when you are engaging your sound designer.

'Production Maintenance' will cover everything from costume repairs, replacements and cleaning to new microphone batteries and gels for the lights, plus any perishable props, food eaten on stage, and the like. Your production manager will be able to give you a fair estimate for these costs based on the size and nature of the show.

The weekly rent you pay for using the theatre, plus contra charges for theatre staff and utilities, should be as per your contract with the theatre; although if a period of time has elapsed since the theatre provided you with a 'sample weekly contra' you should double check that their staff's pay rates haven't gone up in the meantime. You will also need to pay for any 'show staff', which are additional stage staff that they have to bring in over and above their resident staff in order to service the particular requirements of your production. Did you remember to check when signing off the set design how many additional stage staff the theatre would need to engage in order to operate it? This is where that extra flying piece on the set that you agreed to could cost you dear.

The weekly Press, Marketing and PR budget is whatever you want it to be, but it costs several thousand pounds a week just to maintain the most basic profile for your show and you will be competing with some legendarily big spenders in this area.

Our old friend 'Miscellaneous' is where we will find the Company Stage Manager's petty cash float (probably a few hundred quid a week), along with weekly insurance costs (for public liability, employer liability and all your hired and purchased kit), weekly accountancy and payroll costs and any retainers you are paying to production managers, casting consultants and the like. Plus, to be on the safe side, a small 'contingency'.

It is also worth putting a 'recast accrual' into the weekly costs, allowing you to hold back a sum of money from any weekly operating profits to contribute towards the cost of recruiting and rehearsing new cast members if the show is fortunate enough to extend beyond the period of the initial cast contracts. An approximate weekly accrual figure can be arrived at by assuming you will be replacing half the cast and that they will be rehearsing for half the time that the original cast did. Because they are likely to be rehearsing on the set at the theatre, rehearsal room costs won't usually apply (unless new cast rehearsals are taking place on matinee days). The 50% of the cast who you might expect to stay will rehearse as well as perform within their contracted hours, though you will probably need to allow some overtime for them. And of course if it's a musical then you will have to call the band for a dress rehearsal at which you will have to pay for a new set of production photographs to be taken (and subsequently mounted in frames outside the theatre). And talking of 'dress' rehearsals all these new folk are going to require costumes (or at least alterations to existing costumes), wigs and so on. Once you have arrived at an estimated total cost for this exercise, divide it by the number of weeks of the initial cast contracts (say, twenty-six weeks) and put it in the budget as a weekly accrual figure. If you don't make enough money at the box office every week actually to accrue this figure after all the other costs have been paid then don't worry, you probably won't be recasting anyway.

Some producers use a similar methodology to the 'recast reserve' for accruing a reserve fund to pay for getting the show out of the theatre at the end of the run; effectively 'putting by' an amount of money every week for this purpose from operating profits rather than allowing for it in the production budget. This means that if your show closes earlier than expected, or fails to generate a weekly operating profit, you may not have accrued sufficient funds physically to get your show out of the theatre. Given the expense of get-outs, this is a scenario that is clearly best avoided, and it is therefore prudent to include the get-out costs in the production budget rather than as an accrual in the running budget.

Weekly running costs themselves fall into two categories: fixed costs and variable costs. The fixed costs are all of the categories outlined above plus 'fixed royalties' (i.e. regular weekly sums paid to certain members of the creative team for the use of their work). Variable costs usually consist of royalties paid out to those who are entitled to a percentage of net weekly box office receipts. These may include the writer, director, designer, perhaps a star and even a small royalty for yourself as producer. They can also include a share to the theatre if you have been clever enough to persuade them to take a percentage in lieu of rent (thereby sharing the risk with you) or stupid enough to agree to give them a percentage against rent once the production is in profit (potentially giving them a risk-free first call on that profit).

Any payment based on a percentage is calculated on the basis of 'net' weekly box office receipts, which is the money you actually receive once VAT, credit card charges, sales commissions and the ever-increasing list of levies and other annoyances have been deducted. The theatre's box office will very kindly make all of these deductions before handing over the money to you, so at least you know where you stand. The face value of each ticket includes VAT which has to be handed over to the government, and if VAT is running at 20%, and once all the other deductions have been made, a big chunk of your gross box office income will disappear before it even hits your bank account. This can be very misleading when you are looking at what appear to be healthy advance sales figures, which are always expressed in 'gross' (i.e. before these deductions). The 'net down' only occurs once the ticket has actually been used and the sale has 'matured'. The point at which, in other words, the money actually becomes yours. It can be quite shocking the first time you experience this, and it is important that any income projections for the production take this into account.

Like it or not, if you are a theatre producer then VAT is going to have a major impact on your life. Despite continuous lobbying by the industry, and some labyrinthine concessions that can be utilised mainly by building-based companies in the subsidised sector, the government insists on levying a full VAT charge on every theatre ticket sold, resulting in an annual revenue for them of almost £100 million from London theatre alone. This means that all theatre producers become experts at calculating VAT 'on the inside'. If VAT is running at 20% then the VAT taken by the government on a £50 theatre ticket is not 20% of £50 (i.e. £10). It is the smaller sum of (£50/1.2) x 20% = £8.33. If you divide £50 (the gross, or face value ticket price) by 1.2 then you get the net ticket price (i.e. the bit you get to keep) which is £41.67. The 20% VAT that the customer pays to the government is charged on the net price. Net price plus VAT = gross price. The '2' in the '1.**2**' reflects the '2' in the '**20%**', so if the VAT rate is 17.5% then you divide by 1.175 to find the net price before multiplying by 17.5% to find the VAT amount contained within the gross price. This deduction is made at 'point of sale', so it is theatre box office that accounts for it and pays it over to the government.

If you are putting on a West End show then the projected turnover of your company is going to be well over the threshold for registering for VAT, so make sure that you do so at the earliest opportunity. This effectively makes you a tax collector on behalf of the government, and means that every time your company invoices for something you have to add VAT and then hand over all the VAT you have collected to the government on a quarterly basis. To thank you for your services as a tax collector, the government will allow you to reclaim any VAT that you have actually been charged. In terms of cashflow this is done by offsetting the VAT you have been charged against the VAT you have collected. So if at the end of the quarter you have invoiced for £10,000 of VAT on behalf of the government and are reclaiming £8,000 that you have been charged, you will have to write the government a cheque for £2,000. Or if you have invoiced for £8,000 of VAT and are reclaiming £10,000 then they will have to write you a cheque for £2,000.

Amongst your biggest outlays, of course, will be paying people for the work they do. Only a very small number of (usually star) performers will charge you VAT, occasionally via a registered company 'for the services of'. Most members of the creative team, on the other hand, will probably charge VAT. Whilst all of this can have a short-term effect on cashflow it is important to remember that it exists outside of the profit and loss accounting of both your show and your company. Because you don't get to keep the VAT that you charge, and you can reclaim everything that you pay, all of your budgeting should be done 'net of VAT'; in other words without taking VAT into account on either the income or the expenditure side. There are alternative methods of managing VAT for individuals, small companies and charities, but the one I describe is the one that is most likely to be applicable to a West End production company.

Although it feels as if it is you who is paying the VAT on the ticket sale, it is not, it is the customer; and their transaction is not with your company, it is with the theatre box office. This means that you cannot claim back the VAT that is levied on a ticket sale and it does not even form part of your accounting. You will, however, be involved in a complex network of VAT-applicable transactions which you need to keep careful track of, as your cashflow position can be very different from your profit and loss ('p and l') position at any given time.

Once the VAT and other deductions (for sales commissions and so on) have been taken out of your weekly gross ticket revenue you will have to 'collect' this sum from the box office by issuing them with an invoice for this figure. It is at this point that your company actually makes a 'sale' and therefore you have to charge VAT on this sum to the box office. The VAT that you charge on this transaction is not yours to keep but must be handed over to the government. In the other direction, the theatre will charge VAT on services that it provides to you, which VAT you can then claim back from the government. The actual 'settlement cheque' that you receive from the theatre will therefore be calculated on the basis of your gross sales less VAT and other deductions, plus VAT that you charge to the theatre on this figure, less charges that the theatre makes to you plus VAT on those charges. Regular inter-company transactions like this will often be carried out on 'self billing invoice', which means that the theatre will create all the necessary invoices from you to them on your behalf (you may do this yourself when making regular payments to royalty holders for instance).

Technically the only loser in all of this is the customer; the only party involved who cannot reclaim VAT, which is included in the ticket price that they have paid. To avoid becoming paranoid that the government is taking all your money by levying VAT on ticket sales just think of your ticket price as the net price (plus VAT) rather than the gross price. You will of course take VAT into account when setting the gross ('face value') price, but you can't push this price too high or you will put off your potential customers. When theatregoers complain about high ticket prices they usually don't realise how much of the price is going straight out of their pockets into the government's. The fact is, of course, that if the government removed or reduced VAT theatre producers would not actually reduce their ticket prices, so in real terms such a move would be a huge bonus to the theatre industry rather than a small bonus to the individual customer. On the other hand, it could be argued that this levy can be justified so long as the government continues to subsidise the arts; a subsidy from which commercial producers ultimately benefit, via a complex network of co-production agreements with the subsidised sector.

People have been known to lose the will to live when attempting to understand the implications of VAT on theatre accounting, but one day the penny drops and it all becomes remarkably straightforward. In the meantime make sure you have a good accountant and as a rule of thumb, provided you are VAT registered, simply ignore any VAT that you charge or pay out when it comes to budgeting and remember that the price you get for a ticket is after the government has taken their cut directly from the customer.

So, taking into account VAT, as well as various 'at source' deductions which are levied by your landlord, your £100,000 gross box office for the week may well have become something more like £75,000 and it is upon this lower figure that royalties and any other variable payments are calculated. If your royalty holders between them are entitled to 10% of the net weekly box office then your 'variable' royalty bill for the week in question will be £7,500, and at this point you are hoping that your fixed weekly running costs do not exceed £67,500 and hopefully are considerably less (though that would actually be unlikely for a West End show).

To assess the financial viability of your production you need to know the 'financial capacity' of the theatre (i.e. how much money you can take every week if you sell every ticket at full price). Ask the theatre owner for something called a 'Total Seater' and they will provide you with a chart that demonstrates this. There will be a range of prices available in the theatre, from 'top price' seats in the stalls and dress circle to restricted view seats behind a pillar in the balcony. The 'price breaks' (i.e. which seats are sold in which price bracket) are suggested by the theatre management and it is usually best to follow their advice, as it will be based on extensive experience and customer feedback as to which seats in the theatre provide the best views of the stage. Don't forget though that elements of your set design, such as a raised stage or a bridge at the back, may affect the audience's view and compromise the 'sight lines' so a good seat for one production in a certain theatre is not necessarily a good seat for another. There is even currently a website (www.theatremonkey. com) where people write in to share their experiences of sitting in certain seats for certain shows in certain theatres. Although this may seem a bit obsessive at first, it is well worth doing a bit of research on this subject and insisting that the set designer takes sight lines into account to the extent that they may affect ticket pricing.

The amount of money you can take will be reduced if there are seat losses to accommodate an orchestra pit, a stage extension, sound and lighting desks or any other technical equipment. Sound designers in particular have an annoying habit of placing speakers in boxes where there are perfectly good seats to sell. If you have a sound desk position taking up 16 seats and 16 box seats lost to speakers, and granted that these are likely not to be top-price seats, that could be 32 tickets x £40 x 8 performances = over £10,000 of your gross weekly income. Even if you are only turning people away on Friday and Saturday nights that equates to over £2,500 gross per week.

When you request the Total Seater you can ask for examples based on different top prices for your tickets. It's important to set the top price based on an analysis of the top prices being charged for other similar shows, and the quickest way to see what everyone else is charging is to look at a copy of SOLT's London Theatre Guide leaflet, which shows the pricing for all shows currently running. The Total Seater will suggest prices for the less good seats in the theatre based on whatever you are setting as the top price, and the total 'financial capacity' for a performance will automatically adjust accordingly. So if you look at models with a higher and lower top price then all of the other pricing will be proportionately higher or lower. What is important here is that you are not basing your income projections on some sort of average price but on a fixed number of seats at each price (i.e. 400 x £60, 200 x

£40, 100 x £20). There may also be a few 'premium seats' for
customers who like to pay extra for the privilege of having 'the
most expensive seats in the house' (there are always a few!) and
it is important in setting your prices, and indeed in advertising
them, that there is no confusion between standard 'top price'
tickets and 'premium' tickets. The total financial capacity for
each performance is then multiplied by eight performances to
ascertain the weekly gross financial capacity. Deduct VAT and
you are at least most of the way to ascertaining the weekly net
financial capacity. The Total Seater will probably do this for
you, although it will most likely neglect to 'net down' all the
other 'off the top' charges deducted by the theatre for its box
office services and other levies.

Here it is important to remember that the Total Seater
assumes that all seats of whatever price are actually sold at
face value. Unfortunately this is not normally the case in the
West End; outlets such as the SOLT half-price ticket booth
and a number of 'ticket retailers' passing themselves off as the
half-price booth, account for a fair volume of sales, as do the
growing number of discount ticket websites. In addition to which
you will doubtless be offering student discounts, OAP discounts,
entertainment union discounts and Resident Card discounts, not
to mention half-price promotions in newspapers and other media.
Only a smash hit show will be selling all of its tickets at the actual
advertised price. Having remembered all this, you can actually
ignore it, though. Financial projections are based on percentages
of net financial capacity, and the factors reducing that net financial
capacity, be they discounts or a simple lack of sales, are not actually
relevant. All of this of course means that the actual number of
tickets sold is also of little relevance. A half-full auditorium of
people who have paid face value to sit in top price seats is of
considerably more financial interest than a half-full auditorium
of people who have paid half price or are sitting in the balcony.

The next thing you should do is create a chart ('the recoupment chart') that shows how many weeks you will take to recoup your production costs (after you've covered your weekly running costs) if you play to certain percentages of the net financial capacity on a weekly basis. This illustration, along with your budget, forms the core of the information that you will provide to your potential investors.

3. HOW TO RAISE INVESTMENT FOR A WEST END SHOW

'It is a matter of record that of every ten productions that open in the West End, about seven fail to recoup their investment costs. Another two break even, but only one in ten returns a profit.'

– The Theatres Trust *Act Now!* Report, 2003

Every year The Society of London Theatre (SOLT) proudly announces the latest sales statistics for the West End; the millions of pounds that have been spent at the box office, the millions that have (begrudgingly) been handed over to the government in VAT on ticket sales and the further millions that have been generated via theatrical endeavour for 'the London economy'. The big question that these statistics fail to answer is whether or not the productions generating this income were actually in themselves profitable. Unlike New York, where box office figures are published weekly in *Variety* magazine, we are never told which shows generated what income; and because the accounts for individual productions are not a matter of public record, only those people who actually invested in a show will ever find out whether or not it actually recouped its production costs and made money. The box office income for a big, popular musical at the London Palladium can add a very rosy hue to the overall statistics, so whilst SOLT's 'state of the industry' bulletins may give the entertainment unions cause to believe that the endeavours of their members are lining the pockets of theatre producers, the picture from an investor's perspective may actually be very different. And even that big, apparently popular musical at the London Palladium may not be profitable if its running costs are too high. SOLT even used to tell us how many plays and musicals had opened in the West End in the previous year as if this were something to be celebrated; overlooking the fact that for every show that opens another must close. The most encouraging statistic we could be offered is that no shows at all opened in the West End last year, because all those that opened the previous year were so successful that they were still running.

Given the lack of reliable statistical information and the size of the sums involved, raising the money for a West End show is a relatively simple process. With very few exceptions, you will not qualify for any form of subsidy, and corporate sponsors are wary because there can be no guarantee of longevity or market share. A system has developed, however, which enables large sums to be raised from individuals relatively quickly and which allows the producer a remarkable degree of flexibility in how the money is spent. This money takes the form of 'investment' in an individual production rather than in the company that is presenting it. The system is largely self-regulating and its methodology has developed through custom and practice rather than being dictated by any legislation.

The sum of money raised is referred to as the 'capitalization' and is the amount required to finance the Production Budget as opposed to the Running Budget. The capitalization will also include a reserve fund which is intended to 'nurse' the show through any periods of poor business, including typically 'production week', which may see reduced revenues due to performances only commencing halfway through the week, as well as preview weeks where tickets may be offered at a discounted rate. Part of the reserve may also be applied to various deposits you will be asked to place such as those required by the theatre to guarantee the rent. When negotiating with the theatre it is always possible to avoid paying a deposit, and indeed a requirement for a deposit may be considered as indicating that the theatre owner does not feel that your production is sufficiently strong to last the course or that you as a producer are potentially unreliable or under-financed.

And it's not just the theatre owner who will be asking for a deposit. Only a 'Full Member' of SOLT (which you probably won't be) can proceed with a production in the West End without registering a bond (also refereed to as a 'deposit') with The Theatre Council, an entity jointly operated by SOLT and Equity to oversee various regulatory matters. This bond is for the equivalent of three weeks' salary for all of your actors and stage management team. It will be returned to you after your show has closed, but if you run out of cash in the final weeks it can be used to pay the wages and thereby honour your contracts with your employees. Although placing a bond with The Theatre Council is likely to cause a cashflow problem for you, and may effectively create preferential creditors in the event that your production company goes into liquidation, it actually provides a useful security against the stormy financial waters of the West End and it is reassuring to know that, whatever happens, the last three weeks' wages will be paid. Once you have placed (and not needed to call upon) four bonds for four productions, and provided you have become a 'Deposit Member' of SOLT in the meantime (which shouldn't be too difficult if you are actually producing a West End show), you will qualify to be approved by SOLT and the unions to operate your productions without the need to place one. It is acknowledged, in effect, that you have become sufficiently skilled at your balancing act to perform without the benefit of a safety net. A deposit is also required for rehearsal wages, which you will get back once the show has opened.

When you sign a West End theatre contract you automatically become bound by all of The Theatre Council's regulations, and there is no way of avoiding placing these bonds unless you are a full member of SOLT or unless a full member is prepared to vouch for you. This is where co-producing your first ventures with a full member can be a shrewd move. Or, if you are really persuasive, you can get the owner of your theatre (who will also be a member of SOLT) to vouch for you. Remember, though, that if you do not build up a track record of placing bonds with the unions in your own right then you will not get to the stage where you yourself can qualify for 'full' membership of SOLT.

The combined sum of the bonds and 'nursing fund' (together forming the 'reserve') may increase the capitalization figure by up to a third. The total capitalization is then divided into 'units' for sale, typically of £5,000. So, if your production budget is £600,000 and your reserve fund is £200,000, your capitalization will be £800,000 and you will be selling 160 units of £5,000 each to investors. All of this money is placed in a nominated bank account which is used exclusively for transacting the business of the production. Because you are selling units in a particular show and not shares in your production company it is particularly important that this dedicated bank account is (and is seen to be) operated correctly and not confused with any other business that you may be conducting at the time. This enables you to monitor clearly the financial fortunes of your production and enables your accountant and your auditor to report accurately to your investors as to how their money has been spent.

It is very important (though extremely difficult) not to spend any of the capitalization until the full sum has been raised. Technically you should not enter into any binding contracts on behalf of the production until you know that you have enough money in the dedicated bank account to finance the entire production. If the production does not go ahead for any reason then investors will expect their money to be returned in full and if you have already spent some of it then you could be in trouble. This is particularly difficult given that potential investors will want evidence of commitment from your various key players (such as author, star actors, creatives and theatre) before parting with their money, and is just one of the numerous 'Catch 22' conundrums that you will have to learn to deal with as a producer. You will usually end up entering into provisional agreements 'subject to contract' with all parties, with these agreements being triggered provided that the full capitalization is raised within a given period of time.

Once the full capitalization is in the bank (£800,000 in this example) then you can very quickly conclude all the provisional contracts, place any deposits and pay any advances that you need to in order to go into production. You are 'in production' once you start finalising the contracts and spending the capitalization, and from this point onwards you are committed to delivering the project. The 'green light' effectively goes on as soon as you start committing contractually to spending money.

The capitalization should be spent in line with the production budget, which will have been provided to investors in advance of them agreeing to support the project. Most investors will make their decision based on the viability of the budget, so once again your budget is absolutely central to everything that you do. Having said this, the budget provided to investors is deemed to be for 'illustrative purposes' and in reality you have a great deal of flexibility as to how the capitalization is actually applied, provided that the total sum is not exceeded. Generally speaking your investors will be happy provided that each budget heading accounts for roughly the amount of money that you originally said it would. If you end up paying one actor more and another less than in the budget, or if you spend more on sets and less on costumes, this is unlikely to be a huge issue with them. In any event, theatrical investors have remarkably little recourse against a producer if they disagree with his or her decisions. They have trusted their money to you and they trust you to exercise your skill and judgement in spending it wisely. If you betray that trust and fail to do so then they will not invest with you again and you will get a bad reputation in an industry where reputation is everything.

The theatre or their agents provide the box office facilities and bank all of the advance ticket sales income. It is a bold producer who suggests that they share the bank interest thus derived. The net box office income (less the multitudinous deductions that apply to ticket sales) is handed over to the producer on a weekly basis in the week following the week in which the sales 'mature' (i.e. once the customer has actually used the ticket to attend the theatre and the transaction with the customer has thus been completed by actually presenting them with a show). Because the first week's performance wages will have to be paid in advance of receiving the first week's income, the reserve fund may be applied to cash-flowing the production at this point. Although the entire net box office is paid over to the producer 'on paper', the theatre owner will of course take the opportunity to deduct the rent and contra charges before handing it over, effectively giving them a 'first call' on your income. If the total net box office for the week in question does not exceed the theatre's rent and contra then you will be faced with the depressing prospect of having to pay over the difference, and you will know immediately that your show is in trouble because you will not have made enough money to cover the wages and other costs for the week. We have to assume that the theatre and their agents are keeping the advance box office money in a secure account so that it can be returned to the customer in the event that a particular performance or production doesn't take place, or a production ends its run earlier than advertised. The good news for the producer is that the initial transaction is between the customer and the theatre or agent, so if the advance box office money has 'disappeared' for any reason (as it did with the collapse of one of the major ticket agencies a few years ago) then the producer does not technically have any liability to the customer (although the customer will probably blame them anyway).

Provided that the weekly net box office income is not lower than the Weekly Running Costs then the production has broken even for the week, or 'made the break' figure. If the net box office figure is less than the weekly running costs then you will have to apply the reserve fund to 'nursing' the production that week. If the amount of money required from the reserve fund is significant then this is the first indicator that your production is in trouble. This is why it is very important to analyse advance ticket sales in great detail. Although you will sell some tickets 'on the door' the majority of sales in the West End are made in advance. People need to plan their theatre visits, organise travel, accommodation, babysitting, maybe a restaurant; so you get a pretty good idea in advance as to what the financial outcome on each week is going to be. Factors which you can plan for such as school and public holidays and major sporting and public events may well affect the patterns of advance box office sales, as may factors that you can't plan for such as the weather and terrorist attacks. You should work on the basis that, at any given time, your 'netted down' advance box office sales for the next two weeks and your reserve fund are at least sufficient to cover the anticipated running costs of those two weeks.

A production that takes enough money to cover its running costs on a weekly basis can technically run forever in the West End without paying back a single penny of its capitalization to its investors. If it is taking enough to pay the producer's management fee as part of those running costs then it could also make a fairly reasonable living for its producer in the process. However, a middle ground such as this would be an unusual scenario and a West End production usually defines itself as a success or a failure within a few weeks of opening.

What the producer really wants, of course, is for enough income to be generated through ticket sales every week to start repaying the capitalization as well as covering the running costs. In the first instance any surplus is retained in the production account, but once the producer feels sufficiently confident that this pattern is going to continue, a 'distribution' is made to investors of a portion of this surplus. Once again, the investors are in the hands of the producer when it comes to deciding how often a distribution is made and how much of the accumulated surplus is distributed at any given time, but good practice would dictate that a show that is generating a regular surplus against running costs should make a quarterly distribution of most of that surplus. The producer may keep back some money in order to top up or add to the reserve fund, but it is effectively 100% of any surplus that is being distributed to investors at this stage in the process. Each investor receives a share of the distribution in proportion to the fraction of the capitalization that they have provided *'pari passu'* (meaning 'on an equal footing'), so returning to our illustration of £800,000 sold in 160 x £5,000 units, a £5,000 investor would receive 1/160 of the sum being distributed.

The first distribution on any West End production is a cause for celebration. It demonstrates that both the producer's and the investors' faith in the production has been justified and it also justifies the trust that the investors have placed in the producer. It shows that the producer is confident in the production's future, as once those funds have been distributed there is no mechanism for retrieving them on the production's behalf.

This pattern of distributing 100% of the surplus income after weekly running costs continues until the point where the full capitalization (i.e. £800,000 in this case) has been repaid to the investors. Up until this point the production has not made any profit, and the production may well close before the full capitalization has been repaid if initially promising ticket sales begin to fall away. This is why producers have to be canny about when they make a distribution of funds and exactly how much is distributed. Unless sufficient reserve funds are retained in the production account it is possible to make a distribution to investors of surplus income from the early weeks of a production's run and subsequently find yourself unable even to cover running costs in the face of declining ticket sales.

Once the full capitalization has been repaid to investors the production is technically in profit. This moment may occur several months, or indeed years, after the production has opened, during which time the producer's only source of income from the production has been the management fees and office costs stated in the budget; often considerably less than the better paid performers in the production are earning. From the point that the investors' capital has been recouped, 60% of the surplus after weekly running costs is distributed *pari passu* to the investors (so 60% of 1/160 of the surplus per unit in our example) and the remaining 40% of the surplus is paid to the producer. On a hit show this can be a substantial amount of money, but it is statistically highly unlikely for such a scenario to occur and if it does then the money has certainly been hard-earned (and long awaited!) by the producer.

Once the first distribution of actual profit has been made, most investors will adjudge the production a success and consider anything else that follows as a bonus. They will certainly want to invest with this producer again and will most likely follow them into their next project.

The profitability of each production is a carefully guarded secret known only to the producer, investors and any members of the creative team due an increased royalty 'post-recoupment'. The accounts for individual productions are not usually discernable within the publicly accessible accounts filed for each production company. A report published by the Theatres Trust in 2003 claims that seven out of ten West End shows fail to recoup all of their capital, two out of ten do nothing more than recoup and only one in ten actually makes a profit. This means that on 70% of productions investors are going to lose some or all of their money. Not surprisingly, these findings were not widely reported at the time. In fact, although both attendances and ticket prices have gone up since the 2003 report, there is every indication that revenue has not kept pace with increases in production costs; so if anything there is now even less chance of making a profit on a West End show than there was then.

Given that these would not appear to be particularly good odds, who are these extraordinary people who willingly part with their money in support of the many and varied projects of West End producers and who are known, appropriately, as 'angels'? In the absence of any statistical data on this subject, I can speak only from experience.

Investment in West End theatre may be dressed up in the language of the City but most modern-day 'angels' are really the direct successors of the artistic 'patrons' of previous centuries; philanthropic facilitators whose primary motivation is to support creative enterprise, though they do so in the knowledge that they may get a substantial return on their contribution in the statistically unlikely event that they strike it lucky. Although the odds are poor and the timeframe slow the eventual returns on a long-running hit can be substantial, with the potential to make back several times the original investment over the years of the run. Because of the 'high odds/high return' element it is an activity that also attracts people who like a gamble on a racehorse or a game of roulette. As with a racehorse there is the opportunity to study 'form' and take various factors into account before placing your bet. In any event, it can at least be guaranteed that investing in theatre is an experience that will be a longer-lasting and hopefully more pleasurable and intellectually engaging experience than the few minutes of a horse race or the few seconds of a spin of the wheel.

A theatrical investor is 'buying in' to a world of perceived glamour and is becoming a stakeholder in the rollercoaster ride from first rehearsal via first night to final performance. In my experience, the typical profile of someone prepared to invest substantially in theatre would not be a banker or someone who makes a living gambling other people's money on the stock exchange. Such people have an eye for a fast buck and theatre, if it provides a buck at all, does so extremely slowly. A theatre 'angel' is far more likely to be a self-made business person who appreciates what it is like to have to struggle to follow your dream and who is already to some extent a patron of the arts. Not the 'household name' boss of a multi-national empire, but someone who still takes a hands-on approach to the day-to-day running of their business and who enjoys visiting the theatre as a customer. Substantial investors in my own productions have included an Italian art dealer, an Australian waste disposal tycoon, the head of a private tutorial college, a corporate PR guru and a prize-winning chemistry professor. Not to mention the founder of a computer software company who was my valued business partner for almost a decade. To all of these I remain eternally grateful and from all of them I have learnt a great deal about business, art, integrity, generosity of spirit and the importance of pursuing your dream.

Others who may invest in theatre include those who work in it, and friends and relatives of stakeholders in the particular project you are producing. It is usually best not to accept investment from people who are directly involved in a production (such as star actors or the writer) even though they clearly have a vested interest in its success, as this upsets the balance of power with the producer and may give you a sense of obligation towards them that could compromise your working relationship. However, if you have raised a good portion of the capital but not all of it, and particularly if the issue of fundraising has become time-sensitive (i.e. you are about to lose your option on the theatre) then there is no shame in asking those involved to send out a few feelers. A friend or relative of the star actor, writer or director may be more than happy to support the enterprise and it won't cloud your day-to-day relationship with the individuals concerned. I once found myself £50,000 short of a £400,000 capitalization on the eve of a deadline for a West End transfer of a show that was out on tour. I assembled the performers, explained my predicament and that I would not accept any money from them personally. Five out of the fifteen took up the challenge and were able to raise the remaining funds with a few well-placed phone calls. There is no embarrassment in doing this; everyone involved would rather the show went on than didn't, and if there are people in the company who have been in the business longer than you have then they may well be better connected than you are. Some star actors, for instance, have good relationships with regular investors through years of meeting them at first night parties.

The group of people with a vested interest in the success of the show extends beyond the creative team and the performing company of course, and you should not be afraid to approach the equipment supply companies and even your marketing agent for some financial input; if they say 'no' then there is no harm done. If a shortfall means that you risk missing your deadline to conclude your contract with your star actor, and the theatre has no other options on the horizon, then it has been known for particularly cheeky producers to approach their prospective landlords for a contribution. Theatre owners like to make out that they are hard-nosed and will rarely admit that they have succumbed to such an approach.

The easiest part of the money to raise is always the 'last 10%'. Although everyone has the protection that their money won't be spent unless and until the entire capitalization has been raised, people like the idea that their personal participation will guarantee the green-lighting of the project. If producers occasionally use a bit of bluff to get pulses racing in this respect then I couldn't possibly comment, but it has been known for someone to provide the 'last 10%' only to find that another investor then mysteriously 'drops out'. Of course, investors do in reality drop out and there is a big difference between money being pledged and it actually turning up in the production's bank account. The investor is under no obligation to provide funds until they actually decide to send a cheque, and one of the biggest dangers is that producers may count their chickens too early in this respect. It's very tempting to consider the production 'capitalized' and therefore to start the contracting process on the basis of pledges, but you are betraying the trust that the investors who have actually provided funds have placed in you if you do this. Tempting though it can be with all the time-sensitive pressures of theatre production, if you start spending on the basis of a £100,000 pledge and it doesn't materialise then it's too late to return the other investors' funds and you are scuppered. End of lesson.

The best way to meet investors, be they philanthropic business people or people with their own industry connections, is to spend a lot of time in theatres. All theatre investors love theatre, so that is where you will find them. And because investors are often also donors in the subsidised sector, you are just as likely to encounter them at London's larger fringe and Off-West End venues as you are in the West End itself. The most important factor in raising investment is to 'get connected' and the easiest way of doing this is to get a day job, however lowly, that places you in a theatrical hub. You are actually better positioned to meet potential investors if you are selling programmes at a London fringe theatre than if you spend your time rubbing shoulders with stockbrokers in City bars.

Raising money for a West End show from a standing start can be a daunting prospect. The first rule, of course, is not to invest any of your own money. As you probably don't have any money anyway it is even more important not to invest money that you *don't* have, by borrowing cash or mortgaging property. It is a truism that the best way to become a millionaire in theatre is to start out as a multi-millionaire, so it is not a game that you should play yourself. You should also not approach family and close friends for investment; it is awkward and embarrassing, particularly when you lose it all. To get going, try this exercise. Make a list of twenty people you know personally, who are not close family or friends and who can afford £1,000. You have to think out of the box to make this exercise work, and not worry about whether they might actually be interested in investing in theatre. The list might include anyone from your dentist to your old English teacher to the owner of the corner shop. Then, from this list, identify anyone who can afford £5,000. Remember, this means £5,000 that they could spend on anything (a house, a car or a holiday) not necessarily on your show. Now throw away the list. These people are probably not going to be your investors, but it got you thinking, didn't it?

It can be very awkward asking people for money for theatre investment, but the law is actually quite helpful here in that it does everything that it can to discourage you from doing so. Financial Services legislation quite rightly classifies theatre investment as 'high risk', which means that there are restrictions on advertising for it and on sending literature to people if they haven't actually requested you to do so. Being made to jump through these hoops can be a bit frustrating at first, but the decision to invest in theatre is an extremely personal one, based to a large extent on the investor's trust in the producer as an individual, and you are therefore not likely to raise much money as a direct result of advertising or sending out unsolicited circulars in any case. In reality your success in raising investment will be down to your personal powers of persuasion, but be aware that the psychology of the pitch is the exact opposite of the hard sell. Theatre investors don't want to be told how much money they are going to make by investing in your show; they want a fair assessment of how much money they are likely to lose. They will invest if they think you are being fair and honest with them, and this will only be the case if you portray their potential involvement as a way of supporting the creative enterprise rather than a way to make money; you should advise them that they are likely to be better off gambling on the stock exchange if that is their agenda. Any conversation with a new potential 'angel' (unless it's a direct appeal for funds to already interested parties) should not involve an actual request for investment. Instead, the conversation should be structured in such a way that they become interested in your project to the extent that they ask you whether there are any opportunities to get involved.

The first point of communication with any new investor should be verbal, whether it's a chat about what your latest projects are with a potential angel in a theatre bar or an incoming phone call from a contact of someone involved with your show. The investment information is usually only posted to them as a follow-up and at their specific request. Once someone has invested with you they are considered to be on your 'list' and are fair game to receive material about your next project (whether they have won or lost on the first one), unless they have specifically requested not to, of course. Every producer fiercely safeguards their own list, although canny investors make sure that they feature on more than one.

There are of course a number of ways around the Financial Services regulations. Whilst it is difficult to advertise investment in a particular production, there is nothing to stop you from advertising a seminar on 'How to Be a Theatre Investor' as I once did. Following a totally unbiased overview of the pros and cons of theatre investment, the attendees were so shocked that they had not fallen victim to some sort of time-share style hard sell that I was bombarded with business cards as I was packing up the overhead projector, along with requests to receive my next investment prospectus as and when I happened to be producing one…which by pure coincidence happened to be the following week!

Whilst there are legal restrictions on sending out unsolicited investment material for West End shows, the Society of London Theatre does maintain a list of people who have expressed an interest in investing in theatre, and members of SOLT are allowed to mail out to them. This entails delivering hundreds of copies of your Invitation to Invest to SOLT, who then post them out on your behalf without you knowing who they have actually been sent to; occasionally resulting in some interesting telephone calls where these anonymous individuals reveal their identity and allow themselves to be added to your own investors list. Because the scheme is only available to SOLT members it can be handy to enlist one as a co-producer if you yourself are not a member and you want to access it; although generally speaking it does not produce huge dividends (the most I have ever raised from it for a single show is £50,000). Most of the people on the SOLT list tend either to be smaller, more cautious investors without their own industry contacts, or much larger investors who already work with other producers and are just being nosey. Either way, it is a 'blind date' and is unlikely to create an introduction to a meaningful new angel of your own.

As well as providing bursaries to help emerging producers get started in the business, SOLT's Stage One Scheme offers to invest up to the last 10% of the capitalization of West End productions on standard 60/40 investment terms, subject to a cap of between £15,000 and £25,000 (depending on what funds they have available in their kitty at any given time). In this case you really do have to have the remaining 90% in the bank, or at least an accountant who is prepared to vouch that you are good for it. A panel of industry experts will give your budget a 'health check' and set down various criteria such as limits on management fees and producer royalties and an assurance of participation in 'residual' rights. They tend not to judge a project on its artistic merits but simply on whether the figures stack up. If they agree to invest (which they usually do) then it is an indication at least that your budgets and profit illustrations make sense. It is a good scheme that is aimed at encouraging new producers, and the pitch is done on a form so there are no 'Dragon's Den' moments. More established producers with full lists tend not to use it, mostly because they don't need to but also because it involves divulging their show accounts to third parties on the panel (some of whom may be rival producers!).

Because the only way to see a show's accounts is to be a stakeholder in it, producers will often make a small investment in rival productions so that they can keep tabs on what's going on. You shouldn't really send unsolicited investment information to other producers, any more than you should to anyone else, but they are unlikely to grass you up to the Financial Services authorities as in doing so you are gifting them (your competitors) all the key financial data about your production, from theatre rent to star salaries. If they then go on to make an investment they will also find out how much money your show is making and may of course use this information to their advantage, for instance to approach the theatre with one of their own productions if it looks like yours is failing at the box office. Some established producers, of course, genuinely like the idea of supporting the efforts of the 'young guns' and, like 'Dragons', can be an invaluable source of help and advice as well as money.

If you sell a unit or two to an established producer then they technically have the same *pari passu* status as any other investor in your production. However, if you are concerned that you won't be able to raise the full sum of the capitalization yourself then it is common practice to spread the fundraising burden by entering into a fully fledged 'co-production' agreement with another producer or indeed several others. As the economic climate changes and raising investment becomes more problematic, co-production deals are becoming more common, and the typical number of parties involved is ever-increasing. Shows with multiple producing partners have always been a regular occurence on Broadway, where the sums of money involved are much higher, but it is a relatively recent development in the West End.

If a co-producer is responsible for raising 50% of the capitalization then they will usually be entitled to 50% of the producer's share of any eventual profits (so 50% of your 40%). Or you might have two partners, each responsible for raising 25% of the capital (so each receiving 25% of the 40%). It is usual for the producer who has initiated the project to be the 'lead' producer and to have the casting vote on key decisions if a consensus cannot be reached. The lead producer will usually retain the management fees, office costs and producer royalties, though of course shares in these can also be up for grabs if further inducements are needed in order to attract partners. Just as investors are only signing up for the actual production in question, and do not have any ownership of your company or any other projects you might be engaged in, so a co-production agreement does not create any mutual liability between the partners beyond the conduct of the one project. Co-producers are likely, however, to have first option to participate in any post-West End life that the show may have (such as a tour or a Broadway transfer).

An individual investor accounting for a particularly large share of the capitalization (i.e. one who has purchased several units on their own account) may also be brought on board as a nominal 'co-producer'. This can be a double-edged sword. A co-producer who is a theatre professional probably brings no money of their own to the table (they will be able to raise it from their own list) and contributes some expertise to the enterprise (using their contacts to help with casting, etc.). A big investor with co-producer status who does not work in the industry may well have strong opinions about how the business of the production should be conducted but without the necessary skills or experience to back up those opinions. It can nonetheless often be quite refreshing to have a new voice in the mix, and a substantial investor is likely to bring their own business skills to the table which, though not always directly applicable to the operation of a West End show, can sometimes encourage you to question your own working methodologies and to think out of the box. Some investors for smaller but nonetheless significant sums, for instance those 'last ten percenters', who provide the funds that actually trigger the 'green light', may be given courtesy titles like 'associate producer'. The existence of these investors with co-producer or associate producer status on some shows could arguably justify the use of the 'creative producer' moniker to describe 'real' producers. I actually don't think that anyone in the industry has any difficulty in distinguishing producers from investors; and in any case investors may justifiably argue that putting in the money constitutes one of the most 'creative' contributions that anyone can make to the process of theatre production. Only once the money is in place, after all, can the show spring into life.

As well as selling multiple units to large investors, or offsetting portions of the capitalization to co-producers, you may sell fractions of units to smaller investors (for instance a 'half unit', which in our model would cost £2,500). Although it is tempting to agree to any offer you are made, you should think twice before selling too many fractions of units. A large number of small investors can be difficult to manage given that they will all need corresponding with and reporting to on a regular basis, as well as requiring investor perks such as tickets to the opening night performance and party. There was a legendary Fringe impresario who was in the habit of selling £500 shares in the West End transfers of his shows. I worked as his General Manager on one of them, and although you end up with a lot of people rooting for the success of the show it results in administrative chaos; and it takes just as long to explain to someone why you have lost their £500 as it does to explain why you have lost their £100,000. You should also question whether someone who wants to pay £2,500 instead of £5,000 can actually afford to lose it. If a difference of £2,500 is that important to them then it does not sound like this is 'gambling money', which it should be. I have turned down offers of investment of as much as £5,000 from people if I have felt that they are remotely uncomfortable at parting with it, as the implication is that the loss of this money might cause them actual financial hardship. Larger players are likely to be more comfortable generally with the whole concept of a high-risk investment in theatre and are more used to entrusting others to spending their money on their behalf. A small investor has as much right to have their voice heard as a large one, but you have to decide whether you have enough hours in the day to spend the time listening to it.

Small investors sometimes club together to form syndicates, in the same way that lottery players do. This means that the producer only has to deal with the leader of the syndicate as the actual 'investor', but this person has effectively 'sold on' shares in a unit; for instance, five people could each have a £1,000 share in a £5,000 unit. The producer's liability is only to the person in whose name the unit is actually purchased and they are not party to the syndicate leader's agreements with its other members. The members of the syndicate can help and advise each other and are therefore more likely to make correct investment decisions than a small investor acting on their own. Syndicates thus effectively relieve the producer of the considerable administrative and moral burdens of dealing with small individual investors. The theatrical accountant Philippe Carden famously headed up a syndicate in the 1980s (interestingly composed mainly of clients of his who were stage managers) and published the history of their investment experiences over several shows in the excellent book *Investing in West End Theatrical Productions: How To Be An Angel* (now sadly out of print, but usually available on Amazon).

Finally, a word about those legendary impresarios Bialystock and Bloom. The conceit in Mel Brooks' brilliant film *The Producers*, and the subsequent stage musical and the subsequent film version of the stage musical, is that a pair of crooked Broadway producers oversubscribe the capitalization of a new show, meaning that they raise more money than the entire production budget (i.e. by selling '50%' to a large number of investors). They know that if they create a flop and close the show early none of the investors will question the fact that they have not received a distribution and they will be able to abscond with the surplus funds. Unfortunately for them, *Springtime for Hitler* is an unexpected hit and they are faced with the prospect of a crowd of investors each demanding 50% of the investors' share of profits. Although this makes for hugely entertaining viewing, the flaw in the premise is that it is difficult enough to sell investment in a show once over, let alone several times. It is also true to say that this is not an industry that attracts crooks. Misguided fantasists who lose the plot occasionally, but not crooks.

The information that a producer sends to a potential investor, when requested to do so, is often (incorrectly) known as a 'prospectus'. It is actually called an 'Invitation to Invest', and this is the phrase that should appear on the front of the document. Invitations to Invest are usually very similar in style and content whatever the show, and as with most things theatrical the format has developed over the years through custom and practice. There is no legal requirement that they be set out in a certain way, although everything that is actually said within it must conform with the strictures of Financial Services legislation. The received wisdom is that they should not be too flashy, and they usually consist of a few simple sheets of A4, printed in black and white and stapled in the corner. Theatre investors don't like to feel that you are trying to seduce them into parting with their money by presenting them with expensive, glossy documents, and in any case the point you are trying to make is that you need money and that if they give it to you, you will spend it wisely.

Because theatre is classified as a 'high risk' investment, much of what is said in the Invitation to Invest seems specifically designed to deter the recipient from participating. It is certainly not a 'hard sell' and the point of it is simply to present the potential investor with all the facts that they need in order to use their skill and judgement to make up their own mind. In a bizarre way, this reverse psychology probably works in the producer's favour. By stating only the facts and by emphasising the potential downside so clearly you make it apparent to the potential investor that you are someone to be trusted. It is important that there is no hyperbole in the text and that every statement that you make can be legally proven to be true, so your description of your production in this context is likely to be very different from that which appears on your leaflet advertising it to the public.

Following a brief statement to the effect that you are offering units in the production rather than shares in your company and that the document is aimed only at the recipient, you should provide a summary of the project and a list of the key participants (creative team, actors, etc.) and their achievements. You may technically only use the phrase 'has agreed to direct' or 'has agreed to appear in' if you have supporting documentation available on request that demonstrates this. As you are unlikely to have concluded contracts at this stage it may be more correct to say 'has agreed subject to contract'. It is particularly important that you state how long you are intending to contract your star actors for. It is all very well saying that you have a major Hollywood A-lister on board, but if they have only committed to twelve weeks then it is a much less attractive investment proposition than if they have committed to twenty. You should also include a summary of your own CV. It is very important that you don't embellish this. Theatre investors like to know exactly who they are dealing with, as they are taking a risk on you and your integrity as much as they are on the success of the project. If you have co-producers who are responsible for raising some of the funds in their own right then their details should also appear. Investors like to see that the producing entity is your own main operating company and not a 'single purpose' company that you have set up as a vehicle just for a particular production. Using your main company shows that you yourself have faith in the project, although you should take advice on on whether it may prove easier to administer the corporate tax relief scheme for theatre production through a single purpose company. There should also be confirmation that you have obtained the rights to the piece if it is still in copyright. You may need to have borrowed the money from somewhere to take out an option as it would be folly to proceed to this stage without having done so, but as soon as the capitalization is in place you can repay this loan from the reserve fund (or the lender might be happy to convert it into investment units).

The Invitation to Invest will outline the anticipated production schedule, although you should avoid phrases like 'will open on 25 March' as this does not give you enough room to manoeuvre. You should also state where the production is likely to appear. At this point you will probably be in an advanced stage of negotiation with the theatre owner but will not have concluded a contract, making the contracting of the theatre the biggest chicken and raising your investment the biggest egg in the whole circular equation. You should check with the theatre owner whether it is OK to mention the name of the theatre. If their current tenants are unaware that negotiations are taking place which may result in them being evicted then the theatre's owner will ask that you do not actually name it. So you might come up with a phrase like 'We are currently in negotiation for a West End theatre of approximately 800 seats'. This may sound a bit woolly, but at least it gives the investors an idea of the size of theatre you are aiming for and upon which you have based your financial projections. A canny investor may well be able to identify the theatre anyway, based on their knowledge of which shows are currently in what buildings and how they are doing at the box office. The theatre owner is likely to want to keep their options open in case you don't raise all your money, and if you have contracted the theatre before raising the money then the potential investors will quite rightly question your judgement. The investors themselves have the security that if the project does not go ahead for any reason (for instance, you get gazumped by the theatre owner) then they will have their money returned. One thing that is important for them to know is how long you are contracting the theatre for. An open-ended arrangement with the theatre (subject to the usual industry-wide two weeks' notice arrangement) is far more attractive to an investor than a limited season. I have seen a number of projects that have consistently played over the break figure and started to return their capital, but have ultimately failed to recoup fully because they did not book enough weeks in the theatre.

You should make it very clear how much you intend to charge to the production by way of management fees, office costs and producer royalties. This includes the 'lump sum' management fee in the production budget and the weekly management fee in the running budget. At time of writing a weekly management fee would typically be between £2,000 and £4,000, depending on the scale of the project. You can also charge between 1% and 2% of net box office receipts as a 'producer royalty'. The fee is intended to reflect your administrative input and the royalty (which is similar to the director's) your creative input. You can also charge a few hundred pounds a week for office costs. As usual, the size of these sums is dictated only by custom and practice, but it would be a brave producer who suggested that he or she should receive more. Although these fees and royalties sound like quite a good living the problem is that they can only be paid if the money actually exists in the kitty, and when times are hard the producer's weekly income (which is not protected by any union contracts, bonds or deposits) is always the first thing to go. If things pick up then you can always back-pay yourself anything you are owed, but if it has got to this stage then they usually don't.

Following a statement of who will receive what by way of royalties, and the mechanics of any royalty 'pool' that you intend to operate, you should provide some illustrations of the mathematics behind the recoupment process; showing how the total capital is divided into so many units of a certain value, how income is applied first to running costs and then to recouping the capital *pari passu* amongst the investors, and how finally the investors share in 60% of operating profit whilst the producer receives 40%. In the USA the custom is for producers and investors to share profits 50/50, but when one of the big UK production houses attempted to introduce this practice there was an outcry. You should also show what percentage of the capital a unit represents (i.e. value of unit/ value of capitalization x 100 = A) and what percentage of the profit it entitles the investor to (i.e. A x 60%).

The production and running budgets should be attached (a much less detailed version than the one you refer to yourself) and a recoupment chart demonstrating how many weeks the production will take to recoup its capitalization at various percentages of the potential net weekly box office receipts. This is the single most significant financial factor for an investor, and a production that takes a year to recoup at 80% capacity is obviously not as good a prospect as one that takes 15 weeks to recoup at 50% capacity. The recoupment chart also identifies the break figure; the amount of money and percentage of net financial capacity that the production needs to play to in order simply to cover its fixed weekly running costs and royalties. It must be made clear that all financial projections are 'for illustrative purposes only and not a forecast' and that the actual outcome could in reality be very different to the illustrations.

You should also include information about how frequently you intend to account to investors and whether they will have the right to invest in future productions of the same show produced by you. It should be made clear that a dedicated bank account will be used to operate the production's finances, so that they won't become confused with any other business your company is undertaking at the time, and you should give the details of the firm of accountants who will be responsible for preparing the final accounts. There may also be an indication that future productions will pay back a small percentage to the original investors irrespective of whether they invest further. Although it is usually not possible to be specific about what such a percentage is likely to be, these little inducements at least show that you have the investors' long term interests at heart. It is also worth including some information about the tax situation in respect of theatre investments. Your accountant can word something appropriate, but put simply losses arising from investment in a theatrical production can be offset against any profits from investments in other shows; and that's about as good as it gets.

Whilst investors themselves have no personal tax incentive to put their money into a West End show, the production company is able to offset against tax (or in the event of a loss claim back) 20% of 80% of production costs (not running costs) excluding advertising and marketing. This increases to 25% of 80% if the production tours before or after its West End run. Investors have every right to expect it to be made clear that this corporate tax relief is to be accounted in a manner whereby they themselves can potentially benefit from it (i.e. that it effectively is treated as 'income to the production').

When drawing up your Invitation to Invest you have to decide whether or not to make your investors liable for an 'overcall' (i.e. a further contribution) in the event that funds in excess of the initial capitalization are unexpectedly required. More money may be needed due to some unforeseen circumstance such as an actor having to be replaced or simply because the producer has got their sums wrong. In this case, all investors have to be treated equally and their liability limited to a percentage of their original investment (say between 10% and 20%). Although the justification for calling on further funds can be the need to safeguard the existing investment, this can all get quite messy (smacking rather of a Lloyds of London 'bottomless pit' scenario) and thus act as a disincentive to investment in the first place. It is more likely that the Invitation will simply state that there will in no event be an obligatory overcall scenario for investors but that if the reserve fund runs out then more money can be borrowed and paid back as a first call against operating profits. It has to be said, though, that if a production is in the position of borrowing additional funds then it is highly unlikely to be one that goes on to generate a profit of any sort.

In any event, if a production's finances have got into such a mess that existing contingency and reserve funds are insufficient then the financial management skills of the producer will quite rightly be called into question. Whilst you will most likely not include an overcall liability in an Invitation to Invest, a co-production agreement with another producer who has a stake in your share of profits should most definitely include a clause to the effect that they share liability with you for contributing any necessary additional funds, in the same ratio as their percentage share of the original capitalization.

Finally there should be a very clear statement of the risk factors involved in theatrical investment. This is basically a government health warning stating that investment in theatre can severely damage your bank account. It will kick off with something like 'Theatrical production is an inherently risky business. Contributions to the Production will involve a higher level of risk than most other financial transactions and there is no probability, but only a possibility, that contributors will get back the amount which they contribute.' You should also add that although no money will be spent until the full capitalization is in the bank, there is still the possibility that the production might have to be cancelled after spending has started but before it has opened. This is an almost unheard of scenario, and it means that investors simply get back their investment less a *pari passu* share of what has actually been spent to date. It should also be noted somewhere that investors have no claim against any assets of the producer other than those of the actual production for which they are paying.

On the assumption that all of the above has not put off the potential investor completely, an 'Application to Invest' form is enclosed with the 'Invitation', which simply states that the investor is sending a cheque for whatever sum and gives their contact details. If the capitalization is already fully subscribed then their cheque will be returned (unless the show is being produced by Bialystock and Bloom!) It needs to be made clear that investment is offered on a first come first served basis, although the sad reality is that this is unlikely to be an issue unless you are one of the very few established producers whose projects are regarded as such hot prospects that there is a waiting list to invest with them. Such producers are in a position to insist that investors can only stay on their lists if they invest in all of their projects (including the less 'hot' ones) but that is a situation that a new producer can only dream of.

Financial Services legislation requires that the Invitation to Invest is rubber-stamped by an accountant or solicitor 'regulated in the conduct of investment business' (in other words, an expert) or alternatively that the investor is defined by the legislation as a 'high net worth' individual or a 'sophisticated investor'. Getting the Invitation checked over by an expert will cost a few thousand pounds but is a worthwhile exercise, particularly the first time that you issue such a document, as it means that you can be sure you have not made any mistakes in your presentation or phraseology. Nonetheless, you should draft the document yourself (copying and pasting the key phrases from another producer's document if you can get hold of one), as the wording is pretty standard and you don't want to be paying your solicitor more than you have to. The solicitor may well test the veracity of any statements you have made about the production by asking to see supporting documentation such as correspondence with the theatre, the stars of the show and other key players; effectively undertaking a 'health check' of the project on behalf of the potential investors.

Once you are confident that you know how to create one of these documents without the assistance of a qualified expert you can send them out without getting them approved provided that you only accept investment from 'high net worth' individuals or 'sophisticated investors'. If you take a look at the legal definitions of these then between them they pretty well describe the archetypal theatre investor. All you have to do is list the definitions and enclose a form that enables the investor to self-certificate that they qualify. Technically you should not accept an investment if they do not return the self-certification form, but who's to know? As a loophole, it all seems too simple, really.

Although the system for theatre investment is remarkably self-regulating given the sums and the risks involved, the Financial Services and taxation legislation that do impact on it are subject to change, and it is always worth being up to speed with the latest rules, just as you will always be up to speed with the latest union agreements.

Bigger companies with a portfolio of productions have experimented with more grandiose investment models, and the tax-efficient Enterprise Investment Scheme has also been applied with some success to raising funds for West End shows. This involves investors buying shares in a company that then undertakes a number of different investments on their behalf. It effectively disengages the individual investors from the process of selecting the shows that actually receive the finance, but offers them up-front income tax relief to the value of 30% of their investment, as well as favourable taxation arrangements for dealings in the shares themselves. But it does of course mean that errors of judgement on the part of the theatrical stockbrokers concerned can result in the losses from multiple losing investments wiping out the profits from a big winner.

Much is made these days of 'crowdfunding' via the internet, where a crowd (literally!) of *un*sophisticated investors who you have never met pledge small sums towards the financing of your project in return for merchandise items, or indeed slightly larger sums in return for standard investment terms, while the world watches you try to achieve your fundraising target and some savvy internet geek charges you for the privilege. Despite some highly publicised theatre crowdfunding exercises (the first being the ill-fated *Bernadette – The People's Musical*, way back in pre-internet 1990), I can think of few less appropriate ways to raise money for a production. Personally I would rather take my chances sitting on the Strand with a dog on a string and a sign saying 'West End show to support'.

EIS and crowdfunding aside, the methodology for raising investment described in this chapter is the result of decades of finely tuned custom and practice in commercial theatre and is still the most user-friendly if you are putting on your first show. It involves the personal engagement and support of individuals who are both arts philanthropists and sophisticated investors, and in so doing validates both the artistic and the business aspirations of your project. One way or another, all West End producers (with one notable exception) offset the financial risk on their shows to third party investors.

Most importantly, remember that theatre investors are human beings, not just a signature on a cheque. By investing in your show they have placed enormous faith in you personally as well as in your project. It is their money that is facilitating the artistic work. They know that they are unlikely to see it back, let alone achieve a profit, so their decision to part with it and their motives for doing so should be treated with respect. They have made a decision to engage with the journey of your production and they have a right to be made to feel a part of that journey. As well as invitations to the first night and access to purchasing 'house seats' they should receive regular accounts showing the financial position of the show, whether or not such accounts are accompanied by a financial 'distribution' of any sort. They should also receive regular letters keeping them up to date with the overall fortunes of the show including information about any key cast changes and so on. If the production runs into trouble and has to close then investors will be grateful if troubled waters have been flagged up at an early stage rather than receiving the news as a *fait accompli*.

Although authors and directors will most likely retain their right of casting approval throughout the run, an investor (unless also a co-producer) invests only on the basis of the original cast and has no say-so over cast takeovers and other ongoing artistic matters. It is, however, well worth keeping in touch with key investors by phone and over lunch. Whilst they have no right to dictate your course of action their opinions can often be interesting and helpful, and if they have a day job outside of the industry they will be refreshingly inclined to respond to the production as a theatregoer rather than an expert. Conversely, those from an industry background tend to be extremely knowledgeable about how it all works and will have some fascinating insider tales to tell. Above all, it is in your interests to make sure that you develop long-term relationships with investors and build up your list. Theatre investors are well aware that it is a hazardous industry, but provided that they also know that they can trust you, and provided you give them a quality experience along the way, they will most likely invest in your second project even if they lose money on your first. It is also true to say that anyone who is passionate enough about theatre to invest in it tends to make very good company, and is well worth the occasional expensive lunch.

Accounting for West End shows is structured on a weekly basis because of the imperative to cover the weekly running costs (in fact, interim accounts are often referred to as 'Weeklies'). The actual (as opposed to budgeted) running costs are shown (broken down into the budget categories) and set against the net income for the week. Any surplus is referred to as 'Weekly Operating Profit'. From the commencement of performances the production carries forward a massive loss that is the equivalent to the actual expenditure against the production budget (the 'production costs'). The 'bottom line' shows this carried-forward loss less the operating profit for the week, and the adjusted loss is then carried forward into the following week. Of course, if the net income for the week is less than the running costs then the loss will be growing rather than reducing. If the accumulated loss reaches the sum of the production costs plus the reserve fund then the production has run out of money and should close; in which case the entire capitalization (i.e. all of the investors' money) will have been lost. In reality you will also be taking into account any money that is tied up in bonds, as well as the value of advance box office sales; but in any event it is very important that the producer is able to keep their eye on the ball (by analysing forward projections of income against expenditure) to the extent that the timing of the closure does not result in any debt beyond the capitalization.

A happier set of accounts would see the carried forward loss from production costs eventually eroded by a weekly operating profit to the point where the show has recouped its capital and is in overall profit, with weekly operating profit thereafter being divided between the producer and the investors.

Of course the actual cash position of the production may vary considerably from the 'weeklies', because of the existence of bonds, deposits, option payments, a nursing fund, advances paid for equipment hire and accruals made for recasting, VAT, National Insurance (in respect of non-entertainers), pensions and holiday pay. Keeping tabs on the actual cash position of the enterprise is just as important as understanding the profit/loss position, and it may be possible to raise emergency short term loans against the underlying p&l even if the cash position is temporarily precarious. Conversely, it is important to make sure that you are not trading on cash that is actually owed to the VAT office or the Inland Revenue. The sporadic nature of distributions to investors when the production is in profit can also make the cash position difficult to keep track of, and even if the production is in profit it is standard practice to retain the sum originally stated as the reserve in the production account. In the final accounts any unspent reserve remaining, including any returned deposits and bonds, will simply count as 'income to the production' and will be applied accordingly.

Although most productions will quickly establish themselves as 'hit' or 'miss' the financial fortunes of a show can change almost overnight and decisions do sometimes have to be taken very quickly, particularly given the 'two weeks' notice' regime on the key contracts. For this reason it is critical that the producer is fully conversant at all times not only with both the current p&l and cash positions of their show but also with the projected scenario in respect of both for at least the next eight weeks. When important decisions have to be made, such as whether or not to recast or whether or not to extend the contract with the theatre, the accounts and both long and short term projections will be the key factors. Such is the trust that the investors (and indeed everyone else involved) place in the producer that it is the producer's sole decision when to close the show (subject to the relevant clauses in the theatre contract). Often it is better to quit while you are ahead, and closing the show while it is a relatively going concern can sometimes result in higher dividends for the investors than if money that might otherwise have been distributed to them from the pot is used up supporting a declining box office scenario.

If you can see trouble ahead and you think it is not worth spending the money on a recast as you head into a difficult time of year (such as Easter with its series of bank holidays or the summer with its decline in the domestic market) then it can be worth getting out while the going is good and before you actually do start playing well below the 'break'. If you are not actually playing below the break then the theatre owner will have to agree with your analysis in order to release you from your contract, but they may well have a better offer from another producer up their sleeves in any case.

The ability to interpret box office results and to project box office outcomes for future weeks is critical to your ongoing financial management of the production. It's not rocket science, but the large number of different data print-out formats from different box offices can be a bit confusing at first. The advent of computerised box offices means that a wealth of helpful information is at your disposal although it is often shocking just how little the people who actually operate the computers concerned seem to understand about the information they are processing. The most straightforward figures to monitor, of course, are the matured gross and net sales figures for each performance (as against the previous day's and the performance on the same day the previous week) and for each week (as against the previous week). Equally important to the ongoing health of your production is the amount of money actually taken in sales at the box office each day (sometimes referred to as the 'wrap') as compared with the equivalent figure for the previous day and with that of the same day the week before. The daily wrap includes sales made for that day's performance ('door sales') as well as money taken for future performances. The success of a show is often gauged by its 'advance' (the total carried forward gross advance sales figure for performances that have not yet matured). Producers are prone to brag to each other about the size of their advances, although it is important to monitor exactly how the advance is split over future performances; good advance sales stacking up in a month's time may be irrelevant if you can't pay the bills next week.

You will soon come to recognise sales patterns such as those specific to weekends, matinee days and bank holidays, as well as seasonal variations if you are lucky enough to be producing a long-runner. You'll also begin to recognise other quirks; for instance, the gross carried forward advance can drop over the weekend as busy performances mature and the wrap fails to keep pace, and the mid-week wrap can slow down if the forthcoming weekend performances are sold out. All of this information is mathematically interlinked in a way that only really becomes apparent with practice, and if it seems a bit mind-boggling on the page, rest assured that it all becomes self-evident very quickly when you have a living, breathing production on your hands. All of these indicators are your navigational tools as you steer your production through the perilous waters of the

West End and take the crucial decision at the end of every week whether to carry on or to close. Take your eye off the ball for even a moment and you can very quickly find yourself with your nursing fund spent and insufficient finance available to meet your show's running costs.

The final accounts of the production will probably be sent out to investors around ten weeks after the show closes. These should be properly audited and will show the entire history of the production. Investors do not like to be kept waiting for final accounts, particularly if they have lost all or some of their money, and unnecessary delays may make it look like you are trying to cook the books. It is good to add the personal touch of a covering letter of thanks to investors when the accounts are distributed, whatever the financial outcome. The cost of preparing the final accounts, along with any legal assistance you have received in preparing investment documentation, should be included in the production budget.

It is acceptable to include a certain amount of 'development costs' in your production budget if you are producing a new play or musical. This can include such things as script development workshops, play readings, commissioning fees and even hospitality relating to the creation of the piece. All of this may originally have been paid for by borrowed funds, which are then paid back out of the capitalization. Those who have provided such funds will have done so on the high risk basis that they will only get repaid if the production actually goes ahead, and may have been offered a small part of the producer's 40% of profits or the producer's royalty as a thank you for coming in with this essential seed money. Instead of having their loans repaid out of the capital it is legitimate for them to convert them into 'free' units in the show, provided that these sums are shown as part of the production budget and therefore the capitalization. For instance, if someone has given you a loan of £30,000 to finance script workshops for the production, and this sum is shown in the production budget sent to investors as development costs then, if they are agreeable, this person could be awarded six £5,000 units instead of having their loan repaid out of the capitalization. In reality, anyone who has been enthusiastic enough about your project to support you in this way is more than likely to be happy to receive units in lieu of repayment. What you cannot do is to offer them terms on their units that are in any way preferential to those offered to the other investors, unless of course such inducement comes out of your own share.

Although raising hundreds of thousands of pounds may sound a bit daunting at first it's not as difficult as it may seem, provided that you have an exciting project with some marketable talent attached to it. Let's say you are looking for £300,000 to capitalize a small play. If you're starting out on your first West End show then the best first move is usually to persuade a couple of established producers to take 25% each of the capital on '100% terms'; in return for raising a quarter of the capital, each will be assigned a quarter of the Producer's 40% share of potential profits. That reduces your share of potential profits to 20% of the total, but it leaves you with the majority producer stake and means you only have £150,000 left to find. Even though you will be the one actually managing the production, it is reasonable to give your new partners a share of your management fees (and maybe even your producer royalty) in return for getting you off the starting blocks. If one of them is happy to vouch for you then you won't have to lodge payroll bonds, unless of course you specifically want to build up a track record of doing so yourself. They should also have access to the SOLT Angels list, so if you can persuade them to mail the list on the production's behalf then that could put maybe £50,000 in the kitty, half of which should be accountable on your side of the equation (leaving you with £125,000 to find). Once you've raised the rest of the finance then you should be able to get the

last £15,000 of the total capital from Stage One. It's only fair
to account the Stage One money equally with your partners, so
in the meantime you have £117,500 left to find. That's twenty-
three and a half units of £5,000. Let's say you can probably
off-load ten and a half of these to contacts of the writer, actors
and creative team and maybe two to the owner of your theatre.
One of your equipment suppliers may take a unit, and maybe
also your marketing agency; remember, they'll be keen to build
a relationship with a new producer. Now get out there and see
if you can find one single-unit investor and a couple of big fish
for four units each. And then you're done. Fully capitalized at
£300,000. That wasn't so painful, was it? Good luck.

4. HOW TO HIRE
A THEATRE FOR A WEST END SHOW

'If Theatreland did not already exist, it could not now be
created… It is in everyone's interests to ensure that these
theatres remain in the ownership and control of bodies
whose raison d'être is theatre, and not the maximisation
of profit through some other use.'

– The Theatres Trust *Act Now!* Report, 2003

In theatrical circles, a 'West End' theatre is usually taken to
mean one of around forty commercially operated central
London venues which are full members of SOLT and which
for the most part are 'receiving houses' (i.e. do not produce
their own work). SOLT also represents, amongst others, the
major opera and ballet houses, the National Theatre, the Royal
Court, the Old Vic and the boutique producing house The
Donmar. A number of smaller high-profile producing theatres
are 'affiliate' members of the organisation. SOLT changed its
name from the Society of West End Theatre in 1994 in order
to acknoweldge the fact that the building-based part of its
membership extended to venues beyond the accepted definition
of 'West End'. Confusingly, venues such as the Leicester Square
Theatre and Arts Theatre, which are located in the centre of the
geographical West End, are not technically West End Theatres
although producers working in them sometimes style them
as such and given their location it would be difficult to make
objection under the Trade Descriptions Act.

Alongside all of this, London benefits from a thriving and
totally unregulated Fringe, greatly assisted by the number of

publicans who are willing to hire out their premises' cramped back rooms to would-be impresarios. Although *Time Out* magazine has coined the phrase 'Off-West End' to describe a number of reasonably sized and well located non-West End theatres, together with a few high-profile fringe venues, this attempt to corral London's anarchic theatre scene along the lines of New York's strictly union-dictated definitions of 'Broadway' and 'Off Broadway' is really little more than whimsy. In New York, one of the main reasons for the existence of Off Broadway, I am sure, is simply because it is so difficult and so expensive to produce *on* Broadway. In London, when it comes to theatre, just about anything goes; but of the vast range of buildings which play host to an extraordinary variety of work, it is the West End theatres which are iconic.

Although the West End's building stock contains some extraordinary historic gems such as the Theatre Royal Drury Lane and the Theatre Royal Haymarket, much of it was constructed in the nineteenth and early twentieth centuries. Once the ornate facades of these dusty Victorian and Edwardian edifices have tempted audiences through their doors, their decorous interior designs often struggle to distract from cramped seating, questionable sightlines and acoustics and limited front of house space for foyers, bars and toilets. Performers and crew usually do not fare much better, with backstage areas and dressing rooms spartan at best and stage facilities struggling to keep pace with the latest technology. Although these buildings offer a wide range of seating capacities (from the 408 seat Ambassadors to the 2,286 seat Palladium) the vast majority of them are configured as traditional end-on proscenium arch spaces, which severely restricts the nature of the work that can be presented in them.

Hugely expensive to maintain and totally lacking in the customer experience enhancement facilities (such as car parks and restaurants) that are essentials of all modern theatre builds, these anachronistic money-pits occupy some of the most sought-after urban locations in the Western world and owe their continued existence to a great extent to their status as 'listed' buildings. If the government did not obligingly decree that these crumbling monuments to a bygone era of theatre-going were of lasting historical and architectural significance, then the ground that they occupy would doubtless be redeployed to far more lucrative endeavours than theatre production and the entire commercial theatre industry in London could potentially disappear overnight. Listed building status is a double-edged sword, of course, and those West End theatre owners who can actually afford to finance improvements, and to go 'dark' for long enough to carry them out, often find themselves severely restricted by the very legislation that ensures the buildings' continued existence. The planning policies of the two local authorities concerned, Westminster and Camden, also continue to ensure that 'change of use' is not an option.

The Theatres Trust plays an invaluable role in lobbying for the preservation of theatre buildings and advising on planning applications that involve them; although arguably the romantic attachment to these buildings that has successfully been fostered in the British public can sometimes obscure the fact that, however beautiful a theatre building may be as a piece of architecture, it is simply a functional space the purpose of which is to deliver theatrical productions to an audience.

Or is it? If theatre is indeed a collective endeavour where the whole is greater than the sum of the parts then why should it not also include the ghosts of performers and audiences past? What performer would not be spurred on to greater endeavour by the knowledge that they are treading the same boards as Irving or Olivier? What audience would not feel a sense of privilege that they were enjoying an Oscar Wilde play from the same auditorium as the audience that witnessed its premiere? Theatre buildings connect us with our past as well as our future, and for all their frustrating impracticalities and contradictions, these faded *grandes dames* of the West End, with their *faux* glamour and alluring neon-lit facades, lend a theatrical spirituality to any performance that is undoubtedly lacking from 'new build' theatres, for all their technological wizardry and customer-friendly facilities. On one side of the Thames sits the austere edifice of the National Theatre, with its massive foyers, waterside walkways, comfortable seating, restaurants, bookshops, rehearsal rooms, workshops, labyrinthine backstage areas and flexible performance spaces. On the other side, the cramped and crumbling West End theatres stand like beacons in a Dantesque maelstrom of gaudy clip joints, incessant roadworks, grid-locked traffic, drunken office parties, overflowing dustbins, over-crowded pavements, muggers, pools of vomit and discarded hypodermics.

The recent partial collapse of a Shaftesbury Avenue theatre's ceiling during a performance has reignited the conflict between historicity and functionality as regards the buildings in which West End shows are presented. And yet the strange, mystical allure of 'London's glittering West End' will never fade, and there will always be a very special sense of excitement amongst theatre practitioners when they hear that their show is heading there. Unlike on Broadway, it is very rare for a West End theatre to go dark, and there is usually a queue of projects waiting to 'come in to town'.

With a few exceptions, West End theatre buildings tend not to be particularly lucrative assets. They are very high-maintenance, development opportunities are severely limited and their fortunes are linked to the success or otherwise of the shows that they host. Owning a West End theatre therefore usually forms part of a wider business strategy, and a complicated network of freeholds and long and short leases means that the market is a volatile one and that changes in ownership are frequent. It would be true to say that at time of writing West End theatres tend to be owned by 'theatre' people rather than 'property' people, although this has not always been the case. Theatre ownership works on the 'strength in numbers' principle, so most West End theatres are part of a chain. This means that overheads can be kept to a minimum by managing a group of theatres from a central office and moving key staff around between them. It also means that a profitable theatre in the group can support an unprofitable or a dark one if necessary. West End theatres are run as commercial business ventures, although as a business it is extremely volatile and precarious, and theatre owners have in the past made a case that they should receive some form of government support in return for maintaining these historic buildings and accepting the limitations that their 'listed' status places on the operation of their business.

Most West End theatres are technically available for hire, so if you want to put on a West End show then all you have to do is phone up one of the organisations that owns them and ask which theatres they have available and when. SOLT can advise you as to the current ownership status of each theatre building. Once you have agreed on the theatre and the dates you then enter into a hire contract with the theatre owner. They become your landlord and you become their tenant. It is technically no different to hiring the village hall to put on an amateur production, except that the amounts of money involved are much bigger, the stakes are higher and, of course, it is not quite that simple.

Before you sign a West End theatre contract it is worth pausing and asking yourself 'why'? Is your production really suitable for presentation in a West End theatre? Is it physically suited to the space? Will it stand up to scrutiny by the national critics? Is it likely to attract an audience? Have you really got enough money in the kitty? Would your production ultimately be better off in a fringe or Off-West End space, or on tour?

There is no point at all in putting a show into the West End just because a theatre happens to be available. If anything about it doesn't feel exactly right then trust your instincts and step back from it. There will always be other opportunities.

The first problem you will encounter is that over a third of West End theatres are occupied by long-running productions which show no sign of giving up their tenancies. The second is that the 'theatre people' who now own the West End theatre chains are themselves theatre producers, so they will keep all the best slots in the best theatres for themselves. The membership of SOLT is no longer divided between theatre owners and producers so much as between 'producers who own theatres' and 'producers who don't own theatres' (or 'independent' producers), and there will obviously be many agendas at work given that your landlord may suddenly want to take over the theatre you are hiring from them in order to present one of their own projects. It is not a bad business model to be both landlord and tenant (bearing in mind that it is third party investors who pay for the actual productions), and these theatre-owning producers effectively control both the means of production (the shows or, if you like, the 'software') and the means of distribution (the theatres or, if you like, the 'hardware') within the industry. The monopoly principle works well in theatre, and particularly in the West End where the marketplace is limited by the finite number of available buildings. But before you rush out and buy up a load of West End theatre leases remember that those who do this are playing the game at the very highest level and tend to have a wide range of high-end shows in their repertoire to fill those product-hungry theatre spaces. Even they can get badly caught out when shows close suddenly or fail to materialise, and it is true to say that 'the larger they are the harder they fall'. There is no worse nightmare for a theatre owner than a 'dark' theatre where the staff and the overheads still have to be paid, and there are still surprisingly plentiful opportunities for resourceful 'independent' producers to hire West End theatres; even those buildings that are usually associated with work produced by their owners. In any event, most theatre owners will prefer to hedge their bets by filling some of their theatres with their own work and some with work produced by tenants. Ultimately the theatre spaces themselves are essentially 'bricks and mortar', available for hire to the highest (or the most convincing) bidder.

There is a misapprehension amongst some of the public and also, I believe, in some parts of government, that West End theatres are as a matter of course responsible for the creation of the shows that they house in the same way that the major subsidised theatres are. But even if your landlord does have their own producing interests these will be, at least on paper, entirely separate to the operation of their buildings. And although they may appear to be a user-friendly 'theatre person' it's worth considering where your landlord might have obtained the funds from to make these expensive investments in real estate. He who pays the piper ultimately calls the tune, after all; and we are only ever a few carefully choreographed steps away from the tune that the West End dances to becoming the City's.

The fact that SOLT counts both 'owners' and 'independents' amongst its paid-up membership is a significant Achilles heel when it comes to creating coherent policy for the industry and representing its interests to both government and the unions. Over the last ten years there have been significant steps to democratise the organisation and encourage emerging producers to join, helped by a relaxation in the previously draconian membership criteria. Nonetheless, the entrenched interests of 'bricks and mortar' weigh heavily on its political infrastructure, an imbalance that the newly formed League of Independent Producers aims to address. Watch this space.

Because of all these vested interests it is particularly important to make sure that you are not being sold a pup and that your show is not being used to fill in at a duff time of year (such as the summer months) until something better comes along or the owner puts in one of their own shows. Or if your show *is* being used for that purpose then at least make sure that you are aware of this and that you negotiate an appropriate rent deal. There are occasions when a theatre owner will need a show at short notice, at a bad time of year, or as a filler when they have booked something else in advance that won't be opening for a few months. If you have a show that fits the bill then remember that everything is negotiable and that they probably need you more than you need them. Above all, beware of theatre owners bearing gifts. Although it is extremely flattering the first time a West End theatre owner offers you a three-month run on full rent commencing in June, just say 'no'.

Another big problem with booking a West End theatre is timing. In order to attract a good cast and creative team and the investment that you need, your actors, creatives and investors will want some indication that you have a suitable theatre lined up. The theatre owner in turn will want to know that you have a cast and creative team, and most importantly for them the money, before committing to hiring their theatre to you. West End theatres are difficult to book a long time in advance, as the hope is usually that the show which is the current tenant will continue to run (unless it has been intentionally booked in as a 'limited season'). When a production looks like it is in trouble the landlord will start provisional negotiations with a number of potential new tenants, in the hope that one of them will be in a position to provide a replacement at exactly the right moment (sometimes at no more than a few weeks' notice) and without the theatre having to go dark for longer than it takes to get one show out and the next one in. It's a bit like aeroplanes waiting for a runway at Heathrow Airport. For the producer this means that they are constantly having to negotiate on a 'provisional' basis on a number of fronts pretty well simultaneously in order to bring everything together (cast, creative team, finance and venue) at just the right moment. It has to be said that this is not an experience for the faint hearted and that if this sort of thing keeps you awake at night then producing is probably not for you.

This is one of the main reasons why so little work is actually created directly for the West End and why the majority of West End shows are actually pre-produced transfers from other venues or the touring circuit, whose dates just happen to coincide with the availability of a West End theatre. Of course, if your show is such a hot property that a theatre owner can be persuaded to wait for it then you can pre-book a theatre occupied by a failing show for a particular date several months in advance and enjoy the luxury of some planning time. The landlord could then artificially extend the life of the existing tenant's show by offering them a rent discount until you are ready to come in, could fill in the intervening time with a 'limited season' or could choose to go dark for a short but finite period. One thing for sure is that if you have succeeded in persuading a theatre owner to wait for your show in this way then you will be paying them full rent when you do eventually turn up. If you do not have a track record as a producer then it is fair enough for the landlord to expect you to pay some sort of 'holding' deposit, to be offset against your rent, in order to secure the theatre a long time in advance, although this sum should not exceed the equivalent of six weeks' rent.

There is a myth that some West End theatres are 'graveyard' theatres that only ever host flops. It is true that the location of certain theatres (particularly those on Shaftesbury Avenue) can potentially enhance the box office take by up to 10% because of the visibility of their signage and the volume of passing trade; and some star performers will be fussy about which theatres they appear in (no one ever turns down the opportunity to appear at the gloriously appointed and defiantly independent Theatre Royal, Haymarket). But ultimately a West End Theatre is only as good as the show that is in it. Nobody goes (or doesn't go) to a West End show because of the theatre where it's on, and the reputation of a 'graveyard' theatre can be transformed overnight if it becomes the home of a hit. So don't be swayed in your choice of theatre by whether it has hosted a string of hits or a string of flops in recent years. It is far more important that your show fits comfortably onto the stage, that the size of the auditorium suits the nature of the production and that the potential box office receipts are sufficient to recoup your costs. Other than that, if your show is any good then build it and they will come.

The holy grail of West End theatre producing is to book an open-ended run at a theatre of exactly the right size to serve your production's artistic and financial needs, six months in advance of the opening date. Even better if that opening date happens to be early October; when the schools have gone back, nights are drawing in, the weather's getting colder, there are no bank holidays on the immediate horizon, advance bookings for the Christmas period can boost your box office and you stand half a chance of still being on when the Olivier Award nominations are announced. Like the holy grail, however, this ideal scenario tends to prove somewhat elusive.

Everything in theatre is negotiable and the theatre contract is no exception. Although you will be presented with 'our standard contract', and eyebrows will be raised if you question the small print, you should feel confident to challenge anything in a theatre agreement that you don't like. Much of the detail has grown up through custom and practice over decades and remains enshrined in these documents simply because nobody can be bothered to question it. Sometimes a fresh pair of eyes can be a good thing and can lead to unexpected results. Above all, you need to be clear at the outset whether your negotiating position is a strong or a weak one. Do you have a product that will potentially keep a theatre open for a long period of time? Is there more than one theatre landlord interested in your show, so that you can play them off against each other? Are you doing the landlord a favour by filling a 'difficult' slot or bailing them out at short notice? In any event, be aware that negotiations with theatre landlords often have to be treated with a degree of confidentiality, as their current tenant may not be aware that the writing is on the wall for them. It is common practice to use a theatre that you are in negotiation with as an 'illustration' for budget and investment models, but you should never imply that you are going to be presenting your show in a particular theatre until you have the owner's express permission to do so. It is a very small industry; news travels fast, and you must be sensitive to the fact that your good news (your show is opening) is likely to be somebody else's bad news (their show is closing).

The money that you will have to pay the theatre on a weekly basis is split into two sections; the 'rent' and the 'contra'. You will be charged VAT (which you can of course reclaim) on both. The theatre owner will have you believe that the contra is the cost of actually running the building (staffing, rates, utilities, etc.) and is therefore non-negotiable. However, these costs are usually marked up to a certain extent and it is worth querying every element of the detail. It will still be better for the landlord if you are paying a negotiated, reduced contra than if they go dark and have no income at all to cover their running costs. Although the 'dark costs' of a theatre are less than the running costs when it is open they are still substantial. For the landlord a dark theatre is the equivalent of leaving a taxi standing idle with the metre running and is something to be avoided if a deal of any sort can be struck with a producer. On the basis that the 'contra' allegedly represents the running costs of the theatre when it has a show in it, it follows that the 'rent' represents the landlord's weekly profit. The landlord will doubtless have some central office overheads to cover out of the rent and they will also need to accrue funds to cover running costs in any dark periods, but the rent should be a negotiable item and it is always worth questioning the first 'rate card' figure that you are given. In any event, the rent should be considerably less than the contra; although the bigger the theatre the smaller proportionally the difference is likely to be.

The terms of the theatre contract are based on the premise that you are providing the show, the landlord is providing the theatre and you are paying for both. The landlord will provide all of the ushers and bar staff and will be responsible for making sure the building and its fixtures and fittings are cleaned and well maintained. You'll have to warrant to the landlord that you have the necessary rights to present the show and that it does not contain anything illegal; they'll have to warrant to you that they have the necessary licences to present live entertainment. Everyone will have to warrant to each other that they have the necessary insurance policies in place in respect of employees, the public and damage to property.

The theatre will require that you perform a standard eight-show week, usually Monday-Saturday with a midweek (usually Wednesday or Thursday) and Saturday matinee, but it is up to you to set the exact performance times. Evening shows in the West End usually start at 7.30pm, 7.45pm or 8pm and you need to decide what best suits your production, bearing in mind the running time of your show and the fact that audiences may like to grab a pre-theatre dinner at a restaurant beforehand and will need to grapple with the living hell that is the London transport system on the way home. Ticket prices will also be up to you, and you will need to set a top price that reflects the costs of your production whilst being competitive with other West End shows of a similar nature and allowing for the fact that many of the ticket sales will be through discount outlets.

You will normally take occupancy of the theatre as soon as the previous tenant has left, and this may well involve paying premium work rates to crew to get the show in on a Sunday, as your aim is to complete the get-in, technical rehearsal and dress rehearsal as quickly as possible so that you can start generating some income by playing to the paying public. From the moment your contract starts the 'taxi standing with the meter running' ceases to be the landlord's problem and becomes yours. There are very few shows that cannot complete this process in time to open to the public for preview performances in the second half of the first week of the tenancy.

Although it is fair enough to pay a full contra once you take occupancy of the building, you should make sure that you do not pay any rent for the part of the production week in which there are no performances. The contra charge for the get-in period may well in fact be larger than for a standard performance week if your production manager has decided to engage additional temporary get-in crew via the theatre to help unload the lorries and put up the set. There may well also be some theatre staff overtime payments during this period, and it is important that you work closely with your production manager to undertake a cost/benefit analysis of whether the outlay for additional staff working longer hours is likely to be compensated for by the potential revenue from getting the production in front of the public at the earliest opportunity. Despite the inevitable protests of your director and creative team, it is usually the most cost-effective strategy to minimise the number of days that you occupy the theatre at the start of the engagement without actually giving a performance.

Arguably more important than the opening date is the closing date. Most productions aspire to an 'open ended' run as it is easier to attract investment on this basis. A 'limited season' by definition also limits the extent of the potential return to the investors. Even if you are engaging in a limited season (i.e. with a specified end date), it is essential that you are not persuaded by the landlord to 'guarantee' a particular length of run over and above the absolute minimum. Many landlords will, sadly, take advantage of inexperienced producers by implying that the theatre can only be made available to them if they guarantee a run of several months. This is sharp practice, as theatre finance is generally not structured in a way that can sustain running losses over a long period of time, and entering into such an agreement, particularly when the rent for the period is paid up front, is little more than a fast track to bankruptcy. In any event, you should under no circumstances ever guarantee to a theatre owner that you will run your show for more than six weeks.

The key terms to look out for are 'Take-off figure', 'Shortfall weeks' and 'Notice weeks'. The take-off figure, which you provide to the landlord, is the equivalent of the net weekly box office income (i.e. after VAT, credit card commissions and the like) that you need to achieve in order to cover your royalties (for writer and creative team) and your fixed weekly running costs. In other words, the 'break'. For the purposes of ascertaining this figure the production costs which your investors have capitalized are ignored. Either you or the landlord can give the other notice of an agreed number of weeks (the 'notice weeks') following an agreed number of consecutive weeks in which the 'Take-off figure' has not been achieved at the box office (the 'shortfall weeks'). If your production is not covering at least its weekly running costs from the weekly box office income then you will want to minimise your losses and quit as quickly as possible, so it is usual for the producer to press for no more than two weeks' notice (the minimum that you are allowed in turn to give to your actors and other staff) following no more than two shortfall weeks. The production week in which there are fewer performances, preview period where ticket prices are lower and press night week where you will be giving a number of tickets away (and are waiting to assess the critical response) are not counted as shortfall weeks, and these should therefore be listed as 'excepted weeks' (along with other weeks with unusual performance patterns such as Christmas week). On a model where you give your press night in the week after the get-in, week three of the run therefore becomes the first week that can be counted as a shortfall week and the Saturday of week four (once you have the week's box office results in) becomes the first day on which you can give two weeks' notice (notice is usually given on a Saturday).

You have thus in effect that you have guaranteed the landlord that you will pay to occupy the theatre for a period of no more than six weeks; the two excepted weeks at the start of the run plus 'two weeks under and two weeks out'. Your 'reserve fund' in your production budget should be sufficient to nurse the show through this period (in particular covering the losses that you will inevitably sustain in the get-in, preview and press weeks) and in the event of a complete disaster you will be able to draw down deposits you have placed with the entertainment unions in order to cover the last two weeks' wages. Of course the landlord also has the right to give you notice on the same basis, though if a show is struggling in its early weeks but is getting good reviews and demonstrably has sufficient nursing funds available to it then they would be shooting themselves in the foot by enforcing its closure, and you are most likely mutually to agree to keep it running for a while (unless the landlord is particularly ruthless, has been monitoring the way things are going since the show went on sale and already has an alternative lined up). If you give notice to the landlord then you undertake not to present the show in another West End theatre for a given period of time following the closure, which is fair enough. It may sound unduly pessimistic to focus on the terms to be agreed with the landlord for closing the show at the outset of negotiations, but this is where mistakes are most often made, and these terms are fundamental to landlord/tenant dealings in the West End.

You should be as accurate as possible in providing your 'take off' figure to the theatre. Although a temporary strategic advantage may be gained by either exaggerating or reducing the actual figure, the maths work best in the long run if the contractually declared figure is correct. Your landlord may well end up being an investor in your production, or at least is likely to know someone who is, so you should in any case work on the basis that they will have access to your show's accounts one way or another. If your run is open-ended then annual increases in the rent and contra will be specified, and the landlord will retain the right to give you notice under certain other circumstances, such as an urgent need to repair the building or the persistent failure of your star actor to turn up for work. You may have to undertake in the contract that certain 'named artists' will be appearing in the production and state the period for which they are contracted. There may also be contract renewal dates specified which coincide with cast changes and/or new booking periods going on sale to the public.

When you hire a West End theatre it is not technically a 'four walls' deal; you are not actually given the keys, or indeed access to the whole building. Generally the production's use of the space will be limited to the use of the stage and the dressing rooms for the purpose of performances and rehearsals, and only during the standard working hours of the resident staff. The front of house areas, box office, foyers, bars and offices will be reserved for the use of the landlord. All income derived from the cloakrooms and from bar, refreshment and programme sales will be to the sole benefit of the landlord and there is no point in arguing against this, even though most of the content of the programme is provided by the producer. You will get the income from any show-related merchandise that you have created but the theatre landlord will charge you a hefty commission for getting their staff to sell it. Most importantly, the landlord will insist that there is an interval in your production to allow them to maximise bar and ice cream sales. If you fail to provide them with an interval then they will charge you a 'no interval fee' of several thousand pounds a week to compensate them for their lost earnings. Not surprisingly there are very few occasions where an 'artistic requirement' that there be no interval outweighs the financial imperative that there should be one. If your director says that the piece needs to be played without an interval then you should politely suggest to them that they might like to pay the 'no interval fee' out of their royalty.

Although the language of the theatre contract will be such that the box office income belongs to the theatre, the net weekly box office receipts are effectively paid over to the producer, usually on the Friday following the week of performances to which they apply. Unlike many touring theatres, West End theatres are prompt and meticulous when it comes to remitting box office receipts to the producer. The theatre will deduct the rent and contra from the box office revenue before handing it over, and if it is not sufficient to cover these items will send you a bill for the difference. The real shock is the difference between the gross receipts (i.e. the money paid by the customers) and the net receipts (i.e. the money paid over to the producer after various deductions). As well as deducting VAT from the ticket price and handing it over to the government (which is the theatre's legal obligation) they will deduct the value of any refunds, dishonoured payments and third-party agent commissions, which is all fair enough. What is *not* fair enough is that the theatre will most probably charge you a commission for sales made through their own 'ticket centre' and website, ranging from 4% (of what's left after the deduction of VAT) for an individual ticket to 10% for a group sales ticket, *plus* a fixed rate for debit and credit card transactions of another few per cent irrespective of the rates actually charged by the individual credit card companies, *plus* a 'per ticket' charge of more than 20p. This is *in addition* to the booking fees, transaction fees and postage charges (often amounting to several pounds per ticket) being paid by the customer on top of the advertised price. They'll also pocket at least a pound from the customer by way of a 'theatre restoration levy' (irrespective of the actual age or condition of the theatre) just for good measure. Given the state of some of the West End theatres, a little more transparency about exactly how this restoration levy is spent would be appreciated by both their tenants and their customers. A code of conduct, set down by the Committee of Advertising Practice and monitored by the Advertising Standards Authority, at least attempts to encourage clarity in the way that the box office's (or ticket agent's) booking fees are advertised to the customer. But you'll have to scour your landlord's contractual small print very carefully to ascertain the sometimes substantial additional charges that are levied by the theatre from the producer in respect of ticketing.

Somewhere along the line, theatre owners have cottoned on to the fact that the old-fashioned box office with its colourful seating plan charts and pigeon holes full of ticket books could be transformed into a profit centre. This development has been greatly assisted by the concentration of theatre ownership into chains, which enables each owner to operate a centralised phone room selling tickets for multiple theatres; essentially a ticket agent to which all telephone sales are automatically directed and which neither the customer nor the producer has any option but to use. So blatant is this system that some chains even go so far as to set up their central box office resource as a separately identifiable 'ticketing company'. One might expect that the centralising of the box office function in this manner would actually reduce overheads and thereby also the cost of each transaction; but we are repeatedly assured that the extensive investment in computer technology that it entails, not to mention the skills required by an army of unemployed actors pretending that they are answering the phone in the box office at 'such and such a theatre' when its name flashes up on their console, more than justifies the additional charges levied in respect of this 'enhancement of the customer experience'.

The sadness is that when the public complain about the price of a theatre ticket they have no idea just how much is being deducted by way of tax, commissions, charges, fees and levies before the money actually reaches the producer to pay for the show they are watching. As a producer you have some say in the proportion of the theatre's sales commissions that is absorbed by you as a deduction from the ticket price as against the proportion that is paid by the customer as a 'booking fee' over and above the price. The more successful the show is the less of a disincentive to sales these charges will be and the more confident the producer will therefore be to pass at least some of them directly on to the customer. But one way or another there is no escaping them, and either directly or indirectly they represent a significant percentage of the total price that the customer ends up paying for the ticket. By contrast, the small weekly levy that your show will pay to SOLT (in addition to your own membership fee), via yet another deduction from box office receipts, seems like remarkably good value.

As if all this were not onerous enough, the theatre reserves to themselves the income from certain specified seats that are designated as 'private property seats' ('PP seats'); perhaps up to a dozen top price seats per performance in an average sized playhouse. These seats somehow always manage to get sold first and do not show up on the box office statements submitted by the theatre to the producer every week. This means that they do not form part of the calculation of net box office receipts upon which royalty payments are based, so it is writers, directors, designers and star performers as well as the producer and their investors who are losing out. And yet the whole industry remains remarkably acquiescent as the theatre owner quietly siphons off several thousand pounds a week from the box office takings of a show without having to account to the producer for a penny of it. This is something akin to the slots at the side of a fairground arcade's shove ha'penny machine, down which numerous coins mysteriously disappear before they reach the dispenser at the front. There is no denying that West End theatres are cripplingly expensive to own and operate; but it would ultimately be more transparent, and therefore much easier to budget and operate the finances of a show, if the landlords fixed rents that clearly reflected this rather than resorting to these seemingly underhand tactics to cream off a few extra bob at every opportunity from both the producer and the customer. Some theatre owners are worse than others when it comes to all this. You'll soon discover which.

Tedious though it may be, it is worth going through the 'sample contra' that you will be given line by line to ascertain exactly which 'running costs' of the theatre are being recharged to you. The biggest category of recharges will be for staffing; everything from the theatre manager to the stage door keeper, plus of course the resident technical crew ('carpenters' and electricians). Plus employer's National Insurance and pension contributions, holiday pay and so forth for all of the above. Ironically you will also find yourself paying for box office staff. These are not the centralised phone room operatives but the people who work in the booth in the foyer and whose function is to provide a service to the few remaining customers who elect to avoid booking and transaction fees by walking in off the street and purchasing their ticket over the counter. Hopefully they may also pay in cash so that you can avoid credit card charges as well as the central phone room's commission. These staff also organise the distribution of pre-booked tickets to customers who are collecting them 'on the door'. You will also have to pay for utilities, air conditioning, rates, buildings insurance, your Company Manager's telephone usage and Wi-Fi access, pest control, council licences, cleaning contractors and supplies, light bulbs for the foyer, and any number of other items. It is usually worth querying any 'maintenance' charges on the basis that the customer is already paying around £1 per ticket towards 'theatre restoration' and the two headings can sometimes become a bit blurred. It is worth seeing if you can strike a deal to 'fix' the contra charges at a certain level based on the sample contra so that you can budget accordingly and avoid any nasty surprises. This will of course be subject to increase in line with any industry-wide union pay rises.

When it comes to the 'resident' technical crew make sure that your production manager checks exactly what staff the theatre are providing before you sign anything. On paper it may look as if there are sufficient crew provided by the theatre to operate your show on a nightly basis, but the arcane working practices and bizarre division of labour and scheduling protocols that prevail backstage in West End theatres mean that it can almost literally take three people to change a light bulb (one on duty, one off duty and one on holiday). You'll get (and pay for) what you're given at the end of the day, but any additional staff ('show staff') that are actually required to make your production function technically will be a further item on the contra over and above the resident staff shown on the sample contra.

The theatre contract will make provision for working co-operatively on marketing and health and safety issues, all of which makes good sense. If you are taking out advertising for your show then it's important to ensure that the theatre's box office details are correctly displayed (you'll probably also have to display your landlord's corporate logo) and indeed to ensure that the box office computer system has actually been programmed to sell your tickets by the time your 'announcement' press release is distributed. The landlord may be able to make useful databases and mailing lists available to you and may be able to provide further valuable marketing support via media and supplier contacts. On the production side, their resident stage staff can be particularly helpful in ensuring that your set and equipment are installed in a manner that is compliant with current licensing and health and safety regulations and it is worth engaging them in this process at an early stage. For better or for worse, and whatever you think of some of the contractual, financial and working practices involved, your relationship with the theatre and its employees is central to ensuring that your show is a hit. On a day to day basis your team has to interact successfully with theirs in order to deliver the product to the customer, and it is important to remember that the customer's experience is not just of your show but of a whole 'night at the theatre', which will include how well looked after they are by the box office, the bar staff and the ushers. Whilst you can't do anything about extortionate bar prices or cramped, squeaky seats located behind pillars, you can do your best to make sure that everyone working in the theatre feels that they are a valued part of a single team and that they share a sense of personal investment in the success of the show.

All of this is of course taken from the perspective of an independent producer hiring a theatre from a theatre owner. A cynic might marvel at the alternative but increasingly prevalent business model whereby third-party investors have been persuaded by a producer to invest millions in a project which then hands over full rent and contra payments to a theatre owner, not to mention bar, programme and ice cream profits, interest accrued on advance box office receipts and a hefty commission just for selling the tickets. And this producer, who may well be making a weekly management fee despite the fact that the investors have not yet been repaid their capital, happens to be none other than the theatre owner.

There really is no business like show business…

5. HOW TO CHOOSE A WEST END SHOW

'It's urgent that state-subsidised theatres continue to stage work that is not going to find an audience…that's what state subsidy is for.'

– Simon Stephens, playwright

The most important thing about the show you choose to produce (or your 'product' as you will hear it referred to in some quarters) is that you have a real passion for it. This is something that is going to take up a huge amount of your time and energy and it is therefore essential that it is a project that you genuinely believe in and one that you are able to lead with unfeigned enthusiasm. Don't forget that you will probably have to sit and watch it on numerous occasions, and if this is a chore rather than a pleasure then it would appear that you have made the wrong choice. It is amazing how often you will find yourself in the position of considering a project for the wrong reasons; because a particular theatre or star actor is available, because some funding is attached or because you are doing a favour for a friend or someone you admire. Everyone else is ultimately relying on you to make the work happen so there can often be a great deal of pressure to take on a particular production and it can be quite a burden of responsibility when people latch onto you because they feel that you have the skills to translate their aspirations into reality. Just don't allow their dreams to become your nightmare. Your decision to say 'no' to a project is just as important as your decision to say 'yes' to one, and you must be careful not to get into a position where you feel obliged to proceed with a production that you feel uncertain about. You should feel free to express an interest in a project and then change your mind about it without being made to feel that you are letting people down. And if all else fails, you can always fall back on the time-honoured producer's excuse that there 'isn't a West End theatre available'.

There are a number of straightforward practical issues that dictate how likely it is that you are going to be able to take on a particular project. A relatively small cast is always an attractive proposition in the commercial theatre as is an uncomplicated set design, although these are not really your primary consideration as a producer and I always shy away from writers who introduce their new script with the words 'it's very commercial; only two actors and one set'. More important is whether you think it has the potential to attract performers and creative people of calibre and whether the style and subject of the piece will resonate with audiences. Political and social relevance are fleeting attributes, but the basic elements of good storytelling such as romance, humour and jeopardy have an eternal appeal. Mr Shakespeare knew that. Above all, though, be true to yourself. Don't create a piece of work in an attempt to employ a particular star, because a particular writer has previously enjoyed success, or to appeal to a particular market. Create work that you as a theatregoer would want to watch. If this means being counter-intuitive about perceived public taste then be bold and have the courage of your convictions. One of the certainties about choosing your show is that if you set out with the intention of creating a money-making hit you won't get one. Attempting to recreate formulae that have previously been successful is pretty well a guarantee of failure. Virtually all of the legendary hits (*Cats, Starlight Express, Blood Brothers, Les Misérables, The Woman In Black* and *War Horse* to name but a few) are unique creative ideas that did not attempt to follow any kind of blueprint, formula or business model and sprung from the creative energies and passions of those responsible for them rather than a cynical attempt to cash in. If I had a pound for every time someone presented a script to me as 'the next *Les Misérables*' I would have…well, at least fifty quid. Public taste is volatile and unpredictable, and the reality is that you are just as likely to go broke underestimating it as you are overestimating it. The only person's taste who you should always attempt to be true to is your own. The best producers are creative risk takers and your biggest selling point to investors is your own enthusiasm for the work, not a spreadsheet showing them how much money they could make. Your investors will grow to trust your judgement over the years if you demonstrate a consistent track record for identifying and promoting work of quality rather than just jumping on the latest bandwagon.

As soon as you register yourself in the book *Contacts* as a producer you will start receiving unsolicited scripts in the post. It is frankly amazing how many people spend their time writing plays and musicals, and almost equally amazing how few of them are any good. Whilst it is laudable that people put their creative energies into playwriting, no playwright, whether professional or amateur, is ever content for their work to stay on the page. At least if you paint a painting and fail to sell it then you can hang it on your wall or give it to a friend to hang on theirs. But an unperformed play is of no use to anyone and so clearly represents an unfulfilled ambition that the sense of frustration felt by the writer is often all too apparent. When it comes to new writing you are unlikely to be receiving the cream of the crop in any case, as these will naturally gravitate towards publicly funded theatres such as the Royal Court and the National Theatre who have an obligation to seek out and promote new writers and consequently an infrastructure that enables them to do so. The dilemma, of course, is that your post bag may contain a hidden gem and you don't want to risk turning down the next Tom Stoppard. This isn't helped by the fact that a play script is not the easiest of things to read and understand, particularly if you are in a hurry.

Some writers will ask you to return an unsolicited script to them if they send it to you and you are not interested in it, and will provide a stamped addressed envelope for the purpose. I have never really understood this, as you did not ask them to send it to you in the first place, so conferring the obligation on you of ensuring its safe return seems something of an imposition. Also, it is more likely that their work will one day be in the right place at the right time if it is sitting on the shelf in a producer's office. The important thing is to come up with a consistent policy for processing and politely responding to unsolicited scripts; a policy that does not take up too much of your time and energy but ensures that you will not miss the little nugget of gold.

A more fruitful source of performable scripts is likely to be the literary agencies, who you will also find listed in *Contacts*. If you write to them saying that you are a new producer seeking projects for production in the West End then you are likely to receive some work of interest. You may even receive scripts from some quite high profile writers, although you should be wary that these may not necessarily be representative of their best work and may have been doing the rounds of producers' offices for some time. If you think a script (whether requested or unsolicited) may have something to it and you want to explore it further then it's worth getting a group of actors together so that you can hear it read. It is interesting how different a play can seem when you actually hear it spoken, and actors (particularly if they are 'resting') will usually be happy to sit round a table in your office or front room and try out a new play. If you can get a director to work with them for a couple of hours prior to the actual reading then so much the better. Don't feel that you have to turn such a reading into an event in itself; it is purely for your benefit as a producer, and allowing everyone to invite their family, friends and agents just creates unnecessary distractions. No money should change hands, although it is a courtesy to provide refreshments; the actors and director are taking a risk that they may be in at the start of something, or failing that that you will be sufficiently impressed with their work to find another outlet for their talents. You should make it clear, though, that there is no obligation on you to engage anyone who takes part in an informal reading if the project eventually reaches fruition. If you are sufficiently interested in a script to go to the trouble of organising a reading then you should probably ask the writer to attend as well, although this can sometimes give a false impression that you are more interested in their work than you perhaps actually are.

Unlike the subsidised companies, you have no obligation to the taxpayer to seek out and present new work, and it may well be that you would prefer to create a new production of a play that has previously been performed. Any play will be in copyright if the author is alive or has died within the last 70 years, and for a copyright work you will have to obtain a licence from the agent who represents the author. You will also have to pay royalties. If the author died more than 70 years ago then you, along with everyone else, are free to produce their work wherever and whenever you want; although you should check whether the script you want to use is a translation or adaptation that is itself in copyright. The problem with producing work that is not in copyright, although you obviously benefit budgetarily from not having to pay the author, is that there is nothing to stop another producer from putting on the same play at exactly the same time. In practice this very rarely happens, as the process of production takes so long and the marketplace is so small that producers will naturally try to avoid competing with the same titles.

French's indispensable *Guide to Selecting Plays for Performance* lists over 2,000 scripts published by Samuel French Ltd, who deal with amateur performance licences for most (but by no means all) copyright plays in the UK. They will also be happy to give you the contact details for the literary agents representing the playwrights for the purpose of professional performance. French's operate a wonderful theatre bookshop which is packed from floor to ceiling with scripts, and if you are short of inspiration then you can do a lot worse than spend a few hours browsing through its extensive stock. An extraordinary website called Doollee.com is also (at time of writing) an excellent resource, aiming as it does to list every play published or produced in the English language since 1956, and providing contact details for playwrights' agents.

French's and Doollee are invaluable points of reference when it comes to navigating yourself around the playwriting universe, but in reality it is unlikely that a West End project is going to spring from trawling their catalogues. For all the scripts that you are sent by both writers and agents, and despite the extensive resources that are available to you when it comes to selecting plays, it is most likely that your first introduction to a work is going to come through a personal contact. It will often be a theatre practitioner such as a director or an actor who brings a particular script to your attention in the hope that it may be a vehicle for their own talents. These are usually the most fruitful introductions to a new project, as you are not working 'cold' and someone who you trust has already seen something in it. This can be a double-edged sword if you like the script but think it is not suitable for the person who introduced you to it. If it has been brought to you by a household name star actor or a director who will be able to attract a top calibre cast and team then the temptation is always to agree to produce it; but at this point you should pause and ask yourself whether the script itself is really of merit. However popular the cast or however impressive the creative team 'the play's the thing' and critics and audiences will quickly rumble if you are attempting to cash in with a sub-standard star vehicle. You should also avoid getting involved with 'vanity publishing' projects, where a writer effectively attaches a large cheque to their script in an effort to tempt you to produce it, or claims that they can raise all the money if you will only bring your producing skills to the table. In this scenario you will be serving someone else's passion rather than realising your own and you effectively become a general manager rather than a producer.

Once you have identified the play that you want to produce and, assuming that it is in copyright, have tracked down the writer's agent, you will need to obtain a professional performance licence. The idea behind this licence (which is usually drafted by the agent) is that you are effectively buying the exclusive right to put on professional performances of the play in the UK, including the West End. For the period that you hold the licence no other producer will be able to present the play, although there may be pre-existing agreements allowing amateur or repertory productions. The playwright's world is divided into 'Territories' and the territory that you are securing in the first instance is the British Territory (which can usually be extended to include the Republic of Ireland). In order to do this you will have to make an 'option' payment, which is effectively your statement of intent to produce the show. A typical option payment for a play would be a few thousand pounds. Paying this money does not oblige you to produce it but you will not get a refund if you fail to do so. The 'option period' is the period of time you have in which to present the first performance of your production, typically a year or eighteen months. The licence should give you the specific right to produce the piece in the West End (and may actually list the theatres that are considered 'West End' theatres) and should also cover the eventuality of touring in the UK before or after the West End presentation. Once you have opened in the West End and completed a minimum number of 'qualifying performances' you will retain the exclusive rights to present the play so long as there is a 'continuous run'.

The most significant part of the deal with the writer is the weekly royalty payment. This is a percentage of total weekly box office receipts after the deduction of VAT, credit card charges and the myriad of other niggling deductions that are made by the theatre's box office before they hand over the producer's money. This percentage, which is effectively a payment for the ongoing usage of the playwright's intellectual property, generally ranges between 5% and 8% of the net box office income, depending on whether it is a new script by an unknown writer or an established hit. Because of the various deductions made by the theatre before the 'net' figure is arrived at it is important to include a list of these (a 'definition of net box office') with any contract that is based on a percentage of box office receipts. Literary agents sometimes refer to the net receipts as 'gross' receipts, which can be a bit confusing, but in any event they will not argue with the customary (and ever growing) list of deductions being made before the royalty is calculated. Maybe they should.

Payments to the writer are made weekly, usually to their agent, and usually a couple of weeks after the producer has received the box office money from the theatre for the week in question. Such payments should be accompanied by a clear statement of what the total box office receipts for the week in question actually were, so that they can check that your maths is correct. Although your initial option payment is not returnable in the event that you do not produce the play it can be offset against the royalty payments, so you can deduct the value of the option payment from the initial payments to the writer. If the play closes before the full value of the option payment has been recouped then you are effectively in negative equity, but option payments for a play are not usually high enough for this to be an issue, and usually equate to no more than a few weeks' royalties in the West End. Once the play itself is in profit (i.e. once the pre-production costs have been recouped and the investors have been repaid) the royalty to the writer may increase. If this is part of the deal with the writer then they are entitled to receive the same sort of 'profit and loss' accounts that you send to your investors, so that they can be assured that you have correctly identified the week in which the production went into profit and triggered the increase in their royalty. A post-recoupment royalty may be a percentage point more than the original royalty. There may be a further increase in the agreed percentage once the production has recouped twice the value of its original production costs (i.e. at 'double recoupment'). The author of a successful West End play who is on 8% of box office could be earning well over £10,000 per week, which is not bad considering that their own work is usually completed long before the production started (and perhaps several decades earlier if the production is a revival). Given this level of potential earnings it is hardly surprising that there are so many aspiring playwrights.

The playwright will have the right to approve your cast and creative team, probably also the theatre in which the production is presented and possibly even the design of your publicity material, although such approvals should not be 'unreasonably withheld or delayed'. You won't be able to change any of the script without their permission and they may exercise their right to attend auditions and rehearsals and to claim expenses for doing this. The licence will also stipulate the number of free tickets they are entitled to on opening night and the number of tickets that will be reserved for them to purchase at each performance thereafter. The author's billing will be agreed on the licence, including stipulations about the size of type that is used for their name in relation to that use for the creative team and actors. Writers' agents often ask for the print size of the writer's name to be a specific percentage of the size of the title, but this can have disastrous consequences for the design of the poster and should be avoided at all costs. The licence will also allow you to film and broadcast short extracts from the play for publicity purposes.

For an established play there will be a number of 'reserved rights' which the author keeps for themselves, such as repertory, amateur, publication and foreign language, although there should be an undertaking that no other professional productions will be permitted in the territory during the term of your licence. If you are presenting the West End premiere of a new play then you should negotiate yourself a percentage of the author's income from the exercise of these rights in the years immediately following your production, as your production is likely to have substantially increased their value. Interest in a play from repertory, amateur and overseas groups usually increases dramatically following the publicity it receives from a West End presentation. You may also wish to negotiate the ability to acquire rights in some other territories (particularly the USA) if your production completes an agreed number of performances in the West End. Again, you should do this as a matter of course if you are presenting the West End premiere, though in the case of more established plays the rights in other territories may not be available; and if you are presenting a major revival it is worth considering whether the lack of a Broadway option, for instance, makes it a less attractive proposition for you and your investors.

The terms for a play licence in America are governed by something called the Approved Production Contract ('APC'), which is one of the most convoluted documents in the entire international theatre industry. It's OK to agree to this, because basically you have no other option in the USA, where the iron fist of collective bargaining in the entertainment sector makes the various rules and regulations that have developed in the UK look like a sideshow. Do not attempt to read the APC unless you have lost the will to live, and if you end up producing in the USA make sure you have someone on your staff who understands it.

The licence, like all contracts, will usually end with a couple of pages of standard legal clauses. These cover such things as the fact that you can't sub-let ('assign') the rights to another producer without the writer's approval, what procedures to follow if one of the contracting parties defaults or goes bankrupt, the fact that the agreement is binding on their successors (i.e. if the playwright dies their family cannot withdraw the licence) and that it should not be construed as creating a partnership between signatories. A particularly strict-sounding clause will cover the procedures for the serving of notices on each other (a 'notice' is any official communication, usually one requiring remedial action, pertaining to the enforcement of the terms of the contract), and a seemingly innocuous clause will say that the contract is governed by the laws of England. Being governed by the laws of England, which is after all the territory where you are operating if you are presenting a show in the West End, is actually very important, even if you are dealing with people who are based on the other side of the world. These clauses all look a bit dull and are generally cut and pasted from contract to contract, but they are there for a purpose and it is always worth checking that they have been included.

If your chosen play is in copyright then your professional performance licence is one of the single most important documents in the whole process of production and is the trigger for many other things. Contractually you can't raise money or hire a theatre without it (your investors and the theatre owner may well ask to see it), and you would be foolish to employ actors and creative personnel until it is signed. Perhaps the most significant clause, the 'warranty' is one that rarely even merits comment. It is here that the author warrants to you that the work is actually theirs to licence and does not infringe any third party copyrights, and that they will indemnify you against any losses incurred if this proves not to be the case. This means that you are protected from the consequences of any legal claims from third parties arising over disputes about the copyright in the text of the play, and that if you are prevented from proceeding with the production because of a copyright infringement then you can technically sue the writer for damages. In real life none of this ever happens, of course, but that is precisely because everyone knows the importance of this clause. If the play is an adaptation of another copyright work, such as a book or film, then the author must also warrant that they have themselves obtained the rights to the source material and that they are responsible for making whatever payment is required for its use out of their own royalty. The fact that it is adapted from another source should not make the actual royalty payment for the play any higher, and it is up to the playwright to figure out how they are going to split their royalty with the person who came up with the original idea. It is obviously important that the writer's deal for the original material allows them to enter into the full extent of the agreement with the producer, including any overseas options for instance, and however firm the warranty from the writer that it does it is usually worth asking for a copy of the document granting the writer the underlying rights. If a writer brings you an adaptation of a copyright work and expects you to conclude a separate deal with the underlying rights owners then it is usually best to avoid the project, as it often indicates that they themselves have tried to do so and failed.

The fact that a play is adapted from a popular book, film or television programme may of course be one of its major selling points. But it can also be its downfall. You have to consider very carefully to what extent the play meets with audience expectation of how a well-known story should be staged and, in the case of film or television adaptations you have to ask whether it was the title itself or the screen version's casting that made the original popular. A story that has enjoyed screen success because a particular star's performance may fall a bit flat if that key cast member is absent from a stage version.

A licence for a stage musical follows much the same principles as one for a play, except that the royalty figure is likely to be higher, as there are often a number of collaborators involved. The usual starting point for a new musical is 6% (2% each for book (script), music and lyrics) although some of the big 'brand name' musicals can command as much as 12%, which may include a sum payable to the original producer (you'll rarely be told how it's actually divided up). Again, make sure that any underlying rights for source material are 'rolled in' to the agreement and that you are signing one agreement to cover book, music and lyrics.

In the case of a new musical it is worth checking to what extent the music has actually been written, as if you are not careful you will find yourself paying additionally for 'musical arrangements' and 'orchestrations'. It is perfectly possible for the actual music for a new musical to consist of little more than a piano and vocal score. If you are going to have to pay for getting the composer's work finished for them then you need to make allowances for this when you negotiate the licence with the writers.

If the musical is an established one then you may also find that you are bound into a hire agreement for band parts (sheet music for the musicians), and if you want to commission a new orchestration (for instance, for a smaller number of players) then you will need to get special permission to do this within the terms of your licence. Any new orchestrations that are created will generally become the property of the original composer, just as any changes in a script that a playwright agrees to will be assigned to the playwright.

The writers of musicals will usually have an eye on a cut of the potential merchandise sales for the show as well. In this case, you should try to do a deal based on a share of merchandise profits rather than a percentage of income, as the only thing that is more frustrating than a warehouse full of unsold baseball caps when a musical flops is knowing that the composer is the only person who has made money from the five that were actually sold. Merchandise for a successful musical, on the other hand, can be a lucrative sideline for the production, and top of the list of collectable items will be the 'original cast recording'. If you are producing a new musical then make sure that the licence gives you the right also to produce this recording. The wonders of modern technology make this a remarkably speedy and painless process, and even the union agreements are favourably inclined towards it. Bring in a 'hired hand' record producer with a particular knowledge of cast albums to head up the project, and make sure you have some sort of distribution deal in place, even to relatively specialised markets, before you go into production. Even if you have a flop show on your hands you are more likely to shift a warehouse full of cast albums than you are those wretched baseball caps.

Following the boom in West End musicals in the 1980s a great deal of time, effort and money were ploughed into nurturing new musical theatre writing talent, with a plethora of prizes, workshop productions and other incentives on offer to the Andrew Lloyd Webbers of tomorrow. Nothing much came of all this frenzied activity, only going to show once again that talent and inspiration spring up unexpectedly when they are ready to do so and cannot be assisted into existence like genetically modified crops. Prizes were awarded and a number of new shows were workshopped to death, but in the end the Andrew Lloyd Webber of tomorrow turned out to be, well... Andrew Lloyd Webber; and with a few (very) honourable exceptions the West End theatres big enough to host a musical continued to survive on a core repertoire of revivals, compilation shows and the esteemed Lord's prolific output. We are often told that 'musicals aren't written, they're re-written' and that the three criteria for judging them are 'book, book and book'. I usually find that the most important question that needs addressing is 'Why a musical'? Virtually every piece of classic literature now seems to have had the words 'the musical' appended to its title, without any real consideration being given as to its suitability for the genre. In truth, only certain narratives gain from the addition of songs, and identifying them is not as easy as certain composers clearly seem to think. Having said all this, at time of writing there appears to be a genuine glimmer of hope that some emerging new musical theatre talent is finally gaining a foothold in the West End.

No doubt partly due to the paucity of work from 'emerging' musical theatre composers, the 'compilation' show has become an increasingly popular genre, with the music of groups from Queen to Abba packing auditoriums across the West End, some with the wholehearted endorsement of the original artistes and some, notably, without. The compilation show brings with it a whole separate layer of copyright issues, in that the music has to be licensed separately from the script. If there is no script, and the performance can be classified as a concert, then you can perform pretty well any copyright music you like in return for a royalty payment (typically of around 3%) to the Performing Right Society, in its capacity as a sort of universal 'agent' for songwriters and composers. The PRS then divides the royalties between the publishers of the songs, according to what proportion of the show their music accounts for. This system applies even if your performers are dressed like and imitating the voices and moves of the artistes who made the songs famous. Things get a lot more complicated as soon as you add dialogue, characters and a plot to the show, in that you then need to approach the publishers of the individual songs and obtain permission and a licence to include each one. Again, the royalty is divided between each publisher according to the number of minutes of music in the show that they represent, although in this case the royalty for music and lyrics that is being divided up is likely to be higher, typically 5%, which only leaves 1% for the writer of the book if you apply the '6% rule'. Even if the music is all originally composed by the same writer or group, there may be a number of different publishers involved, reflecting different publishing deals that they have struck at different stages in their careers. Publishers tend to buy and sell each other's catalogues, leading to frequent confusion about who actually owns what, and it is even possible for the rights to one song to be split between more than one publisher. The PRS can act as a broker to facilitate the deals with the music publishers for a scripted compilation show, although arguably it is preferable to build your own relationships with them, however convoluted the process may be. In any event, the PRS can be an invaluable source of information on all this, although it is important to clarify with them when you have struck your own deals with music publishers or they will attempt to impose their mercilessly draconian royalty collection procedures irrespective of your protestations that you have already paid for the song rights.

Where the PRS can be particularly helpful is in dealing with sorting out payments for music that is 'interpolated' into plays as opposed to musicals; for instance, if a character is listening to the radio. If a particular piece of music is specified by the writer and is in copyright then technically the writer should have obtained permission to use it and payment for it should be incorporated into the royalty that you pay to them. If a particular piece of copyright music has been specified by the director, however, then it is up to you to obtain clearance via the PRS and to negotiate a payment with them for the composer's work. Typically this will be a very small fixed weekly sum rather than a percentage of box office. You may of course end up having to go back to the director and asking them to change their choice of music, if the piece they have chosen turns out to be unavailable or cost-prohibitive.

If you are producing a musical compilation show which strongly relies on the work of one particular song writer, performer or group, or indeed portrays them, then it is advisable to obtain their endorsement if they are still around and about, or that of their estate if they are not. Although there is no equivalent of the American 'name and likeness' law in the UK, someone whose work you have licensed through publishers or the PRS can find other ways of giving you a hard time, usually via trademark legislation or 'passing off' law, if they strongly object to what you are doing. You are in a much stronger position if you can say that you are the 'official' show featuring the music of the group or artiste concerned. It is worth making a good will payment of up to 2% to secure such an endorsement, even though this has now potentially pushed your royalty payments in respect of music and lyrics alone up to as much as 7% in total.

Producing a new musical of any sort is a major undertaking, extremely expensive and very high risk, and if you want to get more of a feeling for a piece before committing to it, or perhaps want to give your potential investors a bit of a taster of what is to come, then it can be worth giving it a 'workshop' presentation. A 'workshop' is an oddly inappropriate word for a chapter in the theatrical creative process; summoning up images of people brandishing spanners rather than scripts, and wearing overalls rather than leg warmers. Still, we live in a world where you can be sent to 'boot camp' to learn how to become a television pop star, apparently without any intended irony in the use of the word 'camp'. In any event, this is not a 'development' workshop for the benefit of the writers, who will hopefully pretty well have finished their job by the time you get involved, but a producer's workshop to allow the creative team to develop some of their ideas and show you, your potential investors and other potential stakeholders the direction in which they are planning to take the piece. It is effectively an 'audition' for the work itself, a bit like a play reading but on a larger scale. A week of rehearsals culminating in a 'showcase' presentation (script in hand) in the rehearsal room, with some basic movement and choreography, should be more than adequate to get a flavour of it. You'll need to persuade someone to put up some 'seed' money to fund the workshop/showcase process, because whilst actors are usually happy to take part in a play reading in return for food and shelter, you cannot expect them to work for a week without remuneration. Similarly, you will need to offer a small fee to creative personnel such as a director, musical director and choreographer.

You shouldn't spend too much money on the actual showcase presentation. Tracksuits and T-shirts, minimal furnishings and a pianist should suffice. Over-produced musical showcase presentations can actually detract from the piece, and it is important that the viewers (yourself included) can imagine the sumptuous sights and sounds of the final production without the impediment of 'scratch' costumes and settings thrown together for the showcase. If the piece is powerful enough, a 'poor theatre' style of presentation should allow it to shine. If it relies on hydraulic scenery to make its impact then this is the point at which you will find out, and it is probably best in that case to walk away. Whether you facilitate this process before or after you have optioned the piece is up to you, but in any event you will be staging it with the blessing and co-operation of the writers.

If you have actually gone so far as to commission a new musical from scratch then a series of 'behind closed doors' development workshops solely for the benefit of the writers may be a useful, if costly, investment and can enable you as producer to keep tabs on how things are shaping up. It is important that at whatever stage in the process a workshop occurs you do not enter into any ongoing commitment with the performers concerned, and that they sign a disclaimer to protect you and the writer from any potential future allegation that their creative work has been incorporated into the finished product. Any performer who is not happy with this deal does not have to take part, although those who have taken part are of course likely to be near the top of the list for an audition when the show itself eventually comes to be cast. When it comes to the director and other members of the creative team you will probably have engaged them for a workshop on the basis that they will get first refusal if the project actually goes ahead.

If you come up with a concept for a new play or musical then the process of getting a script commissioned is fairly straightforward. Contact a few literary agents and ask if they have any clients who may be interested, or have a look at some new writing on the fringe and see if there is anyone whose style you think might be suited to the subject that you have in mind. You are unlikely to strike up a deal with a household name playwright, but a commission is a great way for a young writer to keep their head above water; although arguably any creative person's work is going to be of a higher standard if they create it 'from the heart' whilst starving to death in a garret rather than to order and for money.

You may well come up with an idea for an adaptation of a film or novel, in which case it will be down to you to secure the underlying rights for the purpose of stage adaptation from the film company or publisher. As with a play script you will probably make an option payment in respect of 'original material' of a few thousand pounds on the basis that it is non-returnable if the project doesn't go ahead but fully recoupable against royalties if it does. You will also need to negotiate a weekly royalty at a level that takes account of the fact that you will be paying a royalty to your commissioned playwright as well. As a rule of thumb, if the commissioned play is based on material by a third party then the total royalty you are paying for the final script should be split roughly along the lines of one third for the original material and two thirds to the commissioned playwright (so, for instance, 2% and 4% respectively). The playwright will expect their own royalty to be that little bit lower if they know that the producer has to take account of some underlying rights. If the idea for a commissioned play comes directly from your own imagination rather than an existing source then arguably you could allow a percentage for yourself equivalent to that which you would pay to a third party for underlying rights. However, this begs the question as to why you are not sitting down and writing the script yourself.

It may also be the case that a writer or their agent has approached you with an idea and a request that you commission them to write it. This means that the writer is passionate about their subject but needs to be able to lock themselves away and focus on the project whilst keeping a roof over their head. If you are able to facilitate a script in this manner then you are likely to end up with something rather good, as well as a young writer at the start of their career who will be your friend for life.

The copyright in a commissioned script remains with the writer and your agreement with them will be a licence to use their work in exactly the same way as it would be for an existing play. The writer will receive a sum of money in advance and then at the various stages of draft delivery and completion. It is up to you how much, if any, of this money is eventually recoupable against royalties. In the commissioning agreement you will need to specify deadlines for the delivery and approval of drafts, and because you are in the driving seat you should be able to negotiate a much longer window within which to launch the project (say, three years) and a structure that allows you to retain the option to produce the work again for a number of years after the first continuous run has finished, by making payments in lieu of royalties. As you would with any new work, commissioned or otherwise, you will make sure that you have the right to acquire the option to produce it in the American territory and indeed everywhere else following an agreed number of performances in the West End. In the case of a commission the number of 'qualifying performances' required is likely to be very low, reflecting the favourable terms that a producer has the right to expect from a commissioned writer. Again, as you would with any new play, you will also get a good cut of their income from their future licensing of the work (to professional, amateur and repertory companies) for an agreed number of years once your own productions have run their course. For a commissioned piece up to a third of the writer's earnings would be reasonable, and you should also make sure that you have the right at least to match any offer to film the script that they received, and that if you yourself don't film it then you at least get a piece of the action if someone else does.

When it comes to play licences, commissioned or otherwise, logic dictates that the more of a 'break' you are giving to the writer the better terms you can insist on for yourself. If you are negotiating a licence for an established classic then it can feel a bit like it's the writer who's doing you the favour and your rights will pretty well be limited to the West End run, and possibly a tour immediately before or afterwards. For a West End premiere you should be able to negotiate yourself a number of the onward options and income participations discussed above. For a commission, whilst you don't actually 'own' the script, your onward options and participations should be extensive. Even with a commission, however, it may be that your intended production never sees the light of day and that your option period runs out. It is quite irksome to see a work that you have commissioned being premiered by a rival producer, but it does happen occasionally and there's nothing you can do about it. Similarly, you may one day come across a touring production of a play that you premiered in the West End but, when you do so and excitedly look up your files on the project, you are more than likely to find that the period in which you had the right to derive income from future productions has just expired.

Although some playwrights will also make a bit of income from the published texts of their work, they make most of their money from getting their plays performed. If you take an option for a play (or a musical, which can be a six figure sum for an established title) then it is not really the option money that they are interested in but the prospect of actually getting their work onto a stage. For this reason a writer's agent is going to want to satisfy themselves that your plans for a production are serious before issuing you with a licence and allowing the work to be taken off the market. Certain writers have producers queuing up to option their work so you may well find yourself having to explain your ideas for a production to their agent in some detail, including who you intend your leading actors to be. The agent's job is to maximise the writer's income, and given that this income is based directly on the number of tickets sold, it is legitimate for them to enquire as to which stars you have lined up to play the leading roles. Not surprisingly, a star actor is unlikely to want to discuss a project with you even in principle if they think that you haven't yet secured a licence to produce the play, so a little tactical bluffing on all fronts may be required in order to move things forward at this stage.

Playwrights fall into three main categories; alive and in copyright, dead and in copyright and dead and out of copyright. Authorial involvement in the production process can be a mixed blessing. Writers of an existing piece will be able to exercise their right of approval over the cast and creative team (such approvals will often not be included in a commissioning agreement). To what extent they do this depends entirely on the personality of the individual involved. Some writers are completely 'hands off' and effectively rubber stamp the producer's choices whilst others will want to discuss casting and creative personnel at length. Always bear in mind, however, that their approvals of your choices cannot be 'unreasonably withheld' and that they are unlikely to be so obstructive as to actually prevent a production from going ahead, as they have a considerable financial interest in assisting it to the point where the audience are buying tickets. An experienced writer's input on casting can actually be extremely helpful. They will know which actors are best suited to deliver their work and, like you, will be wanting to ensure both good reviews and a healthy box office (the latter usually resulting from a combination of good reviews and a marketable cast). They may well also have favourite directors who they know from experience are particularly attuned to their writing. This can be a useful shortcut to bringing a top-notch creative team to the party, but the producer's role in proceedings can be slightly undermined if the director is too much in the writer's pocket.

If the play is an established one then the writer is likely to leave you alone during rehearsals, but the writer of a new play may well exercise their right to attend. Whilst it can be very helpful to have the writer on call to make any adjustments to the script that are deemed necessary as a result of the rehearsal process, it can be inhibiting for the director and the actors if they are around the whole time. The writer is not necessarily best qualified to ensure the smooth transition of their work from page to stage, and their understandable nervousness as opening night approaches can be infectious and can also slow down the process as director and cast are bombarded with last-minute rewrites. Whilst the writer is perfectly entitled to make changes to their own script it is disconcerting if it begins to cease resembling the one that you actually optioned. A skilled director will arbitrate this process in the rehearsal room, and whilst it is essential that you are kept abreast of any changes as they occur it is unusual for a producer to have to intervene in such matters.

Those writers who are dead and still in copyright are represented by their estates, which effectively exercise all of the rights afforded to the writer by the licence. Some estates are extremely knowledgeable about the work that they represent and can be as hands-on in a helpful way as a writer when it comes to the casting and creative team approvals process. Some are not particularly knowledgeable but are still hands-on in an interfering way, which can be extremely frustrating. Others don't seem to care at all about the creative process and just sit back and cash the royalty cheques. In any event, if the writer is deceased then their estate is unlikely to approve any textual changes to the play. Writers who are both dead and out of copyright tend to leave you alone to get on with it.

It is unusual for new plays, particularly those by new writers, to be premiered in the West End, and commercial producers come in for a great deal of criticism because of this. The great thing about being a producer, however, is that you can ignore this criticism because you have a perfect right to produce anything you want to; and provided that you can persuade enough people to share your vision to enable the money to be raised then you are not answerable to anybody. The fact is that the West End is the Wild West. You have no cushion of public subsidy and if you are going to operate in this highly volatile, competitive and risky marketplace then you are going to want to stack the odds as far as possible in your favour. No one is going to thank you for taking a risk with a new play and losing their money when the Royal Court, the National Theatre and other subsidised venues are there to do it for you. What the West End can do, and does brilliantly, is to give new plays which are proven successes an extended lease of life and allow a much wider and more demographically mixed audience to see them once they have completed their limited seasons at the venues that specialise in originating them. If there is a new play that you are particularly passionate about or have commissioned then there are a myriad of avenues available to you for nurturing it into life and routing it eventually into the West End. It's just unlikely that you will actually premiere it there, unless it is by a 'household name' writer or has a particularly big star attached to it. There is no shame in this. It is just common sense.

As a producer seeking work to present in the West End you are not limited to shows that you originate yourself and it may well be that you transfer or remount an entire production that has enjoyed a previous life elsewhere. Work from the tiniest of pub theatres, the Edinburgh Festival Fringe, regional repertory theatres, the big subsidised venues and venues overseas has all found its way to the West End stage, often extremely successfully, courtesy of commercial producers. Most people are delighted at the prospect that their production could be presented 'in town', and there are as many different deals to be struck as there are shows.

If you see a production at another theatre that you would like to take under your wing then the first thing to do is to identify the 'producing entity'. This is the originating producer; the company or organisation which has been responsible for putting on the show and in whose name all of the relevant contracts and licences will have been issued. Once you have identified who it is you should be talking with, all you have to do is pick up the phone and express your interest to them in taking their project into the West End. If they have a hugely successful, well-reviewed hit on their hands then it is likely that they may have a number of such offers to weigh up. Although the financial deal that you put on the table will be a key factor in their decision as to whether to proceed with you as opposed to a rival producer, it will also be important to them that they feel they can trust you both on a business level and an artistic one.

The originating producer will want to be assured that you are a 'fellow traveller' in all respects and will want assurances about every aspect of your plans. How long do you think it will take you to raise the necessary funds? What are your realistic chances of securing a suitable West End theatre within a reasonable timeframe? Are you committed to the cast that you have seen or will you want to bring in different actors (perhaps starrier 'names')? What changes will need to be made to the physical aspects of the production, such as the set and lighting, in order to accommodate it in your preferred theatre, and are there any other changes to the production that you will want the creative team to make? What are your plans for marketing the production? On the other side of the coin, you will need to find out whether the creative team and the actors you have seen are available and interested in taking the production further and, most importantly, if the play is in copyright then you need to ascertain whether the people who have put on this particular production already have an option in their licence to move it into the West End. If they do then you will need to organise for the existing licence to be 'assigned' to you and if they don't then you will need to get their blessing for you to negotiate this separately with the writer's agent.

The deal that you do with the originating producer is effectively a licence to present their entire production and includes similar language to that which is used in the literary licence. You will agree to pay a weekly royalty out of box office receipts to the originating producer, usually of between 1% and 2%. This may not seem like very much, but remember that this income is a risk-free bonus for them and is usually more than welcome. You may also offer them a share of any profits (say 10%) from the West End presentation, which is usually calculated 'off the top' before the 60/40 split between investors and producer.

A significant factor in concluding the terms of this deal will be how much of the original physical production is either available or suitable for use in the West End transfer. The original production may well have been presented in a very different physical space to a West End theatre and it is often the case that it is more cost-effective to build an entirely new set than to attempt to adapt an existing one. The existing set may not in any case be built out of materials of a sufficient standard for West End presentation and may not have been constructed in a manner which lends itself to dismantling and reassembly. Furniture, props and costumes may belong to the originating producer's 'stock' or may have been hired in specially and so may not belong to the production. In any event, your production manager needs to make a full assessment and draw up an inventory of all useable items, as there is no point in agreeing to pay thousands of pounds for what ends up as a pile of matchwood with several key elements missing. It may well be the case that the best solution is to engage the original set and costume designers to go back to the drawing board and create new designs in the style of the original. Of course, this is more likely to be the case if you are transferring the show from a forty-seat pub venue than if you are buying it in from a major repertory theatre, but the issue of certain items being hired in or belonging to stock may occur at whatever scale you are working. And don't forget that there are unlikely to be any understudy costumes, as repertory and fringe theatres rarely engage understudies.

Shows that have been created abroad have a host of other complications attached to them, and again it may well be the case that building an entirely new physical production is actually more cost-effective than transporting the existing one. The costs associated with flying in and accommodating creative personnel who are based overseas can be quite extraordinary, and you also face the million dollar question as to whether you are going to bring in performers from abroad and deal with the myriad of complications that this creates, or persuade the creative team to remount the production with a British cast. Union rules regarding overseas performers appearing in the West End have become more helpful in recent years but work permit regulations for non-European performers remain complicated and the punitive 'foreign entertainers tax' is a major disincentive, although performers can usually get it credited back to them in their country of origin. Whatever the practical issues of bringing in an overseas cast, the decision is ultimately an artistic one, and however tempting the cost savings it is probably unwise to bring in a piece of Noh Theatre from Japan or an ensemble work from the Steppenwolf Theatre Company of Chicago and recast it with British actors.

Bearing in mind the cost of any rebuilds of and 'adapts' to the physical production, you can either offer the originating producer money up front for the purchase of any re-useable physical assets or a larger share of the potential profits in lieu of your use of them. It is best to avoid agreements that involve hiring the physical assets of the original production if at all possible. This sum can be shown in your production budget simply as 'purchase of physical assets' and will form part of the money that you have to raise for the show. Don't spend too much on them, or give away too much profit in lieu of them, as there will be plenty of other calls on your 'transfer' production budget, including potentially a rehearsal period so that the existing actors can be rehearsed into a differently configured set design or indeed so that different actors can be rehearsed into the roles, not to mention the fees you will have to pay to the creative team for adapting and transferring their work. It is often the case, in fact, that a production that has transferred unexpectedly into the West End (i.e. without any pre-planning for the eventuality) can cost just as much if not more than a production that is created specifically for it. You may have to keep reminding yourself that you are following this route because the production itself is a known entity with a track record and therefore your chances of ultimate West End success could be higher.

The originating producer of a production transferred into the West End will have a similar set of approvals as the author, so if you want to make any changes in casting or other personnel then it is best to establish this before negotiations get too far progressed. There will also be an option period which specifies a given timeframe within which the production should open in the West End under your management. It can be worth offering a small advance against royalties in order to secure this option, as this indicates a clear intent on your part to deliver the goods. Like the writer and everyone else involved, the originating producer will want to see their name in lights in the West End and there will be a billing clause that gets their name or brand up there somewhere. The usual phrasing is '*You* present *Their* production of' or '*You* by arrangement with *Them* present'. You should avoid using the phrase 'in association with' as this can be indicative of the fact that the parties are jointly liable for the production as opposed to the reality of the situation which is that one is acting under licence from the other. The 'no partnership' clause in the legal small print on the licence is particularly significant in this respect. In terms of billing, if you are transferring a production created by a prestigious brand-name company such as the Royal Shakespeare Company then their involvement is obviously something that you will want to advertise widely, and you are going to want to encourage the prominent display of their logo on all of your advertising material. On the other hand, if the production has originated at the Old Greyhound Pub Theatre, it may be necessary to take the original producers to one side and tactfully suggest that their branding is kept to a minimum.

Charity law quite rightly restricts the level of financial risk that the flagship subsidised companies are allowed to take outside their own buildings, and there was a time when they thus relied on the skills and gambling instincts of commercial producers and their backers to take their work to a wider audience in the West End. Of late, however, some of these companies have cottoned on to the fact that they can create their own production entities to transfer their work into the commercial arena, thereby eliminating the need to split the producer's share of profits with a partner. The fact that they are able to do this is itself indicative of the growing number of individuals throughout the industry who are making it their business to learn the dark arts of the commercial producer. It would be churlish to begrudge these organisations their entrepreneurial awakening, although it has to be said that it requires minimal entrepreneurial acumen to exploit established box office hits from an extensive repertoire of work created with the benefit of state subsidy. There are, however, still plenty of subsidised companies who welcome input from the commercial sector, and in the meantime we look forward to the global profits from *War Horse* paying off not only the National's debt but the national debt. As legendary Broadway impresario Gerry Schoenfeld famously commented, 'There's no profit like not-for-profit'.

Like the literary licence, the licence from the original producers for the use of an existing production is a key document without which you will not be able to sign up investors or a West End theatre. Once this document has been executed, the processes of production are all pretty much as they would be if you had originated the production yourself. All of the contracts (including those with actors, creative team, theatre and equipment suppliers) will be in your own company's name, the investment will be raised by you and put into a bank account that you control, and overall the liabilities and potential rewards are just the same on paper as for any other West End production.

What is different is that your ability successfully to guide the project into its new home will be monitored continuously by the original producers, and everyone involved with the show will be constantly comparing their experience of working for them with that of working for you. It takes a particular set of skills to keep everyone happy in this scenario and it is important that you become a trusted member of the team rather than be made to feel like an outsider or a foster parent to someone else's cherished project. The people who originated the show will be relying on your skill and judgement to make it shine in its new environment, and the choices that you make will therefore have a wider significance than if you are working on a production of your own creation.

One of the most important decisions you make for your adopted show will be your choice of West End theatre. Of course, the seating capacity is a significant factor in your ability to recoup costs and thereby attract investment, but it may well be that a production that has started life in a small venue will stand a better chance in a more intimate West End space. Virtually all West End theatres are 'proscenium arch' and you need to consider carefully any creative compromises that will be required when transferring a show from a less traditional space. Similarly, any changes in casting may backfire. If the critics previously saw and enjoyed the show with a talented ensemble cast then they may object to the fact that you have parachuted in a Hollywood star in order to boost the box office. Transferring a show that has been a hit in a previous life is nothing like as plain sailing as it may at first appear. A production that appeals to the critics when it is in a converted church hall at the Edinburgh Fringe, and they are seeing five shows a day with regular refuelling stops at the Festival bars, can suddenly lose all of its appeal when presented behind a gold-painted proscenium.

For all of these reasons, it is best to start out with transfers that can be achieved pretty much 'as seen', such as one from a major proscenium arch regional repertory theatre which already has a smattering of star casting in it; though even these can lose something in translation when moved into the unforgiving environment of the West End. Whatever the fortunes of the venture, however, it is important to remember that it was you who had the guts and the vision to give the project a West End life. Don't take a 'back foot' approach with the people who created the show. They will be looking to you for guidance and leadership throughout the whole process and it is important that you have the courage of your convictions. Don't ever ask for, or expect, gratitude from them; but on the other hand don't be overly-deferential. It is you who are the bold risk taker in the equation and, whilst a collaborative approach is always the best strategy in any theatrical enterprise, it is important that all parties acknowledge that it is your energy and enterprise which have created this very special opportunity for the production. Once you have trained yourself, through experience, in the necessary diplomatic, practical and creative skills to achieve a successful West End transfer then you will be well equipped to take on bigger producing challenges.

If you want to avoid the risks of premiering a production in the West End but don't want to share creative control with an originating producer then you might like to try creating your own production in an environment outside of the West End and nurturing it to the point where you feel it is ready to bring into town. In other words, consider transferring your own production rather than someone else's. A production created with this in mind is sometimes referred to as a 'try-out' and there are a number of potential scenarios for facilitating this. Many small fringe theatres are simply available for hire, and if you have a new script that you want to test then this is not a bad option, particularly if you can interest one of the more prestigious venues (which you usually can if you get a cheque book out, whatever their pretentions to a 'programming policy'). Alternatively, you could book yourself a space at the Edinburgh Festival Fringe, which is harder work and higher risk. Your hope will be that you can make some sort of impact in the fringe jungle and that at least a few national critics will see the work and give it rave reviews. If you are sufficiently happy with the audience and critical response then you can start the journey to a West End transfer, but transferring your own project from the Fringe to the West End is just as fraught with difficulty as transferring someone else's in terms of the 'scaling up' process.

Perhaps the best way to try out a production that you want to present in the West End is to convince a regional repertory theatre to act as the originating producer. These are theatres that produce their own work (as opposed to 'receiving' theatres which book in touring productions), and you will find a list of them in *Contacts*. Most major towns have a producing theatre of some sort, which will be financed by a combination of local authority and regional arts council funding. There is likely to be an artistic director, responsible for programming and for directing a number of the theatre's own productions, and an executive director who is effectively the business manager. This is also the arena where you are most likely to find people with the mysterious title 'creative producer'. The key in the first instance is to get the artistic director interested in the merits of your project; the script, the creative team and any casting that you have already lined up. The artistic director is being asked to take a leap of faith that the project you are suggesting will keep the theatre's regular audience happy. It is important to remember that repertory theatres have a much more direct and long-term relationship with their audiences than receiving theatres on the touring circuit and West End theatres, so they will not want to produce anything that might risk calling their artistic director's judgement into question and jeopardising the trust that they have built up with their audience and funders.

One of the best ways to persuade the artistic director of a regional repertory theatre to agree to their theatre taking on your project is to offer them the job of directing it themselves, as it gives them the personal opportunity of having a show in the West End, not to mention a potentially lucrative director's royalty in the future. However strategically convenient this may be, you should only make such an offer if you genuinely believe that they are the right director for the job. If you have already enlisted the services of a director for your project then it is perfectly acceptable to suggest that the repertory theatre takes them on as a 'guest' director, particularly if they are a high profile practitioner whose involvement will impress their audience and funding bodies. Once the artistic director has agreed that the project fits in with programming policy (and you will have done your research on this, so you can be sure that it will!) you will be handed over to the executive director to thrash out a deal.

In this case you are effectively negotiating a transfer deal in advance. All of the terms will be similar to those contained in a transfer licence except that you will be engaging in a 'co-production agreement' and you will be expected to put a sum of money on the table which you will not get back if you ultimately decide not to transfer the show. This amount of money (the 'top-up') should be the difference between what the theatre would normally budget for a production in those weeks of the year and what it will cost them to produce a West End–ready show to your specifications. The top-up payment, which is usually made directly to the theatre and dispersed by them as appropriate, is intended to take account of such matters as your creative team possibly commanding higher fees than the theatre would normally pay and the set most likely needing to be built on a grander scale or to a higher technical specification than would normally be the case. There may also be more people in the cast than they normally account for, and because of this it is important to make sure that they weren't budgeting for a two hander play in the weeks when you are asking them to schedule your production of *Hello Dolly!*.

On the plus side for you they may well budget for a longer rehearsal period than a commercial production, have their own scenery building workshop (this use of the word I *do* understand!) and costume-making departments; and a lot of the costs (such as the full-time workshop staff) will be absorbed into their 'overhead', which is ultimately subsidised. Also important to the equation is that all the performers will be expected to accept Equity minimum pay rates (don't forget that different contracts and rates apply in the subsidised sector) and all the creative team will be on a single fee without a royalty during the run. Performers and creative personnel will be contracted by the theatre rather than you; their agents are used to these agreements with repertory theatres and you will rarely find any resistance to them. If you do, then you may have to include a 'top up' to an individual in your side of the budget, but this is dangerous territory as all the performers will most likely be accepting minimum rates on the basis that they are being treated equally ('favoured nations'), and this is something that you must absolutely never lie to people about.

The theatre will set themselves a box office target for the production based on their usual budgets (including overheads) and income projections for a short run of maybe three weeks, and will cover any loss if this target is not achieved. In any event there will be no further requirement for funds from you, though you might negotiate a share of receipts if they exceed their target. The fact that the box office target does not necessarily require the show to recoup the theatre's own financial contribution to the production can be counter-intuitive to your commercial instincts, but there is a little bit of subsidised alchemy at work here and it is best not to question your host theatre's budgeting methodologies. The important thing is that at the end of the repertory theatre run you wholly own a West End-ready production and that it has cost you less to create it than it would have done from a standing start. In return the repertory theatre has been able to stage a much bigger and more impressive production than they otherwise would have been able to, quite possibly with some impressive star name actors in it working for the 'company wage'; and if the show does indeed have a further life under your management they will receive their 'originating theatre' royalty and the feather in their cap of West End exposure for their work. Everyone's a winner.

Shows co-produced in repertory theatres under these arrangements have the benefit of fitting up, technically rehearsing and generally ironing out the wrinkles away from the financially pressurised hurly-burly of the West End, and are usually all the better for it. With a couple of notable exceptions these venues also tend to create shows that are a good physical 'fit' for standard West End proscenium theatres. If you are taking this route then it is important to remember that the terms of your author's licence must permit you effectively to assign your rights to the repertory theatre for the required period. The author's royalty 'off the top' of box office income forms part of the maths for the co-production deal and is most likely to be paid by the theatre to you and then forwarded by you to the author. The author royalty itself is likely to be at a lower rate for the repertory run than for the West End run and you should really pass on the benefit of such a reduction to the theatre.

Repertory theatres plan their schedules a long time in advance so it is unlikely that you will have a West End theatre lined up for an immediate transfer; and in any case one of the purposes of the 'rep' run is for you to assess whether or not the production has West End potential. Because of this you will need to plan well in advance how you intend to deal with the issue of keeping performers and creative personnel under 'option' for a potential West End transfer after the repertory engagement. In order to secure a commitment you will at the very least have to negotiate West End remuneration 'in the event of' a transfer and specify dates by which transfer options have to be taken up. It is best to avoid paying retainer fees if at all possible. If there is going to be a delay between the repertory season and the West End run then this could necessitate re-rehearsing and recasting (which in turn means re-costuming, new production photographs and other associated costs). You should factor this into your cost/benefit analysis when establishing the financial parameters of the co-production deal in the first place. Of course, once you see the show you may decide to cut your losses and abandon it, in which case all of the top-up money will be lost.

The 'top-up' figure is likely to be a substantial amount of money, though considerably less than you would have to spend on creating the show from scratch. You will therefore need to raise 'seed money' investment for it in the same way that you would for a workshop try-out. This figure (less any small income from a share of box office) is then rolled on into the West End production budget along with any remount costs. Monies spent on the top-up can be repaid to those who provided it out of the West End capitalization or carried forward and converted into 'free' units for them. In any event the providers of the seed money will only be repaid (in cash or units) if the production goes forward. If it does not go forward for any reason then the seed money will have been lost. This may sound like an unattractive proposition for investors, but if the production doesn't work then the repertory co-production model is a far more cost-effective way of discovering this than financing a fully fledged West End production. And if the show does move forward then its chances of success have no doubt been increased by an unpressurised opening out of town, not to mention the fact that the capitalization figure will have been reduced with the result that the recoupment point will arrive quicker. So actually it's a good deal for investors, too.

One important point to remember is that you may not wish the national press critics to review your production before its arrival in the West End. Some of the more prestigious repertory theatres are in the habit of inviting the national critics to their opening nights, so if you don't want them there then you need to make this clear to the theatre at point of contract. On the other hand, if you are confident that your show will be ready then you might think it is worth the risk inviting them in order to create a buzz about it; though in this case do bear in mind that if a national newspaper has reviewed the show 'out of town' they may be resistant to re-reviewing it in the West End. In any event, this is something that you need to strategise properly with your press agent. Make sure too that you minimise on the doubling-up of personnel. The theatre is likely to have resident stage management and technical staff, but you may well have people on your own team who need to learn the show with a view to the future. Again, provided all this is taken account of in budgets and schedules then there will be no surprises.

It's very important with these deals that the theatre has a perceived ownership of the project, particularly for its audiences and its staff, and indeed for the local and national media. Although the billing will be 'by arrangement with' you, you must remember that you are a guest in their building and that you mustn't throw your weight around too much whilst the production is being created. This means that you must have complete confidence in the ability of the theatre's staff to work alongside your creative team in delivering the show to your specification. Part of this 'ownership' will most likely entail rehearsals taking place in the town where the theatre is located. Regional repertory theatres usually have their own rehearsal rooms, which helps with the budget, but on the other hand 'subsistence' payments have to be made to people working away from home. As a West End theatre producer, you will of course be based in London. At least train journeys are good for reading scripts.

If you have negotiated the West End rights for a show then you are also likely to have the touring rights. A pre-West End tour is another good way to run in your show and also to build up some capital reserves for the West End. It can in fact be a worthwhile intermediate stage between mounting a production at a repertory theatre and taking it into the West End. If this is your strategy then you are most likely to book touring dates to follow on directly from the repertory presentation, remembering that as soon as the production leaves the repertory theatre it will become yours and everyone will be contracted to you. This means that the cast will need to commit to a contract with the rep and to a contingent and consecutive touring contract with you immediately afterwards. Receiving theatres tend to have slightly shorter programming lead-times than producing theatres, which works in your favour as it enables you to secure your rep co-production deal and then book touring dates on the back of that once the co-pro details have been finalised. There is still the issue of securing people's services in the event of a hiatus between the end of the tour and the West End opening, but if the rep run has convinced you that the production has West End legs then the tour itself gives you a window of opportunity to negotiate with a West End theatre. The aspiration would clearly be to secure the West End theatre from the week after the tour ends, and this is not as difficult as it might sound.

The touring economy is entirely different to that of the West End. To start with, the agreements governing the engagement of performers are negotiated between the unions and UK Theatre (the trendy new name for the Theatrical Management Association) rather than SOLT. UKT's membership is even more disparate than that of SOLT, representing as it does the interests of repertory and receiving theatres throughout the country as well as those of both subsidised and commercial production companies and a number of other individuals and organisations with interests broadly on the management side of theatre. Smaller touring companies are represented by the Independent Theatre Council (ITC), who operate yet another set of agreements with the unions. The restrictive practices of the West End, which enforce the SOLT-endorsed union agreements via the theatre rental contracts, are less prevalent outside of London so the unions appreciate that they have to offer better deals to producers if they are to be persuaded to sign up to industry standard agreements. This is ironic, given that touring is a far more economically viable business model than presenting shows in the West End.

Although subsidised houses of necessity subscribe to standard agreements, as do most backstage staff at the major receiving theatres, there is a fairly broad interpretation of the industry-approved contracts amongst the wide range of touring outfits that ply their trade up and down the country. If you have aspirations to be a West End producer, however, then I strongly suggest that you toe the line, join UKT (they will welcome you with open arms) and operate their relevant commercial theatre agreements with Equity, the Musicians' Union and the technical union BECTU when your show is on tour. Voluntarily adhering to good practice and civilised wage structures is vastly preferable to having them shoved down your throat, and in an industry as complex as this it is always helpful to have a 'rule book' so that everyone knows exactly where they stand.

Touring is a better bet for commercial producers than the West End largely because it is based on the premise that the theatre pays you to turn up rather than you paying rent to the theatre. There are as many different deals to be done as there are theatres and shows, but if you don't walk away from a touring week with at least enough money in the bank to cover your running costs then you must be doing something very wrong. Potential deal structures include: a 'split' (where the net box office income for the week after VAT and ticketing charges is divided between the theatre and the producer, with the producer typically receiving 75%-85%); 'royalties off the top followed by a split' (where a percentage of weekly net box office goes straight to the producer, nominally to cover their royalty liability, before the remainder is divided between theatre and producer); a system of 'calls' (where the net weekly box office income is allocated along the lines of 'first x-thousand pounds to the producer, next x-thousand to the theatre, next x-thousand to the producer, and so on); or even a 'guarantee' (where the theatre pays the producer a flat fee irrespective of the box office outcome). Guarantees are as rare as hens' teeth these days and something to be cherished. The theatre deals will often consist of a combination of all of these elements, and it is important that you are not bamboozled by their apparent complexities.

As with the West End, the objective is to cover your running costs (including royalties), pay off the production costs and make a profit; so inasmuch as the majority of theatre deals will be box-office dependent you need to be able to compute various projected box office outcomes (netted down of course) into the theatre deal equation, and be sure that the resulting 'producer share' is at the very least going to cover your running costs and make a reasonable contribution to recouping your capital outlay.

There are various financial implications of touring which are absent from the West End budgeting process. It may sound like stating the obvious, but one of the biggest cost considerations of touring a show is the fact that it's touring. The show is on the move, so you need to pay for it to be set up, taken down and transported from venue to venue. The performers and staff also need to get from place to place and accommodate themselves (one principle joy of UKT's agreements with the unions is that you simply pay them a 'touring allowance', so you don't have to get involved in booking digs and the inevitable arguments over the quality of bedsheets and cooked breakfasts). The total 'move costs' always form a substantial part of the weekly running costs, so although a one-week run in each venue is typical it can sometimes be more cost effective with bigger shows (particularly musicals) to park them in the same theatre for two or more weeks.

Although the touring theatres won't charge you rent they will, like their West End equivalents, charge you a contra, but the components of this are rather different. You won't be charged for utilities and basic staffing (they take a risk that their share of the box office will cover this) and the largest items on your bill are likely to be the crew for the get-in and get-out, as well as any additional 'show staff' required to operate your production. If you are presenting a 'concert' show then the theatre will pay the relevant royalty direct to the PRS on your behalf and recharge you through the contra.

Touring theatres will also contra charge you for 'marketing services'. Check what these services include; all too often the agreed contra covers little more than a standard entry in their season brochure, with any further advertising and marketing activity recharged additionally. In the West End the risk is all yours so your landlord is unlikely to take much interest in the marketing of your show, but on tour the risk is shared as per the deal, and you are to a very large extent relying on the local theatre marketing team's knowledge of how best to reach out to their customer base. Of course they can only do this if they are properly informed about your production, so it is down to you to ensure that they have all the information that they need in order to sell your show effectively, including promptly delivered posters and leaflets over-printed with their venue details.

Assuming that your show is intended for the West End then its physical scale and running costs will be such that you will be booking theatres on the 'number one' circuit; the larger of the receiving houses. As is the case when selecting your West End theatre there is a balance to be struck between potential box office revenue and suitability for your product. It is unlikely to serve your purpose to present a two-hander in a vast 2,000 seat barn. Certain receiving houses tend to be associated with certain kinds of work, and it is useful to get onto all of their mailing lists so that you can see what goes where and what your competition is.

It's easy enough to get around the country by train (or plane) these days, so linking touring engagements ('dates') together geographically is not a huge priority, but it is very important that the tour consists of a consecutive run of venues. There is provision in the industry agreements for 'weeks out' and 'holiday weeks', but the basic principle (reasonably enough) is that the people you employ must continue to be paid in any event. As with West End artistes' contracts, you can give the performers two weeks' notice of the end of an engagement (for instance, if you fail to book theatres for the last four scheduled weeks of a tour), but unlike the West End you can't give notice to the theatre (or them to you for that matter) however poor the box office takings.

All of this would be manageable if it weren't for the fact that each venue works to a different deadline for signing off its season brochure, which means that you can be under huge pressure to go to contract on a particular date when you have still not confirmed the theatres for the previous three weeks. Not to mention the fact that it would be folly to contract your actors until you know that you have secured a consecutive tour, but the venues that you *have* pencilled will be clamouring for confirmed casting to go in their brochures. In an ideal world, you are trying to line up say sixteen consecutive venues 'subject to contract', then go back to your actors and confirm their contracts, and then 'green light' the tour dates. The trouble is that your best theatre will inevitably want to go to print with its brochure and announce your cast long before you have lined up the rest of the dates. The theatre's season brochure, which may be published two to four times a year, is by far the most effective marketing tool that these venues have, so always check that there is a good lead time between its publication date and your appearance at the theatre. If you have missed the brochure completely then don't take the booking.

Number one touring venues, like West End theatres, often belong to a chain, so a single negotiation can sometimes secure a large number of dates; in fact you may well find that your potential West End landlord also controls a number of the touring venues you are negotiating with. As with the West End theatres, these chains may be owned or managed by companies who themselves produce, so you may well find yourself in competition with their own productions for the best dates and the best positioning in their brochures and on their theatres' websites and front of house displays. It's important not to be intimidated by the large-scale operators when negotiating your deals with them; they may be big and powerful but they still have an enormous number of weeks to programme at their venues all over the country, and you are helping to solve this problem for them. Despite the fact that it can at times appear that you are battling with entities who are operating from a position of monopoly, it is still perfectly possible to book a tour even if you can't agree terms with a big chain. Many regional venues are still operated independently or directly by local authorities and it may be a better option to do business with these rather than to accept terms that you are not happy with from the big players. In any event, it is important that you examine each individual theatre contract in all of its detail, taking particular care with any that are headed 'standard contract' (there is no such thing!). And look out in particular for the numerous box office and ticketing charges that are usually slipped into the small print and which reduce the net box office receipts upon which your income share is usually based.

If you have never booked a 'number one' tour before then you will definitely need to add a tour booking agent to your growing army of advisors and consultants in order to guide you through this particular minefield. They will charge a set-up fee of a few thousand pounds and then take a small weekly percentage. In order to ensure that they secure you the best possible deals with the theatres, logic dictates that this percentage should really be calculated against the 'producer's share' of income rather than total net box office receipts, although they will usually try to insist on the latter. The tour booker will have a number of clients as well as you, but there is no point in losing sleep over whether they have a conflict of interest in terms of securing you the best dates. The fact that they have a large portfolio of shows to offer means that the venues will take their calls. It also means that they are better positioned to track the routing of other productions, which is ultimately to your advantage.

If you are booking a single tour on your own then it can feel a bit like you are playing a game of Battleships with everyone else who is booking tours. You will often find your route effectively blocked by other shows (to the extent that you can sometimes build up a full picture of your rivals' touring schedules) and then suddenly you'll score a direct hit by finding a venue that has exactly the week you want. Intelligence gathering about the routing of your competitors is incredibly important to the success of your tour booking strategy, and venues are more likely to divulge specific information to a freelance tour booker representing a number of productions. On the other side of the equation, the theatres are dealing with numerous bookers in order to build up a coherent programme of work to present to their audiences. A venue might give your production a 'first pencil' or a 'second pencil' on a date depending on how their negotiations are going with other parties. Given all of this, it is very important that everyone is clear when a deal has actually been concluded, and this should be confirmed through the exchange of a brief memo confirming the headline terms (dates, performance times, get-in schedule, marketing contra and number of crew provided by venue) which then becomes a *de facto* contract pending the signing of a long form agreement for the engagement.

Your tour booker will have all the necessary skills to manage all of these additional spinning plates in your circus act, but don't rely on their input to the extent that you fail to build up a personal relationship with the people who run the touring venues. The contract is ultimately between the theatre and you, and you should therefore at least pick up the phone and put the finishing touches to negotiations before signing it off. It is said that some experienced producers engage in the game of Battleships at a more sophisticated level, to the extent that they sometimes set out to snooker rival producers by deliberately blocking dates at venues that they know their competitors need in order to construct a consecutive tour. It can certainly feel like that when you are starting out.

Whether the theatres' own cycle of brochures is three monthly, four monthly or six monthly, there are effectively two 'seasons' in the touring calendar. The first starts in January (immediately following pantomime), is interrupted by Easter and a number of bank holidays and tends to peter out in the early summer when the domestic audience heads off on its summer holidays. The second starts in September and runs straight through until the pantomime season. This means that if you are tagging a tour directly onto the end of a repertory co-production then you are likely to be looking to schedule your rep co-pro early January or late summer. If you are not taking the co-pro route then there is nothing to stop you from going straight out on tour without a rep season and simply rehearsing the show in a rehearsal room and getting the set built in a workshop in just the same way as if you were going directly into the West End. In this case the first theatre on your tour will have to be persuaded to host your technical and dress rehearsals.

Some star actors will insist that there is a guaranteed West End run if they are going to commit to a tour. It is difficult and expensive to secure a West End theatre sufficiently far in advance to be able to schedule touring dates in front of it, and it also means that you can't bail out of your West End commitment if you change your mind about bringing the show in once you have seen it. On the plus side, if this arrangement helps you to secure top calibre stars for the project then the tour itself may well establish some financial security for the production prior to its arrival in the West End. It's worth bearing in mind, though, that some plays and actors are more popular on the touring circuit than in the West End (and *vice versa*), so you should only link a tour and a West End engagement contractually from the outset if you are extremely confident of both the artistic and financial outcome. If the performers' West End and touring contracts are contingent from the outset then you should technically pay the rehearsal salaries at West End rates, or at least top them up when you get there.

Whether you start your production on the fringe, at a rep or on tour, if you have the West End in mind then it is important to ensure that your licence from the writer includes a West End option from the outset. Some writers will only agree to a conditional West End option subject to their approval of the production when they see it 'out of town'. Don't sign up to this. Your investors will rightly insist that a West End option is in place before they agree to finance the production's pre-West End life.

For investors, a tour is a less attractive proposition than a West End run. Although statistically they are more likely to get a return of some sort on their capital than in the West End, this return is by definition limited by the number of touring weeks that have been booked. Angels don't rely on their theatrical investments to generate a regular income, and in purely financial terms tend to be more attracted to the prospect, however unlikely, of a 'big win' in the West End. Added to which, the bright lights of Shaftesbury Avenue for some reason tend to have a greater allure for them than the doubtless equally bright lights of Sunderland. Investors, like just about everyone else involved, are thus more likely to back your project from the outset if they can be assured of your West End intentions, though you must of course be very careful not to make any undertakings, either written or verbal, that you may ultimately not be able to make good on.

The same basic budgeting principles apply to each scenario, whether you are raising money for a rep try-out, a pre-West End tour or a West End run, or indeed any combination of the above. In each case the budgeted production costs have to be financed in a way that allows the capital raised either to be written off, recouped through weekly operating profit or rolled on into the next stage of the project. And if your investors really don't fancy financing a tour then you could always apply to the Arts Council for a guarantee against loss; particularly if you have a non-star led project of real artistic merit and are co-producing with one of their regional building-based clients. This requires you to demonstrate a projected loss rather than a projected profit, of course, which is counter-intuitive for a West End producer. But if you have the right project, are not in a position to take a risk and are happy to survive on management fees then you shouldn't rule it out as an option.

Just when you thought your life couldn't get any more complicated, it's time to meet your creative team.

6. HOW TO WORK WITH THE CREATIVE TEAM ON A WEST END SHOW

'I personally would like to bring a tortoise onto the stage, turn it into a racehorse, then into a hat, a song, a dragoon and a fountain of water. One can dare anything in the theatre and it is the place where one dares the least.'

– Eugène Ionesco, *Notes and Counter Notes*

Assembling your 'creative team', the people who will supervise the various artistic elements of your show, is a bit like that scene at the beginning of an action movie where an unlikely bunch of misfits is put together to carry out an extraordinary mission. The key player, and indeed the absolute lynchpin of the entire artistic endeavour, is the director. A successful creative dynamic between the producer and the director is at the centre of all the best commercial theatre productions, and choosing the right person for this role is as important as choosing the right show. It may well be the director who brings you the project in the first place, but if it is not then it is essential to do your research before committing to someone you have not worked with before. The power balance between the producer and the director in a commercial theatre production is a delicate one, and managing this relationship is a core skill for a producer. If you are new to producing then getting an experienced director on board to head up your team is a good move, but at the same time it can risk undermining your own position as the creative head of the project. The director may well prove pivotal in attracting a first-rate cast and design team to the project, but it is important that you, who after all have made it all possible, do not become a passive bystander in the process.

Directors who have worked extensively on large-scale productions in the subsidised sector can be used to a different pecking order, where the artistic head of the project is top dog and the administrative elements of the producer's role are carried out by an executive who is there to serve the director's creative vision. They may be used to bigger budgets, longer rehearsal periods and a more comprehensive administrative infrastructure to support the creative process. They often rehearse in the building where the production will ultimately be presented, and in close proximity to the people who are making the sets and costumes. These luxuries, unfortunately, are rarely available to commercial productions. Because of the resources and continuity that characterise the subsidised sector it is easier for a director to build a reputation for artistic excellence, develop long-term working relationships with creative collaborators and start a collection of awards trophies on their mantelpiece. The realities of working in the commercial sector can therefore be a rude awakening.

Like all of us, however, freelance directors have to earn a living, and what the commercial sector can offer is the tantalising possibility, though of course not the certainty, of a long-term royalty income. Productions in the subsidised sector run for a limited time, sometimes in repertoire, and directors are usually paid a one-off fee (unless they happen to be the artistic director of the building). A long running hit in the West End, on the other hand, can put your kids through school if you are a creative stakeholder. Unaccountably, too, the strange, tawdry glamour of the West End even appears to cast its spell over those who have built their artistic reputation working in the subsidised houses. It's great to direct at the National Theatre, but it's magical to see your name in lights on Shaftesbury Avenue. And let's not forget that, whether you are a director, a writer or a star actor, it is only in the West End that they do, literally, put your name in lights. Canny directors skilfully ply their trade between the two sectors, ensuring their artistic reputations through one and their not inconsiderable livelihoods through the other. And who can blame them?

Some directors (usually the older ones) spend as little time as possible in the rehearsal room and entrust much of the business of moving the actors around and debating their motivation to an assistant or associate. Although this approach can seem a bit counter-intuitive at first it actually results in them having more time available to spend on taking an artistic overview of the production. Other directors (usually the younger ones), will happily lock themselves away in a rehearsal room with a group of actors for weeks on end, and sometimes seem to risk losing sight of the bigger picture; that the purpose of rehearsals is to create a performance for an audience. As a method of artistic creation the rehearsal process is particularly odd, and it is important that it does not become an end in itself with the 'process' becoming more important than the 'product'. It is during rehearsals that actors will enjoy their greatest level of creative freedom and self expression as interpretive artists, as they explore and experiment with the text and the character that they are playing. Once the show has opened it is contractually their responsibility to re-create the production 'as directed' eight times a week, and although the experience of doing this in front of a live audience can in itself be a fulfilling one, it is not difficult to understand the attractions of the rehearsal room.

The main problem with rehearsals from a producer's point of view is that they cost money at a time when there is no income coming in to the project. Although all performers and stage management receive the minimum pay rate agreed between SOLT and Equity for the rehearsal period, and not even the biggest of stars will argue with this, the costs mount up when you add holiday pay accruals, rehearsal room hire and other incidental costs. It's taken for granted, of course, that you'll provide an endless supply of tea, coffee, milk, sugar and biscuits throughout the rehearsal process, not to mention some nice pastries at the 'meet and greet' preceding the read-through on the first day. If you don't you will be lynched, but when you do you won't be thanked. I tell a lie. Once, many years ago, an elderly actor with a long but undistinguished career came up to me at the end of the first day of rehearsals and said 'Well, that went well; and thank you so much for those lovely croissants this morning.' I have long since forgotten the play we were rehearsing, but I will never forget that small courtesy.

If what is cooked up between the director and the actors in the rehearsal room is not what you wanted then you only have yourself to blame. Just as a good director has the knack of giving actors creative ownership of their work whilst achieving exactly the outcome that the director has envisaged, so a good producer will give the director ownership whilst achieving exactly the outcome that the producer has envisaged. Directors who have worked mostly in the subsidised sector can be a bit suspicious of the producer's role at first, and it is easy for the producer to become characterised as the paymaster rather than the ultimate creator of the project. It's all too easy to get bogged down in arguments about casting, lack of rehearsal time and limited production budgets and to forget that the shared goal is the creation of a work of art. Once directors have overcome their initial suspicion of commercial producers and their agenda, I know for a fact that many of them very much enjoy having their boss as a creative collaborator; someone to run their ideas past and to share their hopes and fears about the progress of the project; someone to help them untangle their problems, to act as a sounding board and to take ultimate responsibility for the outcome.

And collaboration, of course, is the key. Particularly experienced directors know how to get the best out of producers, just as good producers know how to get the best out of directors. One certainty is that you won't get anywhere as a producer if you play the 'he who pays the piper calls the tune' card. If you want something on stage doing your way then you need to have a good reason and a good argument; you need to be able to tackle an artistic debate head on. You have to be as persuasive on the subject of Hamlet's motivation as you are on the subject of why the director should accept half their usual fee. Of course, if you don't know your stuff then you will quickly be rumbled, but if you haven't done your homework on the play or musical you are producing then you should question why you are doing it in the first place. Your director and indeed all of your team must trust your artistic vision as much as they trust in your financial and administrative acumen. You can't be passionate about something that you don't understand. I may wear a suit and you may wear a leather jacket, but that doesn't mean we can't have a meaningful discussion about Ibsen.

It is very important to respect the director's status with the actors and the rest of the creative team, and not to challenge or undermine their vision in front of others, particularly in the rehearsal room. If you have concerns about the way things are going artistically then a quiet chat over coffee in your office is usually the best way. It is critical to the successful progress of the project that the producer and the director are seen to be singing from the same hymn sheet at all times and it is particularly important that you restrict any comments to actors about their performances to 'darling, you were wonderful' or similar. A producer 'noting' an actor can have catastrophic consequences, as you may unwittingly be contradicting something that the actor concerned has been told by the director. As you are their boss they probably won't argue with you, although they may disagree with you. Chaos and confusion worthy of *A Servant of Two Masters* is all too likely to ensue. This is not to say that your instincts about what is right and what is wrong in an acting performance won't be absolutely correct, and it is often the case that the producer notices things that the director has overlooked. But notes should always be given to the director, and argued and debated with them if necessary, before being passed on to the actors by the director. A good director will then give the note to the actor as their own. If the director attributes the note to the producer, even if they make it clear that they endorse it, the actor may suspect that the director disagrees with it. It is often the case that actors don't appreciate just how creatively hands-on a producer is actually being behind the scenes.

In any event, however involved you are it is usually advisable to steer well clear of rehearsals. Go to say hello to everybody on the first day. Give a stirring speech and introduce the director to make their own stirring speech. You should always speak first. That puts the director at the top of the bill but gives you ultimate ownership of the project in the eyes of those present. Listen to the read-through of the script and pray that everybody is as you remembered them from when you were casting the show and that the leading lady hasn't put on two stone. Some actors will have learnt all their lines and some will barely be able to string two words together; neither fact is an indicator either of their work ethic or of the way in which their performance will turn out. After the read-through it is usually best to make yourself scarce for the rest of the rehearsal process. It doesn't look good for the director if the producer is seen to be breathing down their neck, and in any case if you are doing your job properly preparing all the other aspects of the production then you really shouldn't have the time to be hanging around at rehearsals. And if you don't trust your director enough to get on with it then you have chosen the wrong director. The director will keep you up to date with progress in the rehearsal room and, if they are any good, will involve you in any key artistic decision-making. Daily written reports from the stage management will keep you informed on the nitty gritty such as whether an extra vase of flowers is needed on the mantelpiece in Act Two, Scene One. You'll in any case have regular production meetings with all the key creative players in the final weeks of the production process as all of the elements of the production begin to come together under your ultimate supervision.

The next time you go into the rehearsal room will most likely be for the final run-through before work moves to the theatre (sometimes styled the 'management run'). It's actually very useful to have a fresh pair of eyes at this stage, and the arrival of the producer should create a *frisson* which will be absent if you have been a regular visitor throughout the process. The director should be keen to receive your notes and comments after this run-through, and if you are good at your job then you will have plenty to give.

Matching the right director to the right project is an important skill of the producer, and you will find that certain directors work at their best with certain styles and *genres* of work. Some excel with small-scale work and others are at home with large scale epics. Some are particularly associated with the work of certain playwrights. Like actors, they don't like to be 'typecast', however, and tend to appreciate the challenge of an opportunity to work outside of their comfort zone. And as with actors, if you give them the opportunity to do so the results can be either triumphant or disastrous. Musical theatre direction, in particular, is a specialised skill; and although everyone has to start somewhere it is a high-risk strategy to take on a director for a musical who has no experience in this particular field. For these reasons it is very important to do your homework. Ideally you will have seen at least one of your preferred director's productions, but failing that you will have studied their track record and the critical response to their work in detail. The director is your creative partner on the production's journey and it is essential therefore that they are a fellow traveller and share your artistic vocabulary. Equally importantly though, and easily overlooked in the hurly-burly of assembling your creative team, is whether you get on with the director on a personal level. A mutual respect, an ease of communication and a shared sense of humour are essential prerequisites for this key relationship; and this is just as important when you are considering transferring an existing project from another theatre as when you are creating one from scratch. It may sound obvious, but if you and the director don't get on well together then you are unlikely to be able to create great work together.

One of the reasons that you need to get on well with your director is that you will probably spend most of your time arguing (behind the scenes, of course, not in front of the actors or the other members of the creative team). The biggest bone of contention is likely to be casting. There is a popular misconception that directors cast on talent and producers cast on marketability. Nothing could actually be further from the truth. Producers tend to be extremely good judges of acting talent, and in any case when that talent converts into five-star reviews that is the best marketing your production could possibly have. Conversely, directors who have elected to come over to the Dark Side and work in the commercial West End will have their eye on a long-running hit just as much as the producer. The problem that they both face is the ticket-buying public. We will examine issues surrounding 'star casting' later on; but the fact is that, whatever the merits of your production in its own right, you exponentially increase the chances of your show becoming a West End box office success if it is cast with star actors. Directors know this as much as producers, so the casting arguments are not, as is usually supposed, about 'talent versus stardom'. They are simply the same arguments that any two people would have about which actors have the greatest talent and which will sell the most tickets. Fortunately there are plenty of actors out there who possess both qualities, however evasive they may seem at times; but nonetheless the debates between producer and director about who is the right actor to cast in each role will go on far into the night. These debates are a critical test of the relationship, and if anything approaching a consensus can be reached on this centrally important issue then just about everything else will follow.

Whether you have hunted down a director whose work you admire, or whether they have come recommended by the author or someone else who you trust, the key factors in getting them to sign up will be whether they like the script and whether they like and trust you. For just about everyone else involved in the project the criteria are likely to be whether they like the script and whether they like and trust the director. In any event, your director will be a key factor in encouraging actors and other practitioners of calibre to put their names to your project, particularly if you yourself are relatively new on the scene as a producer. Equally, a director who is perceived to be weak or inexperienced may well be a deterrent, however highly their work is regarded. Young and emerging directors have a world of opportunity to ply their trade and develop their skills on smaller-scale projects and on the fringe, and as assistant or associate directors in the subsidised sector. But the choppy, pirate-infested waters of the West End are better navigated by pilots of maturity and experience. Don't worry if your director is more experienced than you are; you still have every right, as the project's initiator, to be an equal partner in its creative realisation, and you will learn a lot from watching a really good director at work. Given the shared journey of the producer and the director, and the gentle blurring of the lines between their roles when it comes to the creative process, it is not surprising that some of the most enduring creative partnerships in the industry are between producers and directors.

The design team (set, costumes, lighting and sound) is the next link in the creative chain. The director will often want to work with people who they have worked with before, as this gives them an understandable comfort factor and reassures them that their creative vision will be realised. It's important, though, that the producer has some say in this matter and is not simply presented with a *fait accompli* by the director. Like directors, certain designers tend to work best in certain *genres* and on certain scales. Proscenium arch theatres require a specific set of skills. If you have seen a designer's work that you like, and you are convinced that they are right for your project, then you should fly the flag for them with your proposed director. If you are unhappy with the outcome of this particular argument then it does not bode well for your working relationship with your director, and strategically it may actually be better to switch directors at this stage rather than designers.

It is crucially important that you are ahead of the game with all aspects of the design process. The set design, in particular, can have a critical impact on both the artistic and the financial outcome of the project. The producer, director and designer should sit down right at the start of the process and ensure that they are all broadly on the same page. The designer will then work with the director to create a detailed concept for the show, which may well be presented to the producer in the first instance as a set of 'artist's impressions'. Provided everyone is happy, a 'white card model' (the clue's in the name!) will be created by the designer (or their assistant) to show how the set works physically. Finally, a detailed, full colour, model will be made (on a 1:25 scale) and presented to the producer. All the way through this process, the protocol is that the designer is presenting their ideas for the approval of the producer (it is taken as read that they have collaborated with the director in the creation of the design to the extent that the director is happy with them). This is therefore your chance to speak out; to comment on, challenge and provoke debate about what you are being presented with. If you are not happy with any aspect of the aesthetic (be it the brown wallpaper in the kitchen scene or the raised platform at the back of the stage) then say so. The design process is another context in which your valuable fresh pair of eyes can really help people to see the wood for the trees. Who has the casting vote? No one. It is all about argument, persuasion and consensus, and provided you are talking sense then your opinion is as important as the designer's and the director's. You need to have the confidence, if necessary, to explain to a designer who has been following a creative brief from their friend the director, and has been slaving over a meticulously detailed model box for weeks, exactly why it doesn't work and why they need literally to go back to the drawing board. Having said all this, rejecting the set design is a sign that you have failed as a producer. If your instincts in appointing the director and the designer were right, then the designer will score a bullseye with their first model box presentation.

Lurking somewhere in the room during the model box presentation will be your production manager. It is their job to keep a discrete eye on proceedings from a practical and financial point of view. It's probably best not to comment on such matters yourself, as it undermines your position as a valued creative collaborator, and characterises you as a Scrooge rather than a facilitator if your concerns are seen to be budgetary. A good production manager will step up to the mark and fight your corner for you in this respect, but it is vitally important of course that you know exactly what your production manager is talking about so that you can ensure that they haven't missed a trick when you compare notes afterwards. The set build is the area of the production process that most frequently goes over budget. You pretty well know how much it costs to rehearse a certain number of actors for a certain number of weeks and how much money you have agreed to pay the creative team.

And it is up to you exactly how much or how little you spend on advertising and marketing the production in the lead-up to opening. But accurately budgeting the process whereby the set design evolves from a model box, via a set of scale drawings, and a construction process in a workshop, to a full-scale physical structure on the stage, is a real skill that relies on a successful interface between your production manager, the designer and the workshop entrusted with the build.

You yourself should be confident to ask questions about sightlines. Is all of the set fully visible from all of the seats (or at least the top price ones)? There can sometimes be an issue with items that are positioned too far upstage, particularly when viewed from the balcony, and many West End theatres have overhanging circles which means that the top of the set is not visible from the rear stalls. By the time you are looking at the final set model you should know which theatre you are going to be hiring, so the model should be presented inside a black box which represents to scale the opening of its proscenium. This will give you a rough idea of sightlines in relation to the proscenium arch itself, and there are computer programmes available that can work out in more detail the line of vision from individual seats. Your designer, or at least their technical drawer, should be conversant with these. It may sound obvious, but it is always worth double checking that the black box surrounding the model is a representation of the correct theatre. I know of a case where it was not, and the consequences for sightlines were disastrous. Your concern with sightlines may be dressed up as a purely creative one, but of course there is also a financial impact if you have to reduce the price of seats because of restricted views of the set.

It's perhaps better though to let your production manager question the price of individual elements of the design. A skilled production manager will have a good sense of the potential cost of what is being presented and in particular of the materials that have been specified. They should also be able to flag up any health and safety issues at an early stage; adjusting a set that has already been built in order to meet health and safety requirements can be a costly and time-consuming process.

As far as the installation of the set into the theatre is concerned time is money and every man-hour counts. Your production manager will therefore be making an initial judgement, based on the model, as to whether the set can be installed successfully during the time allocated for the get-in. They will also be assessing how many crew it will take to operate during performances. A large number of 'flown' pieces or trucking units is indicative of a large stage crew, again with long term financial consequences. Automation can cut down the number of crew required, but carries its own budgetary burdens in terms of kit and staffing; and if it malfunctions can be responsible for your show grinding to a halt completely or, worse still, for some quite nasty injuries. If there is a possibility of a tour before or after the West End then there will also be the question of whether the set is designed to be put up and dismantled easily and how many 45-foot lorries it will fit into. The production manager will be asking all of these questions and more on your behalf, and will give you the verdict on the set from their own perspective once the creative team have left. Any subsequent alterations to the design for reasons of practicality or cost should then be negotiated with the design team by the production manager, to avoid you as producer being the villain of the piece – though the team of course are no fools and know that the production manager's views are fully endorsed by you.

Once the design is approved a set of detailed technical drawings are created to enable the workshop to build it. It's good to take a look at these drawings and to have them explained to you. There is no shame in not fully understanding what you are looking at, but something may leap out at you that you had not noticed before. Construction workshops are commercial enterprises who will pitch to the production manager for the job, and the contract to build the set will be awarded according to various criteria including cost, speed of delivery and quality of work. If you are lucky enough to be co-producing your show with a subsidised regional producing theatre before transferring it into the West End then you may have the luxury of a fully resourced, fully-funded in-house workshop at your disposal.

Throughout this process the clock is ticking. The set model needs to be in rehearsals on the first day so that the performers can see the set that they will be acting on, and plans need to be available so that the stage management can mark up the acting area on the rehearsal room floor. Workshops allocate particular time slots to particular sets, so if there is any delay in delivering the plans to them then they have to engage additional staff in order to stay on schedule and this costs extra. All of this is your production manager's headache in the first instance, but you need to know what is going on and how it all works so that you can ask the right questions at the right time.

Set models are beautiful, hand-crafted things, and there is sometimes a round of applause when the designer creates a little moment of magic by lifting a black cloth off their latest creation to reveal it to the assembled actors on the first day of rehearsal. They make wonderful museum exhibits and are always evocative of the time and the place in which the production was presented, effectively encapsulating the spirit of a show in a way that no photograph or film ever could. For all the advances in computer graphics there is no substitute for a set model when it comes to getting a feel for the design concept for a production. And it is not only the models that are at risk of being replaced by computer graphics but the sets themselves. A vogue for the use of projection in set design (some of it now even in 3D), not to mention the fact that cloths tend now to be printed rather than painted, is putting many of the traditional scenic crafts at risk of extinction in much the same way that CGI is increasingly replacing more traditional skills in the film industry. It may be argued that the aesthetic of printed or projected scenery sits more comfortably with the computer games generation, but my own view is that if you want to see a film then you should go to the cinema. The smell of wet paint as the last brush-strokes are applied to the set while the audience queues outside for the first performance is all part of the magic. Just as an animatronic 'animal' can never be a substitute for the spectacle of a human-operated puppet because it has no heartbeat, so a set that has not had the benefit of human contact in its decoration is somehow immediately soulless. Nonetheless, projection is rapidly establishing itself as the 'must have' stage design component so it probably won't be long before the set model simply consists of an array of blank screens. Projection has a budgetary implication, both in terms of the hire and installation of the equipment and its ongoing operation, and although it is fairly straightforward to execute in a West End context, if you are planning for your show to have a touring life then it is not always a particularly user-friendly option when it comes to presenting it in venues of different shapes and sizes.

Also present at the model box showing will be the lighting designer. Just as a director is likely to recommend a set designer, so a set designer is likely to recommend a lighting designer, as the way that a set is lit can be absolutely critical to its aesthetic. At the presentation the model box itself will probably be lit by nothing more than a couple of standard lamps, but the lighting designer will nonetheless be able to get a feeling for the scale of the set, its colour palette and the materials it is constructed from; all essential knowledge for the successful execution of their own craft. They will also want to know what space is available amongst all the scenery to hang the lanterns that actually shed the light. Most theatres offer a number of metal bars which hover in the 'flies' above the stage; and the production manager will have to arbitrate between the lighting designer who will want to hang lights on them and the set designer who may want to hang bits of scenery on them.

Theatre lighting technology has changed beyond all recognition in the last thirty years, with the advent of computers representing, as ever, a mixed blessing. 'Intelligent' (i.e. moving) lights have the ability to refocus themselves into any number of configurations (and colours) in the course of a performance. This has radically cut down the number of actual lanterns involved in any lighting design, but means that a new generation of computerised 'moving light programmers' has evolved who get paid a handsome daily rate during the fit-up at the theatre. It also means that when anything goes wrong with the control desk during a performance there is often nobody in the building who has a clue what to do about it. It has to be said that advances in lighting technology, unlike advances in projection, have had an entirely positive effect on the sophistication of the stage pictures that can be presented to an audience. The only slight niggle is that the sequencing and timing of each cue is pre-programmed, so that the person operating the lights simply presses the 'go' button over and over again when instructed to do so over their headset, and without any real creative engagement with what is happening on the stage. And of course what is happening on stage is a live performance being given by real people that is not pre-programmed. This begs the question as to what happens if an actor accidentally cuts a minute of material from a speech that is covered by a three-minute lighting fade. Of course there is a manual over-ride, but this presupposes that the lighting operator hasn't by then slipped into a catatonic trance. And if the director or lighting designer decide to make any changes after the show has opened then you have to call in, at vast expense, an army of computer geeks with machines that go 'ping'. I once saw a lighting designer sitting in a theatre auditorium in London focus a moving light hanging in an opera house in Germany via his laptop. There's really no answer to that.

Ideally your set designer will also design the costumes, as this is an easy way of ensuring a synchronicity between the principal design elements of the show, but designers who work in both disciplines are an increasingly rare breed, probably due to the evolving skills base required for set design. The processes of costume design and making remain reassuringly old-fashioned, however, the most recent innovation being the sewing machine. Costume design is a wonderfully eccentric art, and until we get to the point where they are projecting 3-D costumes onto naked actors (well I guess it would speed up quick changes!) there will always be a demand for it. Again, the set designer is likely to want to work with someone who is known to them, as a successful dialogue between set and costume design from the outset is essential to achieving a consistent overall 'look' for the production. The lighting designer is also going to take an interest in the colour palette and material of the costumes. The main question that your production manager will be asking, however, is whether the costumes are to be hired, bought or made. If hired then the cost will form part of the running budget, and if bought or made then it will be in the production budget. Ultimately it may well turn out to be a combination of all three. Bespoke costume 'makes' are an expensive investment but are of course essential if the design is unique or if practical problems such as quick changes or the need to execute a high-kicking dance routine require clever solutions. If the show is intended to have a long life in the West End, or a life beyond it, then making or buying a stock of costumes may well be a worthwhile investment, not forgetting that they will have to be altered or replaced when new actors take over the roles or when they wear out. If it is a short run, and a good match can be found from a hire company's existing stock without compromising the design, then hiring can be a better option.

Your production manager will discuss all of these options with the costume designer and suggest a course of action that balances the artistic, practical and financial needs of the production. The 'Head of Wardrobe' will then supervise all the measurements and fittings of actors (which can sometimes take huge chunks out of the time allocated for rehearsals) under the watchful eye of the costume designer. Actors can sometimes be a bit resistant to wearing hired or second-hand costumes, but giving the frocks a good clean and popping them into Harvey Nichols bags normally does the trick.

Props and furnishings will generally come under the remit of the set designer, who may delegate this part of their work to a specialist props buyer acting under their instruction. If any bespoke props are required then a specialist props maker or workshop may be engaged. Props and furniture budgets can easily get out of hand on plays with period settings, but a good props buyer will earn their fee through their knowledge of where to source at a good price all those little knick-knacks (or at least things that look like them) that lend an air of authenticity to a set. Wigs and facial hair (and make-up on some large scale musicals) all need designing, creating and maintaining, and on a big show can account for significant financial outlay both in terms of pre-production and running costs. Wigs and make-up obviously have to synchronise well with the costumes, so the people responsible for them may well be suggested by the costume designer. Given that 'looks' are an important consideration in the casting process, actors have an obligation not to change their physical appearance without your permission once you have engaged them. Suddenly shaving their heads, getting a visible tattoo or eating lots of hamburgers and putting on weight is not permissible. On the other hand, if you want their own hair worn differently than it was in the audition then you will have to pay for it to be cut and/or coloured, maintained throughout the run and then at the end of the contract restored (as far as possible) to its original style.

The design team is completed by the sound designer. For a play this can involve little more than helping the director select a few pieces of apposite incidental music and getting them cleared by the Performing Right Society (PRS). If the cast includes performers (film actors for instance) who are not sufficiently schooled in the gentle art of vocal projection then there may be some discrete 'float microphones' at the front of the stage to help enhance the spoken word. At the other extreme, a play may include a repertoire of zany sound effects, the creation of which is, I suspect, the part of their job that sound designers enjoy most. The art of the sound designer really comes into its own with musicals, where the voices of performers wearing battery powered radio microphones has to be balanced with the amplified musicians in the pit via a mixing desk that looks like something from the Starship Enterprise, and then fed out through speakers placed at strategic points in the auditorium. There is also room for a bit of alchemy in the sound mixing process involving the use of pre-recorded vocal tracks at key points, usually triggered by the musical director from the pit. Although much of the sound operation of a show is pre-programmed, the operator, unlike their counterpart on the lighting desk, is making choices on the night which affect the audience experience. The sound mix has to take into account all sorts of variables such as the number of people in the auditorium and the condition of the performers' voices. A good sound operator is therefore crucial to the successful execution of the sound design.

For obvious reasons the sound design can make or break a musical, and the most important (and difficult) thing to achieve is that the auditory experience is exactly the same from every seat in the house. In musicals there will always be the great debate about where on an actor's head a radio microphone is best placed in order to achieve the desired sound quality without detracting from the 'look' of the show, although audiences seem willing enough these days to suspend disbelief sufficiently to ignore a head microphone worthy of Madonna hooked over the ear of a nineteenth-century aristocrat. West End theatres generally do not have much in the way of in-house lighting and sound equipment so you will have to include the hire fees for all this kit in your weekly running budget. And don't forget to budget for regularly replacing all those short-lived and ecologically unfriendly radio microphone batteries.

Most lighting and sound designers will at some point attempt to situate large pieces of kit in positions where seats should be. Such seat losses (or 'technical kills' as they are somewhat graphically known in some quarters) are to be avoided where at all possible, in just the same way that speakers, lanterns and bits of set should not be positioned in a manner that obstructs the view of the public and therefore reduces the price that it is reasonable to charge them for their seats. Again, you should send your production manager in to do battle on all such issues, as it is not appropriate for the producer to be seen to be involving themselves in niggling financial matters, particularly when the creative team may feel that such concerns are compromising their work.

Musicals bring with them an extended creative *dramatis personae*. The choreographer is likely to work closely with the director on the overall staging of the production in addition to creating the actual dance routines. Like the designer, they are therefore likely to be someone who the director has worked with before. A kind of creative shorthand grows up between directors, designers and choreographers who are used to working together, and although it is your absolute prerogative to break up a team and introduce new blood it is often best to adopt an 'if it's not broke don't fix it' policy. The upside of using an existing team is that you can be pretty sure (though by no means certain!) that they will share a vision for the show and get along with each other in the process of making it. The downside is that they can form a sort of 'creative cabal' from which the producer feels excluded. It is easy for the producer to slip into the role of an observer rather than a contributor when the core creatives on a project have a long track record of working together.

It is helpful to involve the choreographer in meetings from the early stages of the production. Not only is the dance style often the defining feature of a musical, but they will constantly remind the rest of the team to allow for the practicalities of staging dance numbers. The set needs to have enough floor space to accommodate the routines, the costumes need to be in a style and material that is easy to move in, and if the numbers are particularly energetic then some of the vocal tracks may need to be pre-recorded. If you've ever watched a show and wondered how the performers managed to sing so accurately whilst leaping round the stage executing energetic choreography, well the fact is that they probably didn't.

The number of people involved in the music department on a musical production will vary hugely according to what state of readiness the music itself is in. With a classic musical it should simply be a case of hiring a good musical director to supervise the cast vocal rehearsals and band rehearsals and to conduct the band in the pit every night. If you're lucky, the musical director will also choose the band players for you (meaning that you don't have to get involved with a band 'fixer') and may even play the first keyboard ('keys one'). The assistant musical director (usually 'keys one' if the musical director does not play in the band and 'keys two' if they do) will probably also be engaged for the entire rehearsal period to help teach the music to the cast, and will deputise for the musical director in the event of their absence for any reason. There may also be an additional rehearsal keyboard player (probably the person who played piano at the auditions).

This is all in an ideal world. If the show is a new one, or if it needs re-orchestrating (for instance for a smaller line-up of musicians than featured in the original production), then you may well need a musical arranger, an orchestrator and a copyist, all of whom may try to convince you to pay union rates 'by the bar of music' for their contribution. You are also likely to need a musical supervisor to co-ordinate their work and communicate it to the musical director and band. If you think this is an excessive number of highly paid people just in order to get the music onto the music stands in the pit then you're right, it is. And we haven't even mentioned the electronic keyboard programmer.

Casting a musical is hard work, and there will be endless debates between director, musical director and choreographer about whether acting, singing or dancing skills should take priority in the casting of each role. Performers who excel in one discipline can often be embarrassingly inadequate in the other two, and those advertising themselves as 'triple threat' tend simply to be mediocre in all three. It becomes even more difficult when you add to the selection criteria the commercial imperative of star casting and the necessity for members of the ensemble to understudy principal players.

Given that what audiences remember most about a musical tends to be the singing, the dancing and the set and costume designs, it is often assumed that the director (who is, after all, responsible for the 'acting') is something of a back seat driver. Nothing could be further from the case. The large number of different elements and disciplines that need to be brought together successfully in a musical mean that a strong overall vision for the piece is absolutely crucial. The role of director and choreographer is sometimes combined if a show is particularly dance orientated, but in any event someone needs to be responsible for the artistic overview. Getting it absolutely right in every department is a rare achievement, but when it works the results can be extraordinary. And equally when it doesn't they can be disastrous.

Negotiating the creative team's contracts with their agents is made all the more difficult by the fact that often the set designer and choreographer will know that the director has 'asked for' them, the costume designer and lighting designer will know that the set designer has 'asked for' them and the sound designer will know that the musical director has 'asked for' them. 'A' won't do it without 'B' and so on is a favourite negotiating tactic, but you mustn't let this either push their fees over your budget figure or put you in a position of taking on people who you don't want to work with. The creatives may also stipulate key personnel over whose appointment they should have approval or at the very least the right of consultation. In the sound and lighting designers' cases it may include the production engineers who install the equipment, the staff who operate the equipment on the night and even sometimes the actual equipment suppliers. In the costume designer's case it may include the people who make the costumes and the wardrobe supervisor, in the set designer's case it may include the choice of workshop where it is built, and so on. A separate budget is allocated for the creation of the model box, which is then paid to the set designer who may make the model themselves or subcontract the work under their supervision. Your production manager should advise you of the required schedule for the delivery of the model box, and this schedule should be included in the set designer's contract.

With the exception of the musical director, who is paid through the weekly payroll at a negotiated rate in any event higher than that earned by the band members, the deal with each of the creatives is split into two elements; the fee for the actual work (in the production costs) and the royalty for its continued use (in the running costs). There are agreed minimum rates and contract wordings for engagement of creative personnel negotiated between SOLT (on behalf of producers) and Equity. In reality, however, directors and designers are freelance creative artists who are perfectly capable of negotiating fees that reflect the value of their services, and the idea that they should be represented by a trade union is frankly bizarre. They obviously think so too, as they also have their own guilds and associations which they more appropriately belong to. In any event, you shouldn't pay below the agreed SOLT/Equity minimum rates, and nor would you want to if you are going to stand any chance of attracting the calibre of people that you will need in order to create a successful West End show.

The director will receive the biggest fee and royalty, usually followed by the set designer (or sometimes the choreographer if dance is a major feature of the show). As with the writer, the royalty is based on a percentage of net weekly box office receipts (i.e. a percentage of income 'off the top' rather than a share of profit). A fee for a director for a small West End play will typically start at over five thousand pounds, and royalties tend to range from 1.5% to 2%. You then work down from there with the fees and royalties for the other members of the team. Lighting, sound and costume designers may well be persuaded to accept a fixed weekly sum of a few hundred pounds instead of a percentage. If the show is a 'transfer', and is not being created specially for the West End run, then West End fees may be reduced according to the actual amount of work involved. Again, technically there are industry approved protocols for such calculations, although common sense is usually the best starting point for transfer fee negotiations.

Although creative fees are paid as a lump sum rather than by the week, the figure arrived at should be a fair reflection of the actual time involved in preparing the production. It is permissible for members of the creative team to be involved in preparing for other projects whilst they are working on yours, but their contracts will state a period of 'exclusive services', usually from the start of rehearsals until press night for director and choreographer, and from the start of the get-in until press night for the design team. The contracts will also say that the fee is deemed to include remuneration for auditions (for the director and choreographer) and planning and production meetings, all to be scheduled at mutually convenient times. There is likely to be a clause in each creative's contract to the effect that they have a general duty of care for maintaining standards in their respective departments once the production has opened, but it is important that you appreciate that the royalty that you pay them is for the continued use of their intellectual property and does not oblige them actually to attend performances after press night. In fact, it may be necessary to agree a 'day rate' of a few hundred pounds for any attendance at performances and any consequent rehearsals and notes sessions with the cast and/or on-site technical staff. Obviously it is your hope that the creatives will pop in to see the show every so often in any case, but the day rate is agreed in the event that you actually request them to do so, and that when you make such a request they are in fact available.

The initial fee for direction, choreography or design is likely to be paid in three equal instalments; the first on signature, the second on the first day of rehearsal and the third on the day of the first preview performance. Having stipulated the fee for the creation of the work (the equivalent of a commissioning payment, if you like) the contract will then go on to state the terms for what is effectively a licence for its use. Fundamental to this is the concept that the actual copyright in the work remains with its creator and that they are permitting you to use it on an exclusive basis in return for a royalty payment. As with a writer's contract no changes in the work will therefore be permitted without the creator's consent. A non-returnable but fully recoupable advance against royalties may also be thrown into the mix as an inducement to accept a slightly lower fee. With variable (i.e. percentage) royalty holders you need to be a bit careful about this, because you could be left in negative equity if the show does particularly badly at the box office or closes early. Because of this, the reality is that these advances will be set at a few thousand pounds; a nice boost to the cashflow of those concerned but well out of the danger zone as a gamble on your part.

Other clauses in creative team contracts will include 'billing' on posters and other marketing material. At this point you should check your licence from the playwright, as this may well make stipulations about the size and positioning of their own billing in relation to that of the director. Once you've sorted out the size and position of the director's billing everything else should fall into place logically. Creative team billing is usually always 'below title'. Set designers usually come before costume designers in the pecking order and lighting designers usually come before sound designers. If you are putting on a big musical then the number of people who need billing can be mind-boggling; usually the musical arrangers and orchestrators and even the casting director. If you want guidance on this then the best thing is to take a look at the 'billing page' inside the front of a programme for a big musical produced by an independent producer (rather than one of the big production houses which may use more in-house personnel).

Billing is important to people and costs you nothing so can be a useful negotiating tool, but make sure things don't get ridiculously cluttered, particularly if you are also billing a number of co-producers in the small print at the top of the poster. In any event, you should be very clear about where billing will actually appear. It is legitimate to restrict it to the official ('folio') poster for the show, the billing board on the front of the theatre and the billing page of the programme.

Also be very careful about whose billing 'triggers' whose. If the costume designer has to be billed wherever the set designer is billed, and the set designer has to be billed wherever the director is billed, then you can quickly find yourself in a position where you are obliged to bill everybody everywhere. Billing is never as straightforward as it appears.

Creatives will want free tickets for the first night and the ability to purchase 'house seats' for subsequent performances. They will also want to be able to reclaim expenses for costs incurred in fulfilling their duties. Clauses relating to expenses need to be extremely clear to avoid any misunderstandings further down the line. Some of the team may be from outside London, in which case you are likely to provide them with hotel rooms and train tickets rather than reimbursing the cost of them. Standard class rail tickets should be fine but the quality of hotel rooms will be the subject of endless debate, and if someone needs to be accommodated throughout the entire rehearsal process then it is usually better to find them a self-catering apartment. If the creatives are from overseas then you will need to pay for flights (try for super-economy, but you may have your arm twisted to provide business class) and there may also be a requirement for a cash *per diem* for food and incidental expenses. Using that whizz kid director from New York suddenly doesn't seem like quite such a good idea after all. Even if your director is travelling from outer London, you still have to be very clear as to whether a travelcard is a legitimate expense on top of the agreed fee; after all, most people (including, it has to be said, the actors) pay their own way to work. You must also make sure that you have the right to film short extracts of the show for publicity purposes without the need to make any further payment to the creative team, as well as an 'archive' video for reference purposes.

Although your deal is that you can use the copyright work in the direction, choreography and design of the production for any performance that you pay the agreed royalty for, and that the creatives are not permitted to licence their work (which you have, after all, also paid a fee for) to anyone else, much of their contracts will be taken up with provision for future presentations of the show after its run in the West End. Before you spend too much time on this you should check that the terms of your licence from the writer actually give you the ability to present the production after its West End run (i.e. on tour or on Broadway). The first principle here is that whenever and wherever you present the production again the original creative team have the first option to provide their services for a fee to be negotiated in good faith. If any of them don't want to do it or are unavailable when the time comes then they will continue to receive their royalty but you will have the right to appoint someone who they approve of to recreate their work. In this event, the person who recreates their work would generally receive a fee but not a royalty; though you might like to include a provision for the original creative to reduce their royalty so that you can budget for a small weekly payment to someone who recreates their work in the future. You also have to decide whether in this event the creative concerned will continue to receive their original billing or will be demoted to 'original production directed/choreographed/designed by'. It may seem a bit tedious to have to make all these provisions for an unknown future at this stage in the game, but it is worthwhile in order to avoid misunderstandings further down the line. This also begs the question as to what actually constitutes a 'production'. For instance, if you produced a Noël Coward play six years previously, to what extent are you obliged to use the same team if you decide to put it on again? In the absence of any specific contractual stipulations, a good rule of thumb for ascertaining this is whether you are trading off the critical reputation of the previous production and whether you are performing it on the same set design. If the answer to either of these questions is 'yes' then you should offer to re-engage any of the original team who have a first option.

One important point to make in the creative contracts is that you have the right to 'assign' both the obligations and the benefits of the contract, meaning that you can effectively sell the production to another producer (one of your co-producers for instance) provided that they continue to honour all the terms that have been agreed. This is particularly important if the contracting entity on the producer's side is a single purpose company, as you may well want to sell on the production to another company that you yourself are involved in. Obviously the creative team do not themselves have the right of assignment, or chaos could ensue.

Some creatives will attempt to stipulate in their contracts that you are obliged to engage various 'associates' to assist them in their work. There is nothing wrong with the principle of them delegating some of their duties, and these people may of course be the ones who go on to recreate their work in the future. But the people you have engaged to head up the project creatively must retain overall responsibility for the results, and you should not get involved either with the engagement or the payment of their assistants. That is up to them. For a long-running musical you may eventually engage a resident director to work alongside the company manager, the dance captain and the musical director in maintaining the show; but for most plays the Company Manager should be more than capable of keeping things ticking along, supported by the occasional visit from members of the original team. In any event, resist the pressure, which will be considerable, to engage more people than you actually need to get the job done.

The reason I have dealt with creative team contracts as a group rather than individually is that they all work on the same basic principles. They also need to synchronise in a way that reflects the realities of the particular production in hand, for instance with regard to approvals and billing stipulations. For these reasons it is much better to use your own contract pro forma rather than an 'industry standard' one. Don't forget to put in the legal clauses at the end relating to English Law and so forth; you can borrow most of these from a play licence if you need to. Get a solicitor to check over your creative team contracts the first time you issue a batch, but draft them yourself or you will end up paying unnecessary legal fees.

If you are negotiating with the agents of the creative team for a production that you want to transfer to the West End from another theatre then they will assume that you are at a tactical disadvantage because you may not be in a position to replace any of them. Doing so would be time-consuming and costly, and in any case they may well have signed 'first option' agreements with the existing producing entity. More importantly, it is probably their work that has made the project a success with audiences and critics to the extent that transferring it appeals to you in the first place. The exception to this is if the piece is a small fringe production, in which case it may be both prudent and contractually possible to replace some members of the creative team who may not have the necessary experience to take things forward to the next stage. Such discussions have to be handled with extreme sensitivity, but it would be very unwise, for instance, to engage a designer for a West End project if they have never previously designed for a space larger than a studio theatre. Generally speaking, though, if you inherit a ready-made creative team then they will assume that they are in a strong negotiating position. For all the bluff and bluster of their agents, however, remember that it is probably more important for them that their work gets seen in the West End than it is for you. If you go into the negotiations with this in mind, you can quickly reach a reasonable compromise. The most important thing is that you all stay friends at this early stage in your new creative relationship.

Once you add together the royalties to the writer, the director, the choreographer and the designers, plus any royalty due to an originating producer, plus a nominal couple of per cent for yourself, you could easily be looking at a total royalty outlay of more than 14% 'off the top' of the weekly net box office income before you are able to apply any funds to covering the weekly running costs. This percentage may increase by a few percentage points post-recoupment, as writers and most creatives will ask for their contracts to specify an enhanced royalty rate after this point (i.e. once the full pre-production costs have been repaid to the investors from any weekly surplus income and the production is thus in profit). Anyone on a post-recoupment deal will be entitled to receive the profit and loss accounts for the production in the same way that investors do, so that they can verify that you have correctly identified the point at which the production recouped its capital. If you don't want to share this information with your creative team then you can agree an increased royalty after a fixed number of weeks. This way there is a lot less paperwork flying around, and if the production actually recoups prior to the fixed number of weeks you have agreed then you win financially as well. And if it recoups after the fixed number of weeks then they win. Better still, try to get away with not building in any increases at all.

Because royalties are a 'usage' payment and not remuneration for ongoing work being carried out on the production, it seems more than reasonable that those who benefit from them should help to ensure the production's long-term financial stability by only taking a percentage of the box office in 'winning' weeks. This system, known as a 'royalty pool', is frequently used in America and is proving increasingly popular in the West End, particularly for musicals. It is in fact one of the very few pieces of American theatrical custom and practice that I can wholeheartedly recommend. Being an American model it is of course very complicated, but it is worth considering nonetheless. It works on the principle that the royalty holders 'trade in' their percentage of net box office income in return for an agreed fixed sum per percentage point (usually a few hundred pounds). This minimum guarantee in lieu of royalties is then paid irrespective of the show's fortunes. In the happy event that the show makes a weekly operating profit over and above its running costs then the weekly operating profit is divided at an agreed ratio between the royalty holders as a group and the repayment of the capital; say, 30% to the royalty holders. The royalty holders then divide this sum between them *pari passu* according to the number of points they hold in the pool. So if the author gets 8 points and there are a total of 14 points in the pool then they receive (8/14)x30% of weekly operating profit against their minimum guarantee. The percentage allocated to the royalty holders may increase post-recoupment (to, say, 40%). This system is designed to facilitate recoupment on large-scale shows with high running costs and multiple royalty holders, and an agreed fixed weekly allowance towards amortisation (i.e. recoupment) of production costs is usually added in to the running costs before the calculation of the split of weekly operating profit. Of course, if the show is a rip-roaring hit then the royalty holders may eventually end up receiving more money than they would on a straight royalties 'off the top' deal; but if that is the case then everyone's a winner and you are unlikely to begrudge them. Alternatively, you can cap their earnings at (or slightly above) the weekly equivalent of what they would have received under standard royalty terms.

This system doesn't necessarily work to the benefit of all shows, particular smaller ones where the underlying mathematical equations are markedly different, so it's important to do the calculations and see if it can really help you before applying it. A royalty pool only works if everyone agrees to it on a favoured nations basis, so either the terms for a pool have to be written into creative contracts from the outset or at the very least an 'in principle' agreement has to be made by everyone to participate in one if required to do so. Remember that if you operate a royalty pool then you will have to provide those involved with regular profit and loss accounting demonstrating the financial outcome on each week, though actual payouts are often calculated on aggregated accounts over four-weekly periods.

The physical creation of a West End show is quite rightly subject to stringent health and safety regulations, and your design team is likely to ask for it to be stated in their contracts that whilst they acknowledge a professional duty of care in this respect, it is you who is actually responsible for ensuring that their work is compliant with all of the latest legislation. In practical terms it will be your production manager who takes on this task, although as the employer it is you who is ultimately liable for the correct implementation of H&S law. You should therefore familiarise yourself with at least some of the basics of what is going on in this area of your operation, and in doing so it is very important to disentangle the reality from the myth. Unfortunately the very legislation that is intended to make it possible for all of us to carry out our work in a safe and healthy environment is often interpreted and applied by frustratingly over-zealous jobsworths in a manner that prevents us from carrying it out at all. The implementation of this area of legislation increasingly finds itself the victim of a perfect storm created by a combination of the 'cotton wool' society, local authority bureaucracy and paranoia created by the boom in 'no win no fee' accident litigation. As a wise old safety consultant once said to me 'It's called 'Health and safety *at work*'; not 'Health and Safety *stopping you from working*'.

On the other hand, working in theatre is actually fraught with danger and it is entirely appropriate that the relevant rules should be properly enforced. To this end, the most constructive requirement of H&S regulations is that all of our activities should be properly risk-assessed. Filling in these documents is time-consuming and may sometimes feel like a combination of box-ticking and stating the bleeding obvious, but it is a good discipline and forces everyone to focus on the matter in hand. There is always a huge pressure in theatre to get everything done as quickly as possible, and with the best will in the world the individuals responsible for rigging technical equipment and putting up scenery are not always over-blessed with appropriate qualifications. From the moment an actor walks out onto the stage they are placing themselves directly underneath several tons of technical equipment and scenery that are suspended in the air above them. It is right and proper that all concerned take a pause for thought to ensure that this highly unusual working environment is actually safe.

Anything involving working at height is particularly likely to send the H&S enforcers into a frenzy. This once resulted in a bizarre exchange where I was advised that I had to put an unsightly fence along the front of a bandstand situated at the back of a stage in order to prevent band members falling off it and onto the stage. I pointed out that the distance to the stage was actually less than that which the actors would have faced from the front of the stage to the floor of the pit had the band been situated in the pit, and questioned whether the logical extension of this thinking was that we are soon going to see rails installed on the front of stages to stop actors falling off. A compromise was reached. Similarly, there is an ongoing debate about the use of 'tallescopes', aluminium ladders on wheeled frames that lighting people get pushed around the stage on so that they can point the lights in the right direction ('focus' them). Suddenly the edict came that these could only be used if the lighting person concerned came down from the ladder before it was pushed along and then climbed back up it when they reached the next light, which rather defeats the object of the exercise and increases the get-in time for a show by several hours. I make no comment on the rights and wrongs of this, and I gather that a compromise was eventually reached, but my theory is that it was all a conspiracy by the manufacturers of self-focussing moving lights.

Whilst the safety implications of working at height are clearly a serious issue, H&S regulations extend into all areas of your operation. A raft of recent legislation means that your ever-expanding list of responsibilities now includes the hearing of the people who work for you, which has given rise to a whole new industry based on the monitoring of the noise levels created by shows; musicals in particular, of course. Your budget for a musical should thus now include an allowance for noise monitoring consultants, individual hearing assessments for everyone on stage…and ear plugs.

The ear plugs are intended for the performers rather than the audience, of course, but judging from the proliferation of warning notices facing an audience when they walk into a theatre these days we will doubtless soon be responsible for supplying the audience with them as well. Recent collectors' items include a notice I saw displayed in the foyer for a production of The Who's rock opera *Tommy* stating 'Please note that this performance contains loud music', and one for a production I won't name which stated 'Warning. Contains nudity, strobe lighting, smoke effects, smoking, gun shots, loud noises and adult themes', to which someone had added '…and bad acting'. Smoking, by the way, is (currently) perfectly legal on stage in England (if specified in the script) though not in Scotland, Wales and Northern Ireland; so good luck if you are touring a Noël Coward play throughout the UK. The exemption in England was hard-fought by the theatre community so don't let any interfering venue managers or licensing inspectors tell you otherwise. Obviously you are not going to ask an actor to smoke if they don't want to, but if the script states that a character smokes and the actor is happy to do so (after all, it can be the only cigarette they get to enjoy all evening now that smoking is banned in dressing rooms), then the government is effectively censoring the playwright's work if they don't allow it. In practical terms, cigarettes containing herbal tobacco tend to stink the place out, and no one has yet succeeded in creating an entirely satisfactory prop cigarette that actually makes it look like the person is smoking.

The major inconvenience faced by audiences in certain West End theatres is actually none of the above, but the patter of tiny feet as the resident mice scurry about their business. I once received a complaint that a mouse had given birth in the aisle during the interval of a show, with customers having to navigate their way around the happy event in order to reach the bar. The manager's denial that there was a vermin infestation in the theatre would have carried more weight had two mice not been scurrying across his desk behind him as he spoke. Theatre cats used to deal with all this, of course, but there are now inevitably H&S objections to keeping cats in public buildings. One despairing theatre owner was even driven to announce that they were going to solve the problem by introducing free-range snakes into their theatres. Fortunately the date of the press report was 1 April. What a delight, though, that a real live mouse has taken to making regular appearances on stage during performances at St Martin's Theatre, home of *The Mousetrap*. I saw the show recently but his understudy was on.

7. HOW TO CAST
A WEST END SHOW

Though people who act,
As a matter of fact,
Are, financially, amply rewarded,
It seems, when pursuing their calling,
Their suffering's simply appalling.
But butchers, and bakers, and candlestick makers
Get little applause for their pains.
When I think of miners
And waiters in diners,
The query forever remains:
Why must the show go on?

– Noël Coward

In any 'strengths and weaknesses' analysis of live theatre as a viable business enterprise, the fact that it requires dozens of human beings to deliver anew the same product eight times a week would be at the top of the list on both sides of the equation. Like any human beings, theatre people may be ill, late for work, distracted, on holiday or otherwise not in peak condition (or indeed even present) to carry out their work to the standard expected by the paying customer. It is a minor miracle that every night all over the West End the requisite number of box office staff, stage door keepers, ushers, bar staff, stage crew, flymen, carpenters, electricians, sound desk operators, projection and automation operators, wardrobe staff, stage management, actors and many others all succeed in being in the same place at the same time and interacting to create effectively exactly the same theatre-going experience as occurred in the same place at the same time the night before.

Of all the skills that combine to create this experience, that of the actor inevitably takes centre stage. Entrusted with the realisation of the writer's and director's vision, and yet artists in their own right, their role both on and off stage is one of contradictions and conflicts. Watching a skilled Berkoff ensemble or Live Theatre Newcastle's *Pitmen Painters* deliver the goods, or one of our leading thespians eat up a Shakespeare lead, is a thrilling and never-to-be forgotten experience. But then equally so can be watching an army of musical theatre graduates in a high-tech rock opera, or a miscast Hollywood A-Lister getting away with it simply because of who they are. Somewhere in the middle of all this, those who have decided on acting as a career path have to stay sane and stay solvent. It is, admittedly, not the easiest of lifestyle options. Actors have the ability constantly to amaze, in both art and life, and it is this unpredictable element at the very heart of what we do that ultimately gives live theatre its excitement and edge as an art form. Dealing with the 'actor factor' can be dispiriting and uplifting in equal measure, but the one certainty of being a producer is that it will account for a great deal of your time and energy.

'Who's in it?' is the first thing anyone will ask when you announce that you are putting on a show. Unless you are fielding one of the few 'brand name' ensemble groups who can sell tickets on the basis of reputation, it is an unusual West End production that does not require a sprinkling of stardust at least in its initial casting in order to grab the attention of investors, theatre owners and, above all, audiences. The role of the producer in this dynamic is often misunderstood. Most producers I know, if allowed to exercise their own tastes and priorities, would gladly cast their productions on the basis of talent alone. However, as the initiator and facilitator of the uniquely constructed creation that is a West End show, the producer is obliged to bow to the economic necessity of inducing both investment and sales through star casting. This places a focus on the role of the actor in the overall dynamic that is both unhelpful and unhealthy, creating an agenda around actors and their casting that is not part of the artistic process and which means that they carry a burden of responsibility for the economic outcome of the project above and beyond their role as an interpretive artist. It is only fair of course that this added responsibility should be recognised with both financial recompense and an element of control over the context in which their performance will be realised.

Casting a West End production can be a daunting and frustrating process and if you are new to it then it is worth engaging a freelance casting director, who will charge an up-front fee and may also ask for a weekly retainer (although the latter is an American practice that is to be discouraged). Just because you have a casting director on board does not mean you can't be hands on with casting, and it is important that you develop your own relationship with the actors' agents by dealing with the actual negotiation of wages and contracts yourself. Where a casting director can be helpful is in coming up with ideas and opening doors. Sadly, if you are a new producer then it is a fact that the agents are more likely to pick up the phone to an established casting director than they are to you. As with many of the specialist experts you engage to help you put the production together, you are buying into their experience and contacts, so the longer they have been around the better. Some casting directors concentrate on particular areas of work, such as musical theatre, film or TV, so you should establish what their particular specialisation is before taking them on. Don't forget, though, that a good knowledge of the performers who work in film and TV can come in very useful when casting theatre.

It may be that your project is a 'star vehicle'. A particular star may have come to you with a script that they want to do, though performers are not always the best judge of plays so you should tread carefully if this happens. Or maybe you have discovered that a certain actor is available and interested in stage work. Or maybe you have simply found a play with a leading role that you think will attract a performer of calibre. From Roman theatre through Shakespeare, via Garrick and Irving to Judi Dench, the public have always been attracted to the theatre by star performers. Star casting is a minefield, however, and star vehicles can sometimes resemble a freak show with no one really caring whether the actor in question is performing Shakespeare or standing on stage reading aloud from the telephone directory.

In 1995 Ralph Fiennes played Hamlet for the Almeida Theatre at the Hackney Empire, starting a rush of Hollywood A-list casting that saw everyone from Nicole Kidman to Madonna treading the boards in London. Like all such trends it was ultimately self-defeating, and what was initially viewed as a novelty that helped to drive sales eventually became an essential ingredient in the mix; producers were not only expected to provide investors and audiences with star casting but were regarded as having let them down if they failed to come up with a Hollywood 'name'. There came a point where you couldn't walk down Shaftesbury Avenue without colliding with half a dozen Oscar winners. One of the great attractions of the Hollywood contingent for theatre producers is that they don't actually need the money, so striking a financial deal is not that difficult; provided you can get past their army of agents, managers, publicists and attorneys and work out exactly who you are supposed to be doing the deal with.

Appearing on stage allows a film actor to reconnect with their audience and indeed with their craft. Screen acting is not really proper 'in the moment' acting, benefiting as it does from multiple takes, cue cards, stunt doubles, camera angles, musical underscoring and clever editing. It is no wonder that hearing an audience's appreciation and applause is something that an actor craves after years of being shouted at from behind a camera. Appearing on the London stage, where Shakespeare plied his trade, also brings much kudos amongst their celluloid peers, and an Olivier Award sits nicely in the trophy cabinet alongside the Oscar.

Although a Hollywood actor should cost no more than a UK-based star name performer in terms of their actual weekly wage, there are a number of other issues to consider. As well as the cost of flights, accommodation and *per diems* for the actor and their entourage (bringing the family to London is all part of the thrill) there will be cars to and from the theatre and possibly a requirement for security staff. Hollywood actors do tend to imagine that the stage door will resemble a film premiere every night, with uniformed police struggling to keep the frenzied crowd back behind metal barriers. West End audiences actually tend to be fairly restrained in this respect; and apart from a few genuine fans and the occasional outburst of teen hysteria for certain 'heart-throbs', autograph hunting tends to be limited to a rather strange breed of anoraked 'star spotters' who wait patiently and quietly in all weathers to get their cherished memorabilia signed and add another trophy to their collection.

The main problem with engaging film actors on stage is scheduling. Filming schedules are notoriously unpredictable and it is often difficult for them to identify suitable windows of opportunity. And when they do so, they are unlikely to agree to a length of engagement that makes any real economic sense in terms of recouping the production's capitalization. Not surprisingly, having checked in to a dressing room that is a quarter of the size of their usual on-set Winnebago, taken their first night bow to a standing ovation, been reviewed by *The Times*, been assessed by judges from the various awards panels and taken the family to the Tower of London, the attractions of performing eight shows a week in a city with London's average rainfall soon wear a bit thin. Canny agents will also be pressurising them to get back to LA and start replenishing their bank accounts. Frustratingly for commercial producers, the film actor's desire for a short engagement along with the fact that their agenda is dictated by kudos rather than cash means that they are likely to be particularly attracted by offers from smaller 'brand name' producing houses such as the Donmar. A smaller auditorium may also be a comfort factor in terms of delivering a performance for an actor returning to the stage after years spent working in film, whilst a commercial producer is inevitably more likely to offer the more daunting prospect of a larger theatre. The combination of a big star, a small theatre and a short season can be particularly frustrating for theatregoers when it comes to ticket availability, and the only real winners when this happens are the ticket touts.

Sometimes frighteningly low on the 'Hollywood star casting in theatre' agenda is the issue of whether they can actually do the job, which may be regarded as open to question given that the acting discipline they work in is so different from that of live stage performance. Thankfully the answer is usually 'yes', mainly because actors tend to be aware of their own limitations and no one is going to risk their reputation by walking out in front of hundreds of people and making an idiot of themselves. The breed of film actor that is happy to take to the stage usually started their acting career in the theatre and is fulfilling a long-held desire to return to it. Those who have done nothing but film would usually quite rightly regard appearing on stage as too much of a risk. Stage acting is an extremely demanding craft, both mentally and physically, involving practical issues such as vocal projection, negotiating a raked floor and timing quick costume changes, as well as the debilitating effects of adrenalin and stage fright.

Former television stars, again often actors who started their careers in theatre and know how to deliver a theatrical performance, can make a very good living headlining in commercial touring productions but tend to be less of a box office draw in the West End. There is also still a rare and cherished breed of actors who are *bona fide* stage stars without major film or television credits and who West End audiences (but usually not touring audiences) will pay to see. And then there are a multitude of media celebrities who dabble in acting and who will sell thousands of tickets for the local pantomime but would be laughed out of town if they appeared in the West End. It seems, in fact, that certain so-called 'names' can actually be a deterrent to ticket sales. If you are new to all this as a producer then it is very easy to make mistakes, but your casting director should be able to guide you expertly though the balancing act between the perceived box office popularity of a performer and their ability to deliver a credible leading performance. It is important to remember in all of this that the critical verdict on a production will hang largely on the success of the leading performances and that the critics, and indeed audiences, will quickly rumble you if your casting agenda does not serve the work as well as the box office.

The likelihood is that your production will not be relying on a single star name but that it will include a number of headliners and featured players in its cast. Most West End show budgets are structured to accommodate two or three star salaries, so start by identifying which roles are the ones most likely to attract star players. This is not always as easy as it seems. We all know that the actors playing Lady Bracknell in *The Importance of Being Earnest* and Shylock in *The Merchant of Venice* will be the stars of the production despite the fact that the roles are not the biggest in those plays. In fact, in some plays, the biggest roles are also the dullest and a star will want to play the role that the audience goes away remembering, irrespective of the word-count. It's always good if there can be both male and female stars on the bill, although playwrights are not always accommodating in this respect.

If you are embarking on your star casting process from a standing start then make a list of the one hundred actors you would like to play each of the star roles in your production in an ideal world. This 'fantasy list' (which usually includes Meryl Streep or Robert De Niro) is a good starting point for focussing your thoughts on the 'type' of actor you are after. If you can whittle this list down to ten names, having now taken into account the likelihood of them actually agreeing to do it, then you are moving towards a position where you can start sounding people out (at this point Meryl and Robert tend no longer to be on the list, though it's always worth a try). Although every star actor is of course approached on the basis that they are the producer's 'first choice' it can be instructive once you have completed casting to go back to your original list and see how far from it you have strayed.

If you are producing your first show, and the agents of the stars you are after have never heard of you, then this is where you send your casting director in to break the ice. The first question is whether the actor is actually available for the dates you have in mind; the 'availability check'. You might even avoid mentioning the project at this stage, as you don't want word to get round that every actor in town has been checked out for (and turned down) a particular role. If they are available, then your initial selling points to the actor are the role, the script, the writer and the director. Most actors don't like being typecast, and it can be an added incentive if the role takes them outside of their usual comfort zone. Film baddies like to play goodies and *vice versa*, television detectives don't like to play detectives on stage and musical theatre stars always want to try their hand at 'straight' acting. However, this can be a mixed blessing at the box office as audiences tend to know what they like and like what they know. A big star who is familiar to the public in a particular genre or role-type can flop if they stray too far from their audience's perception of them.

For a top star it is worth indicating that there is some flexibility in the dates and even the choice of director. If they can be persuaded to read the script then a copy should be emailed to the agent as well as posted or couriered. It's important that the 'reading copy' is user-friendly and it is usually better not to send the published version of a script but a specially typed-up and bound A4 version. Don't be surprised if you get a lot of 'window shoppers'. Some agents like to impress their clients by inducing the largest possible number of availability checks and script submissions even when they know them to be working on something else and not really available. Some will even go so far as to insist on a firm offer before passing on a script or arranging a meeting. Don't be drawn by this; such offers are almost always declined and are just helping the agent to keep up their quota of offers. If there is serious interest then a read and a meet will always precede an offer. At the other extreme, agents will sometimes not even pass on your expression of interest for fear of distracting their client from the lucrative business of film and television.

If you do get a bite then set up a meeting between the actor, the director and yourself. Offering a role to an actor sight unseen, however big a star they are, is extremely risky. They may have put on weight since they were last on television or have strange ideas about how the role should be interpreted. With a star performer this meeting is a 'chat and a cup of tea' and is not styled as an 'audition', although you may 'kick the script around a bit'. If it's a musical then the musical director may also be present to 'check their vocal range'. It is important that you are at the first meeting as otherwise the actor and director may form a bond that excludes you and it can then be difficult to regain your position in the creative process. At this meeting the actor is auditioning you and the director as much as you are auditioning them, and it is important that there is a mutual respect and understanding as well as a shared vision of both the piece and the role. A proper star will be more impressed by your understanding of the script than they will be by any obsequiousness on your part.

Some people believe that key introductory and creative meetings should be held in restaurants. Personally I have always found that eating and talking is not a good combination, and that if I am attempting to impress a Hollywood star then doing so whilst trying to avoid spilling spaghetti down my shirt does not usually produce the best results. And you are also unlikely to be in a position to kick the script around or check someone's vocal range between courses. If for some reason you do have a burning desire to conduct your theatrical business in public, then there is no better place to do it than the Ivy Club. I noticed that advance publicity for this book said that I would divulge 'how to book a table at the Ivy'. Well, the answer is actually quite simple; as with any other restaurant just pick up the phone. Tired of being gawped at by the public, many of the great and the good of theatreland have abandoned the historic eatery in favour of a private club that shares its name, shrewdly set up next door by the same management. Here they can enjoy excellent food and a relaxed ambience whilst happily gawping at each other to their hearts' content and leaving the tables they formerly occupied at the original Ivy Restaurant available for the enjoyment of the hoi polloi. It's easy enough to join the Ivy Club; they even offered membership to me.

If the meeting goes well, wherever it's held, then you should proceed to an offer; but if you feel on reflection that this particular performer is not right for the role or that they may be difficult to work with, then you should have the courage of your convictions and look elsewhere, however tempting it might be to see their name on the bill. Of course you will consult with your director, your writer and any other third party with casting approval before actually making an offer.

In the course of making the financial offer to your star actor several other factors will be discussed, in particular the length of contract. The actor's agent will always want a shorter contract so that they can get their client back into higher-earning film and TV work and the producer always wants a longer one so that they can sell more tickets. The venue will also be discussed; is your chosen West End theatre suitable for the project in the actor's view?

Another issue of great importance is billing – the prominence given to the actor's name on posters and advertising. If you have hooked a big star then 'first position above the title' is the obvious place for their name to appear and where they will expect it to be. But if you are in negotiation with other stars of similar status to play other roles in the production then it is important to get all of your ducks in a row before agreeing a billing order. You don't want to give away first position and then discover that you have the option to engage an even more impressive star in another role. In one legendary West End production the billing outside the theatre for the male and female co-stars had to be reversed on a weekly basis, as a contractual compromise over who received the cherished first position.

A star will always want to know who else you are considering for roles in the production, not only to find out who they might be working with, and whether they are people who they get on with, but also whether they are likely to steal their thunder when it comes to 'top dog' status. If there is more than one starring role then negotiations can be undertaken on a 'favoured nations' basis to allay such fears. This means that you guarantee that no party will receive preferential treatment in terms of money, billing, length of contract and so on; although another party can, if you wish, receive exactly the same treatment. It also means that you have to be pretty sure that Robert De Niro isn't about to phone up expressing an interest in one of the roles.

The least stressful scenario for a producer is when a decision is made to offer all the actors in the company the same money (a favoured nations 'company wage'). This practice is more common in the subsidised sector than the star-driven commercial sector, and is usually indicative of an existing ensemble company being transferred in to the West End from somewhere else. It often means that half the company are actually being paid less than they are worth in commercial terms and half are being paid more than they are worth, but it is a great shortcut when it comes to the negotiating process and at least means that everyone knows where they stand from the outset. Billing disputes can often be resolved by offering alphabetical billing (particularly useful if the star you are really wanting to sell has a surname beginning with the letter 'A'); and for those who are not at the top of the bill, appearing at the end of the list preceded by the word 'and' is considered to have a certain cachet. It is not good practice to tell the agent of an actor you are negotiating with exactly how much another actor in the show is earning, but you can say things like 'no one is earning more' or 'only two people are earning more'. In any event you should always work on the basis that all the actors in the company will know exactly what each other's deals are by the end of the lunch break on the first day of rehearsals, so do not ever agree to a deal of any sort on the basis that the actor concerned 'promises not to tell' the others. It is also essential to avoid giving any actor, however starry they may be, casting approval over the other roles. It can, in any case, be very difficult to cast the remaining leading roles in a production which is quite clearly a vehicle for one particular star performer, as other performers will feel that they will be counted as 'also rans' by the critics and the public.

Agents will make out that the biggest deciding factor in their client agreeing to do the job is money, but that is only to be expected given that they make their own living from a percentage of the actor's wage. Your heartstrings will be tugged upon time and time again as you are told that so-and-so cannot possibly live off £3,000 per week, that they are 'insulted' by your offer and that they have the opportunity of much more lucrative work elsewhere. To which the answer must always be 'I am sorry to hear that. No offence intended. If I were you I would take the other job, then'. Theatre will always be the poor relation to film and television; ironically the very media that give a performer mass public recognition and make them marketable to theatre audiences in the first place. The deciding factor with actors is actually more likely to be whether they like this particular role in this particular production of this particular play; so provided that you are offering a fair market rate you will always be in with a chance financially. Sticking to your budget figure to the extent that you would rather let a star actor slip through your fingers than offer them more than you can afford to pay is one of the most difficult disciplines you will ever learn as a producer. Agents will take merciless advantage of a new producer's need to add credibility to their project by overcharging for the services of a star client, so do beware of this. Check with your casting director and other producers what a fair weekly fee is for a particular actor, check that this is in line with your budget, then make your offer and stick with it. If you panic and over-pay then you are doing yourself, and indeed other producers, no favours in the long term. Having said this, you may like to humour the agent by offering 20% less than you are actually prepared to pay so that they can 'talk you up' and impress their client with their negotiating skills.

If you are dealing with a genuine star who you feel will add real value to the box office and impress your investors then you could consider offering a share of box office receipts as well as a weekly fee. After all, it is only fair that an actor whose name has brought increased revenue to the production should benefit from it. It is also a good test as to whether the agent themselves believes in the 'pulling power' of their client. A true star who is a genuine draw will accept a relatively low fee and a share of the box office receipts, as they will be confident from experience that they can make money this way. Any percentage offered on this basis should not be 'off the top' like a royalty but should be on weekly net income in excess of a certain figure. If you calculate the weekly income figure that triggers the percentage participation as the weekly break-even point plus a bit towards recouping the capitalization then you can't go far wrong. As for the percentage itself, do the maths and offer a percentage of the excess that enables the actor to double or maybe even treble their basic fee if you play to financial capacity. Just give them the figure rather than detailing how you have calculated it; if the agent knows their business then they will have a good instinct as to whether you are playing fair. You must be clear, though, that the actual percentage you are offering is of any excess income over the agreed figure and not on total box office income. The agent may well argue for a fee set against a percentage of total weekly revenue (i.e. £X or Y% of net box office, whichever is the greater) but it is safer from your point of view effectively to offer your star a share of the weekly operating profit.

The best agents are actually remarkably skilled at balancing all of the agendas involved in a negotiation and have a good sense of the difficulties of putting together a West End show and the financial imperatives that drive the process. Provided Hollywood isn't beckoning, they usually want to close the deal as much as you do, because for an agent, in most cases, an actor earning something and being seen in a role by critics and casting directors is better than an actor sitting at home earning nothing. When you start having heated debates about whether their client will be in 'number one' dressing room then this is usually a sign that negotiations with your star are reaching a conclusion and that you are at last about to clinch the deal.

As the brunt of every 'resting' actor's frustration about lack of employment, the agent's role is not an enviable one but it is, nonetheless, an essential one. All of the actors' agents are listed in *Contacts*, and they range from large companies employing dozens of people to small boutique agencies and individuals working from their front rooms. Even in the large companies individual agents operate their own lists, and actors tend to be loyal to a particular individual rather than an agency so will sometimes travel with their personal agent from company to company. Some agencies believe that their client lists should include a range of performers whilst others specialise in television actors or 'triple threat' musical theatre performers who can act, sing and dance (at least in theory). Some will only take on big stars and will refuse to represent understudies and others will recruit direct from drama school showcases. Although actors will often think that the solution to all their problems lies in changing their agent (if changing their promotional photographs for the fourteenth time hasn't helped, that is), a long-term relationship with a good agent tends to be an essential factor in a successful career path for an actor. The fact that an actor has been taken on by an agent who you as a producer trust effectively means that an initial selection process has taken place. For this reason it is far more likely that an actor with an agent will be selected for an audition than a self-represented one. Some actors, through no fault of their own (and very occasionally by choice), find themselves without an agent on either a temporary or a permanent basis. In the unusual event that you shortlist an unrepresented actor for a role it is both difficult and dangerous to negotiate with them directly. Not only does it sully the creative relationship that a producer should enjoy with an actor but it can easily lead to 'misunderstandings' and a suspicion that the producer has in some way exploited the situation. Agents do a lot more than just close the deal; they act as a point of contact between the producer and the performer throughout the engagement on all sorts of issues, often bringing great diplomacy and problem-solving skills to bear.

Some agents can seem a bit aloof or even rude, especially when you are a new producer hot on the trail of one of their star clients. You will often find that they are incredibly difficult to get hold of and that you spend a great deal of time talking with one of their long-suffering assistants. However, you have to remember that they do have to deal with a lot of timewasters, and if you stick with it then the relationships you develop with agents over the course of your producing career will be some of the most important and long-lasting in your working life. As well as being quite robust, agents can often have a wicked sense of humour; both essential prerequisites for dealing with the 'actor factor' on a daily basis. They can be arguing with you hammer and tongs down the phone one minute and charming you over a drink the next. And they will always, without fail, be out for lunch between 1pm and 2pm.

In response to the frustrating tendency of audiences not to trust the producer's judgement about casting unless they are familiar with a performer from screen appearances, the theatre industry has created a whole new phenomenon; the television 'search for a star' series. This has revitalised musical theatre casting in the same way that the influx of Hollywood stars boosted the casting of West End plays for over a decade. These programmes allow the audience to buy into the idea that they are 'creating' a West End star in the same way that *Britain's Got Talent* propels some hapless amateur into the showbiz limelight. The basic flaw in the concept is that whilst a shelf-stacker from the Isle of Wight may well be able to acquit themselves admirably playing the spoons whilst juggling budgies, they are unlikely to be able to sustain eight shows a week in a West End leading role unless they have some serious training and experience behind them. This problem is addressed in the initial 'selection process' as the audience good-naturedly overlooks the fact that the shelf-stacker in question just happens to be a drama school graduate with a rigorously trained musical theatre singing voice, or indeed a professional performer of some years' standing with a relatively impressive CV who just happens to stack shelves when they are 'resting'. Subtle subliminal messaging, along with the ability of the professional judges to 'save' certain candidates who the public have rejected, slowly and gently manipulates an outcome which ensures that the 'people's choice' of star for the latest West End Musical production is actually up to the job.

In the course of the competition, the West End show in question receives the sort of sustained publicity that even the starriest of Hollywood casting could not hope to bring to it, indeed to the extent that the television channels concerned are constantly forced to justify their position in respect of 'product endorsement'. But more importantly producers can now for the first time cast performers in the leading roles of West End shows on the basis of talent alone, and the public will flock to buy tickets because they have themselves invested in these performers and feel some sense of ownership towards them. They have 'created' their own television stars (with a little gentle professional guidance), and now they are happy to buy tickets to go and see them in a show. The conceit is a brilliant one, and everyone is a winner; the producer, the television station, the public and, of course, the talented but previously unknown performer concerned.

An interesting side-effect of involving the public in the casting process, and of seeking their comment and endorsement along the way, is that they now feel empowered to pass judgement on just about every aspect of a production. Theatre audiences used to limit their letters of complaint to the fact that the bar prices were too high, the taps in the toilets weren't working or the actors weren't speaking loudly enough. All fair comment no doubt; but basically they trusted you and your team actually to put on the show. These days, buoyed up by the fact that they personally chose the star of the latest hit musical via a premium-rate phone line, they will email lengthy critical essays to the production company with the aim of getting their money back simply on the basis that a show is not to their liking. Suddenly everyone's an expert. It's a fascinating and bizarre level on which to engage with your customers, but I'm not sure that it's necessarily a healthy one.

If you can't afford to produce a bespoke television casting show to find your star, or you feel that the format doesn't quite fit your new production of Ibsen's *The Doll's House*, then it is down to you, your telephone and your list of potential performers, with your casting director contributing ideas to the list and forging the introductions. Although theatre will always be the poor relation to television and cinema in most agents' eyes, the West End still retains a certain faded glamour and is regarded as a good gig; at least compared to touring or a summer season in a seaside town. For 'serious' actors, though, appearing at the National Theatre, the Royal Court or the Almeida is often regarded as a more credible career move than Shaftesbury Avenue, and it has to be said that despite the lower rates of pay for leading actors, these venues do tend to offer a better working environment. So if you are producing a play rather than a musical then you will not only be competing against television and film for leading actors but also the major subsidised houses and boutique producing theatres.

The process of casting is a long and frustrating one. There is little pleasure in it and on some days it feels like the acting profession is equally divided between the ones you don't want and the ones you can't get. If you are working against a deadline, due to the availability of your preferred theatre or director for instance, then your hand may be forced and you may end up with a leading performer or performers who don't entirely strike the balance between marketability and suitability for the role. Before committing to this 'second best' scenario it is worth seriously considering whether you would be better off cancelling or postponing the project rather than risking compromising it with lead casting that does not instinctively feel exactly right to you. But as you are a producer, you will probably consider this option for all of five minutes before deciding to plough on in any case. Within a week you will have convinced yourself and everyone else that the casting decisions you were forced into were actually a stroke of genius, and you will just have to hope that the critics and the public agree with you.

If casting the star roles is difficult, casting the supporting players and ensemble is also something of a minefield. For this part of the process you will need the assistance of Spotlight, a directory where virtually every professional actor advertises their services with a photograph or two, some vital statistics such as height, playing age and 'voice character' and a summary of their career to date. Annually updated, this indispensable aid to casting used to be published only in book format, but the fact that it required a forklift truck to deliver the numerous hefty volumes meant that the internet version was warmly welcomed by producers and postmen everywhere. Now available online it has something of the feeling of a dating website, as you type in the various characteristics of the role you are seeking to cast and survey the resulting 'matches'. It also allows you to send out mass e-mails to agents, or to your own tailored lists of agents, detailing the roles that you are looking to cast. The agents then respond by submitting the Spotlight pages of any of their clients who they deem to be appropriate. It's all done at the push of a button and is extremely efficient, although work experience students in agents' offices can be a little trigger-happy with the submissions, sometimes suggesting major stars for third spear-carrier, or actors who are clearly not available for your dates due to existing widely advertised commitments. Spotlight submissions, even the good suggestions, are often made without the knowledge of the actor concerned, so the first question to ask is always whether they are actually available and interested.

The existence of Spotlight online has reduced the number of paper CVs from actors that used to arrive at production offices by the truckload (leading to a moral dilemma over what to do with all those stamped addressed envelopes). Actors' CVs, whether paper or electronic, carry the same degree of truthfulness as in any other profession, though in an industry where 'looks are everything' the accompanying picture is often as important as the words that go with it. Some actors need to understand that this does not mean that 'good looks are everything' and that there are as many different types of role as there are types of people. Making yourself look sultry and sexy in a photograph when in fact you are ugly and overweight does not in the end help you to get work. Your deceit will be uncovered long before you are actually offered a job and will only annoy the director who will have called you in for a sultry, sexy role. In the meantime the ugly, overweight role in the same play will have gone to someone else who was more honest about what they had to offer. There are also roles for all ages, so making yourself look younger than you are is no advantage either. Hair length and colour can always be changed, of course, and it is the producer's right to require this (at their own expense), so making a big feature of a particular hairstyle in your Spotlight photograph is an unnecessary irrelevance.

When it comes to star casting, Spotlight is a great way to remind yourself who's out there and check which agents they are with, but you should not actually solicit submissions for star roles via Spotlight. Stars and their agents tend to respond better to a direct approach and even a call to a friendly agent asking what stars they have available at the moment can pay dividends. It's unusual to land a 'big fish' in response to a Spotlight casting breakdown (if one is submitted then it's usually that work experience kid getting the wrong end of the stick again) but it does very occasionally happen that one comes up in the net. A few mega-stars turn their nose up at the idea of actually listing their achievements in Spotlight, on the basis that everyone should know what roles they've played and shouldn't need reminding; so ironically a photograph accompanied by a completely empty page is a sign of a true star (at least in their own eyes). And don't be misled by the number of actors who describe themselves in Spotlight as 'leading' actors; these are not necessarily star performers but simply actors who believe themselves to be suitable for leading roles rather than 'character' roles such as comedy maids and bearded old seafarers.

Apart from the 'blank page' brigade, the list of roles played on the actor's Spotlight entry will usually show a mix of stage and TV credits. The former, broadly speaking, establishes that the performer concerned can act and the latter that they might be known to a wider public and in some way marketable; although it is a golden rule that all working actors of a certain age at some point will have appeared in *The Bill* and all younger actors will at some point have appeared in *Hollyoaks*. If an actor has appeared in a 'long-running television drama' and doesn't clearly state that they are a regular or leading character over a number of series, then it is worth checking on IMDb (the Internet Movie Database) which will tell you exactly how many episodes they have appeared in. IMDb also clocks all TV appearances as 'themselves' on chat programmes and the like, which can be another good indicator of a particular actor's marketability. The deluxe version of IMDb ('IMDb Pro') also features a 'star ranking' system which uses various criteria to give a global profile rating to every known screen performer. It can be disappointing to discover that the A-list superstar you are negotiating with is listed as number 5,310 but it can be instructive when they demand more money than you have already agreed to pay to number 3,408. These ratings can change dramatically on a day by day basis and it is quite fun (and a wonderfully distracting waste of time) to monitor this 'stock exchange' of talent. In short, you should definitely subscribe to both Spotlight Interactive and IMDb Pro. Your casting director will have access to these resources and you don't want them to be one step ahead of you. In fairness, I should point out that in addition to Spotlight there are a number of other websites and publications designed to communicate casting information to the acting profession. Also in fairness, I should point out that Spotlight is the only one that really matters when it comes to casting West End shows.

Even using these tools, and given the high levels of unemployment amongst the acting profession, casting the non-starring roles is not as easy as it should be and can be both time-consuming and frustrating. At this level you are not competing with the lure of lucrative television and film contracts, although such is the power of television as a potential career enhancer that the slightest sniff of even a bit part on TV is likely to divert an actor's attention away from a West End offer. More significantly though, for those committed to making their career on stage, the subsidised companies sometimes offer higher rates of pay to jobbing actors than the commercial ones. It can be difficult to explain this to actors, who only need to hear the words 'commercial' and 'West End' to assume that you are rolling in money when in fact your livelihood is not underwritten by the state and you are constantly struggling to raise every penny you can get.

Once you, your director and your casting director have waded through the vast number of electronic submissions for the non-leading roles that have arrived in response to your announcement to agents via Spotlight Interactive, and once you have drawn up your list of those who actually fit the bill and are of interest, it is time to start the audition process. It's important that you examine the CVs carefully as agents will sometimes sneak in a six footer for a role that is specified as 5'6', a fifty-year-old for a role described as 'mid 20's' or even a male actor for a role described as 'female'. The casting director can now keep themselves busy making the calls to the agents to offer auditions to their clients. At this point you will discover that a large number of the people you are interested in, if they are not already committed to another job at the time of your contract, are not available because they suddenly remember that they are getting married, are on holiday, have childcare issues or are in the middle of moving house. If you shortlist about twice as many as you actually want to see then you should nonetheless end up with a fairly decent crop.

The casting director will spend a lot of time and energy setting up and running the auditions. This is not work that you have time to do yourself, although it is fairly straightforward administrative stuff, so don't be fooled into thinking that they are actually justifying their fee by doing this. It's that key call to Robert De Niro that you are actually engaging your casting director for. It is probably best to leave the first rounds of auditions to the director (and choreographer and musical director if your show is a musical) but it is nonetheless important that you are engaged with the process, as auditions are the first point of contact that most performers have with a production company and the manner in which they are conducted will reflect on you personally. By the time your director is actually meeting actors in audition you should have weeded out the timewasters, the window-shoppers and the honeymooners, so it is safe to assume that the vast majority of actors who turn up actually want to be in your production, and indeed that for some of them being offered this role in the West End could be a life-changing experience.

It is important that all auditionees get the opportunity to be fairly assessed and are given quality time by the director (and musical director if appropriate). Dance auditions are normally conducted *en masse* (*Chorus Line*-style) but it is still important that everyone feels that they have had their opportunity to show what they can do. Make sure that the physical environment is user-friendly, that there are waiting rooms and places to get changed as well as easy access to toilets and refreshments. A bright, clean, airy space will bring the best out of people and put a spring in their step. Also make sure that it is clear to people what the system is; whether they are seeing the director, the musical director or the choreographer first, and whether they are free to go once seen or need to hang around to be seen again. It is important that auditions stay on schedule (as auditionees may have day jobs to get back to or other auditions to go to), and that everyone knows in advance what will be required of them and whether they need to prepare anything or dress in a particular way (i.e. for dance).

Acting is an insecure lifestyle and it is easy to forget how important the opportunity to audition can be for a performer, so even if you are running to a strict timetable everyone should feel that they have been treated with respect and had their chance to shine. Some directors are much better at creating a feeling of well-being at auditions than others, but ultimately it is you as producer who is responsible for the quality of the experience. A shrewd director will make a note of anyone who might be useful for a future role even if they do not fit the one they are actually auditioning for, so even if an actor is rejected the audition won't necessarily have been wasted. Sometimes a director will spot that an actor is actually more suited to a different role in the same production, so an offer will not necessarily be for the part that they actually came in for.

It is good practice to let the agents know the outcome of the audition even if their client has not been successful. However, if you have seen hundreds of people and do not have the time or resources to do this then you should not lose sleep over it. The old adage 'Don't phone us, we'll phone you' still holds and the assumption will be that if they do not hear from you within a few days then they have not got the job. It is important not to say 'no' to any candidates until a role has actually been accepted, as you may need to go to a second or even a third choice. An agent may call for feedback, particularly if the client is new to them, and in this case it is always important to tell the truth (at least as far as is possible without being offensive). Saying that you were 'really impressed' with someone when actually you weren't is misleading to both the agent and the actor, and if there are areas for improvement then it is important for a performer's development that they know what these are. My four top audition tips for actors are; don't be late, don't say that you are ill or have lost your voice (the panel will be able to tell and will give you credit for battling on uncomplainingly), don't say that you haven't had time to prepare (even if this is the case) and don't spend ages briefing the pianist before delivering your song. The last thing a producer or director wants to do is to engage an actor who doesn't turn up on time, is prone to sickness or vocal problems, doesn't do their prep or generally faffs around. An auditionee displaying any of the above traits risks being discounted immediately, irrespective of their talent.

The 'open audition' (i.e. anyone can just turn up and queue to be seen) is now largely a thing of the past and is usually only used as a publicity gimmick. A few of the big long-running musicals will occasionally advertise open casting calls in *The Stage* newspaper, but otherwise a widely advertised 'could you be the new Elvis Presley?' audition is more than likely to be an excuse to get the television cameras along filming the colourful queue of Elvis lookalikes. The problem is that the proliferation of 'anyone can be a star' television programmes has led people to believe that this really is the case, and whereas in the past one could expect a certain standard at an open audition these days just about anyone is prepared to try their hand at it, even if you put 'experienced professionals only' or similar on the advertisement. Having said that, I was once involved in a

West End show where two brilliant young leading actors were discovered from an open audition which had in all honesty really been set up for publicity purposes with little expectation of finding any real talent.

Following the first round of auditions, the director (in consultation with the musical director and choreographer if it's a musical) will make a shortlist of two or three candidates to be recalled for each role. At this stage it is important to establish with the agents what the rate of pay is that you are offering. A bit of banter on the subject of remuneration with the agent of a *bona fide* star is all well and good, but life is too short to be haggling over an extra £50 a week for a performer when there have literally been hundreds of submissions for the role. Anyone who attends a recall audition should have indicated a willingness to accept the role if offered and at a given rate of pay. At this point the producer should take an active role by joining the recall audition panel and being a significant voice in the final decision-making process.

Somewhere between the top star who has to be hunted down and gently coaxed into the role, and the chorus line who are selected from hundreds of hopefuls, are the actors whose name may appear on the billing below those of the stars and in smaller print, and who may have a bit of a following in their own right and add some commercial interest or a touch of class to the overall package. They may have auditioned 'by invitation' against two or three others, and they may have been the subject of a bit of a pay haggle with the agent. These performers used to be defined by the fact that they could negotiate themselves a few hundred quid a week more than the ensemble players, but this financial status has been eroded by large increases in the union minimum rates in the West End. These days, once you have paid your chorus line and your spear-carriers, there really is not enough of the pay pie left to afford these more senior players a pay differential of any significance.

You will probably need to have your star actors in place in order to secure your investment and even your theatre, as although you are offering rent to the theatre owner they have a vested interest in the commercial success of your show and may be weighing your offer up against one from a producer who has actually succeeded in securing Robert de Niro. You must always be up front with performers' agents about exactly where you are up to in this chicken-and-egg process and you may have to do a deal 'subject to contract' whilst you get all the other pieces of the jigsaw into place. This is where you have to be extremely careful about knowing when you have actually concluded a deal with a performer. If you have agreed dates, role, venue and money with an agent by telephone, email or fax then you have a legally binding agreement whether or not a contract has actually been signed. If the deal is provisional in any way then this should be made clear at all times and any written exchanges should be marked 'subject to contract'. This protocol works both ways, and if an actor pulls out of a deal following a clear verbal agreement then you have the right to pursue them for compensation. Because it can take a while to draft up and issue a final contract it is important, in order to avoid any misunderstandings, that you issue (by post and email) a brief memo stating the headline points of the deal as soon as they have been agreed. Although these memos are rarely counter-signed and returned they act as a record of the deal as mutually agreed, and if no queries are raised within 24 hours then it is safe to assume that your understanding of arrangements is the same as the agent's.

If you are asking an actor to wait for other elements of the production to fall into place before concluding the deal then their agent may ask you to pay some sort of retainer fee to keep them available. It is best to avoid this if at all possible, particularly as you may not have any money in the bank at this stage and will have to borrow such a sum against the likelihood that you will eventually raise the capital for the show. If possible it should just be left that you have a 'first option' on the actor's services and that they have the right to come back to you and ask you to sign up and pay up if they get an alternative offer of work. If you are not ready to go at this stage then it may be that you have to wave goodbye to your hard-won star or bite the bullet and fork out for a retainer (which you can recoup from the production budget under 'development costs'). Apart from the star names that you require to hook the investors and the theatre, the rest of the casting, for featured roles and ensemble, should not take place until your project is well and truly capitalized, contracted and under way. All of this requires nerves of steel and an advanced diploma in plate-spinning, combined with an absolute clarity and honesty when dealing with all parties.

Actors occupy a strange position somewhere between freelance artistes and employees, and this dichotomy is reflected in everything from their tax status to the way they approach their work and the way they interact with producers. Once the casting process is over and the offer has been made and accepted the actor/producer dynamic can occasionally change beyond all recognition. Instead of the creator of an extraordinary opportunity for artistes to exercise their talent you can suddenly find yourself cast in the role of the capitalist exploiter of their alienated labour. Odd, given that when I last dipped into *Das Kapital* (which was admittedly some time ago) it seemed to me that the concept of alienated labour was predicated on the fact that the worker is actually adding 'surplus value' to the product in economic terms rather than living (albeit indirectly) out of the pockets of philanthropists/investors. This sudden reassignment of your role from creator to exploiter can be quite upsetting the first time you experience it but, like many things in theatre, it is best taken with a large pinch of salt. One of David Hare's characters asks, 'What is theatre, but a low drizzle of persistent complaint?' If as a producer you are going to maintain your optimism and dynamism then you have to develop techniques for blocking out that drizzle.

Ironically, in this most creative of environments, facilitated by the producer and generously supported by the patronage of investors, you will find yourself in the position of having to manage a 'workforce' that has chosen to organise itself along the lines of factory employees. It is a world of union meetings, 'overtime' payments, parental leave, holiday entitlement and grievance procedures, all fuelled by some expert professional trades unionists, that seems very much at odds with the process of collaborating to create a work of art. Actors, who are prone to enjoying a bit of role play, will happily cast themselves as aggrieved blue-collar workers between applying their make-up and doing their vocal warm-ups. But it is important not to take any of this personally. It is not intended maliciously, and often stems from a lack of understanding of the role of the producer. 'Industrial relations' are not helped by the fact that backstage conditions in certain West End theatres remain Dickensian, something which you of course have no control over; or by the fact that the producer will often be referred to as 'the management', a misleading phrase which only serves to reinforce 'them and us' stereotypes.

Much as they may be happy to talk about their work, there is a limit to the amount of time that producers can be expected to spend explaining exactly what it is they do, and drama schools must surely take on at least some responsibility for educating young performers on how to get the best out of the dynamic with their future employers. And while they're about it they could usefully spend a bit less time teaching their students how to find their 'motivation' and a bit more teaching them how to fill in a tax return and explaining to them how to go about booking digs. It is a constant source of amazement to me how ill-prepared for the exigencies of life drama school graduates can be, and I always advise young performers to complete a university course before attending drama school if they possibly can, if only in order to get something closer to a taste of the 'real' world. The 'world owes us a living' attitude that seems to be instilled by certain drama schools, along with the cotton wool society that has grown up of late and the chip-on-the-shoulder trades unionism that occasionally rears its ugly head in the theatre industry, inevitably have a deadening effect on the creative process. Older performers are less likely to get involved in all of this nonsense, and the demise of the 'rep' system, where the youngsters learned every aspect of their trade first hand from their older and (we trust) wiser colleagues, is rightly lamented. Stars, of course, tend to rise above the 'drizzle of complaint' completely. But then again they can usually afford to.

So is an actor a freelancer or an employee? They organise their own tax and National Insurance on a freelance basis and yet the language of their contracts defines them as employees. They rightly demand to be treated as collaborative creative artists and yet their union insists on characterising them as 'workers'. An artist has the right to ask 'What's my motivation?'; an employee's motivation need be nothing more than the pay cheque at the end of the week. In 1907 when music hall performers went on strike (the first example of industrial action in the British entertainment industry) the hall owners were aghast that people who they regarded as close professional colleagues had so publicly turned against them. The scars never healed and the strike clearly marked the beginning of the end of what arguably remains the most popular form of live entertainment in British history.

For better or for worse, the emergence of Equity in 1930 has meant that acting is unusual as a 'profession' in being represented by a trade union rather than a professional association. As a union it finds itself acting on behalf of the widest possible range of talents, skills and personalities; from delightful old thesps and knights of the realm to young chorus boys, from Shakespearian maestros and millionaire Hollywood film stars to triple-threat drama school graduates and jobbing 'character' actors. This diversity means that the concept of 'one contract fits all' is a complete fallacy. Hotly pursued stars, and even 'featured role' performers to an extent, can in reality dictate their own terms and conditions and their own fees. The principal function of the collective agreements negotiated between Equity and SOLT is thus to ensure minimum terms and pay rates for chorus members and other supporting players, and in so doing they arguably give these performers a collective negotiating position that is disproportionately strong. These hard-fought agreements (which, let it not be forgotten, theoretically protect the producer's position as much as the performer's) nonetheless create a useful infrastructure for the operation of the industry as a whole, providing a level of conformity about such issues as number of performances per week and required notice periods which permeates all the way through to investor agreements and financial recoupment models. A level of self-regulation is important in order to maintain confidence in an industry that could so easily otherwise degenerate very quickly into chaos, particularly when the underlying financial infrastructures are so precarious. But when the official industry definition of an 'actor' is 'A Performer who is neither a Booth Singer nor a Supernumerary' the dead hand of the committee room is all too evident.

It used to be the case that only performers who were members of Equity could work in the West End, but in 1988 this last bastion of the closed shop was swept away by Thatcherite union legislation. The industry is all the healthier for this development. The benefits of union membership for performers should be self-evident, but whether or not an actor is actually a member of Equity you are still obliged to issue them with a union-approved contract. The SOLT/Equity Agreement is enforced through the theatre hire agreements, so when you sign a contract with a West End theatre you are obliged to use it, along with SOLT's agreements with the Musicians' Union and the technical union, BECTU (the 'Broadcasting, Entertainment, Cinematograph and Theatre Union' – thank goodness for acronyms!). You should get hold of copies of all of these agreements from SOLT as soon as you decide to commence production, as they are an invaluable point of reference in preparing your budgets.

Although the initial deal memo is sufficient to secure an actor's services, every actor you engage, whatever their status, will receive from you a signed copy of the short pro forma contract which signs both parties up to the full terms of the SOLT/Equity Agreement. The Agreement itself is in booklet form and you do not need to supply a copy of it; you may legitimately assume that the performer (or at least their agent) is aware of its content, and you should arrange for a copy to be available for reference at the place of work. Star actors are also likely to receive a covering letter from you confirming any additional terms that have been agreed, such as billing position, dressing room allocation and very occasionally a car service to and from the theatre. Don't worry if you don't receive signed copies back; performers often fail to return their contracts. They are still obliged to turn up if their agent has agreed the terms of the engagement.

In order to gain access to the downloadable actors' contract pro forma (as opposed to the collective Agreement booklet to which it makes reference) you have to register your production with The Theatre Council and become an 'approved manager'. And in order to become 'approved' you will be asked to place the salary bonds for your performers. When you sign up to the SOLT/Equity contract both you and the actor are agreeing to a number of important principles. The Agreement which governs the contract is renegotiated and updated every four years so it is essential that you are familiar with the terms and conditions in it. Most importanly, you must never pay less than the agreed minimum rates for working in a West End Theatre. A list of these rates can be obtained from SOLT but they increase every year in April by an agreed amount so make sure that your budgeting takes account of this. West End theatres are divided into three categories, according to seating capacity, for the purpose of determining the applicable minimum rates, so bear this in mind when choosing your theatre. The pay rates are based on an eight-show week, usually Monday to Saturday evenings with two matinees, although provision is increasingly being made to allow for Sunday performances on the Broadway model, a scheduling innovation which pre-supposes that West End theatregoers are happy to go along with it. If Sunday is played then another day (usually Monday) is taken as the day off.

After the financial provisions, the most important clause in an actor's contract is the length of the engagement; and the most significant point about this clause is that whilst it commits the actor to appear in a production for a fixed number of weeks it allows the producer to close the show at two weeks' notice without compensating them beyond the actual length of the run. This is without doubt the single most important contractual stipulation in the producer's favour and is absolutely central to the operation of the industry. This simple piece of good sense at the centre of it all, which effectively acknowledges that the actor and the producer are sharing the same precarious journey with respect to the fortunes of the production, more than makes up for a great deal of the nonsense that is to be found elsewhere in the SOLT/Equity Agreement. Generally speaking, if you have an open-ended contract with the theatre rather than an agreement for a limited season then you will aim to contract an actor for a six-month period in the first instance, bearing in mind that the recasting process is a costly one. You may of course only be able to contract some of your leading players for a shorter period, so at some point the cast members on longer contracts may find themselves re-rehearsing with new performers in the principle roles. In any event, synchronising artiste contract dates with theatre contract dates in a manner designed to minimise re-rehearsal and re-advertising costs is an important part of the strategic management of the production from the outset.

The SOLT/Equity Agreement specifies hours of work; both the hours between which work may take place every day and the total number of hours that can be worked each week. This is only really important when rehearsals are taking place, as an actor who is engaged on a West End show and who is not rehearsing will typically work no more than a twenty-eight hour week, (allowing 35 minutes for the 'half hour call' before the show and 15 minutes to get changed afterwards), albeit at what may be regarded as anti-social hours. Actors wishing to undertake other performing work (for instance television appearances) whilst under contract to you must seek your permission, but they are free to pursue other paid non-performing work without advising you.

Much of the rest of the Agreement is taken up with endless discourses on such matters as overtime, holiday entitlement, work on public holidays, working time regulations, parental leave and incapacity pay, as well as interventions on such issues as the necessity for an adequate rehearsal period, for costumes to be cleaned and for scripts to be provided to actors, plus handy hints on how to conduct auditions and what footwear to use on a raked stage. Somewhere towards the end of all this is a brief mention of the fact that it is reasonable for the producer to expect the artist to perform as directed and in a 'diligent and competent manner'.

An unnecessarily complicated set of disciplinary and grievance procedures makes dispensing with an actor once you have engaged them virtually impossible (arguably a fair enough *quid pro quo* for the producer-friendly two weeks' notice clause) so it is particularly important to ensure that the performers you engage are of an appropriate standard and temperament for the task in hand. 'Turned out not to be as good as they appeared to be in audition' is, unsurprisingly, not on the list of offences leading to potential dismissal for gross misconduct. Any disputes arising from the engagement of performers in the West End are generally settled by arbitration rather than by law, and this is inherent in the Agreement. Cases are heard by a sort of mock 'court' convened by The Theatre Council, which comprises representatives of Equity and SOLT and whose decision is regarded in the industry as binding. This element of self-regulation saves money for both parties and means that the case is being heard by a panel of experts rather than lawyers uneducated in the arcane employment practices of West End theatre. Generally the system works extremely well and the outcomes obtained are well-judged and equitable.

When contracting your cast it is essential that you make proper provision for understudies. Regional repertory theatres usually take a risk and operate without them so this needs to be factored in if you are transferring a show from one of these venues. Understudies are effectively a form of insurance that the show will go on, and although it is very much in your own interests to ensure that there is adequate cover in the event of illness or holiday, the contract with the theatre will oblige you to engage them in order to protect those all-important ice cream sales. For this reason you'll also need them if you take your show on tour. Right at the start of the process you need to sit down with the director and work out how the understudy cover plan is going to work. The plan can involve giving understudy responsibility to actors playing smaller roles as well as engaging 'walking understudies'; these are additional members of the performing company who don't actually 'walk' but have the thankless task of *sitting* in their dressing rooms all night just in case the call comes. In musicals, where performers are apparently more at risk of stubbing their toe or losing their voice than in 'straight' plays, there will often be a first and a second cover for the principal roles as well as an army of 'swings'.

There is ongoing debate about whether adding understudy duties to the existing duties of a performer warrants additional payment and indeed whether going on and performing a role as understudy justifies a premium. The result of such payments can be that performers with multiple understudy roles actually earn more than some of the people they are covering. It is certainly the case that the understudies, who are called to extra rehearsals during the run of the show, are often the only members of the company working the hours for which they are actually contracted. For the time being, look out for such payments when budgeting, and remember to include them during the rehearsal period if duties have been allocated at point of contract, paying particular attention to what you designate a 'leading' role for the purposes of understudy cover.

Walking understudies, who are unique amongst performers in that they are entitled to give notice to the management after a period of time, are usually engaged to join the company towards the end of the rehearsal process. In any event, the skill is to create an understudy plan that utilises the minimum number of additional performers, particularly 'swings', without risking jeopardising the production. 'Swings' are all-purpose dancers who step in to fill gaps in the chorus line (often when the gap is caused by the performer concerned themselves going on as understudy in a leading role); but user-friendly choreographers are perfectly capable of staging numbers that can accommodate gaps in the line-up and thereby reduce the number of swing performers required. I take my hat off to understudies, many of whom diligently prepare their roles and never experience the catharsis of actually performing them, and I have seen some extraordinary examples of them saving the day in thrilling showbiz tradition. The terms regarding their engagement in the SOLT/Equity Agreement, however, account for a great deal of the unnecessary twaddle in that august document.

Although there is no obligation to refund ticket money if an advertised artiste is replaced by an understudy, audiences are becoming increasingly savvy about this and have a moral if not legal right to see the performers who they have actually paid to see. Some (usually older) performers will take this obligation to their audience to an extreme, battling on through illness and pain to ensure that their public is not let down. Other (usually younger) performers will take the night off if they feel even slightly unwell. We now live in a world where it is deemed perfectly acceptable to expect the public to buy a ticket for a major West End musical where up to a quarter of the advertised cast may be off sick or on holiday at pretty well any time. Given that the producer has to pay for sufficient understudy and swing cover to fill those gaps the budgetary implications of all this are substantial, and of course there is a knock-on effect on the ticket price for the customer. One of the incidental benefits of touring from a producer's perspective is that actors go off sick a lot less than in the West End (proven statistical fact). Even if you are a bit under the weather, going to work is clearly a more attractive proposition than spending your evening listening to your landlady's life story in digs in Sunderland.

Featured child performers (i.e. actors aged under sixteen) in the West End are entitled under the SOLT/Equity contract to be paid 50% of the relevant union rate but generally end up costing more than adult performers, because of the need for chaperones and the licensing authorities' insistence on alternating between a number of performers. There are as many different child licensing regimes as there are local authorities in the country, and although the theatrical West End is governed by Westminster and Camden Councils, each child's performance licence will be issued by the authority where the child concerned actually lives. The whole thing is a minefield of half-baked union regulations, confused employment law, rampant local government bureaucracy and well-meaning but over-cautious child protection legislation, and is best avoided if at all possible; or at least until good sense, consistency and clarity prevail. There are also union rates for 'booth singers' and 'supernumeraries'. Booth singers are performers who boost the chorus vocals by singing off stage; a deliciously old-fashioned idea which turns a blind eye to the existence of recording technology. Supernumeraries are background artistes (i.e. extras) who make up the numbers in crowd scenes and who do not qualify for professional actors' minimum pay rates; but it would be a brave producer who negotiated the trade union red tape, and accompanying negative PR, and actually fielded these in a West End show.

Stage Management are also engaged by the producer under the SOLT/Equity Agreement although there is a separate set of clauses relating directly to their work and they have their own contract pro forma. Recruiting a strong stage management team is critical to the smooth running of your show on a daily basis and these are key appointments which you should take the time to get right. Your production manager will usually be the person directly responsible for recruiting stage management although it is important for you to get involved personally.

The Deputy Stage Manager (DSM) is responsible for running the show in performance and is located at the 'prompt desk' (usually stage left) from where they give all the cues to the different departments (lighting, follow-spots, sound, music, automation, stage crew, flying, etc.). The DSM has a major health and safety responsibility inasmuch as it will be their judgement call as to whether it is safe for a cue to be given and whether to abort it if it is compromising safety (for instance if an actor has suddenly moved into the path of a piece of scenery that is being flown in). They work from a 'prompt copy' of the script which they will have meticulously marked up during technical rehearsals with all of the 'stand-by' and cue points in the show. The prompt desk is the theatrical equivalent of air traffic control, and can look a bit daunting with its multiple video screens, head sets and cue lights, but as a producer you should be conversant with how it operates and take the time to get a guided tour of one so that you know exactly what your DSM is contending with. The one thing you don't want the prompt desk to be used for is giving a prompt, but if necessary it is the DSM, reading from the prompt copy (known as being 'on the book') who will do the honours. In rehearsals the DSM is responsible for running the rehearsal room and 'marking out' the floor in coloured tape with a diagrammatic representation of the set that the actors will be working on.

The senior member of the Stage Management team is the Company Stage Manager (CSM) who is ultimately responsible for the delivery of the show on a nightly basis. The CSM is effectively the front-line manager of the production and it is their job to ensure that the actors, stage management, band and crew are in the right place at the right time and to organise any substitutions in the event of non-availability for whatever reason. They are responsible, in liaison with the production manager, for the schedule of work both during rehearsals and once the production has opened and for keeping a record of everyone's working hours so that they can prepare the weekly payroll. It is obviously very important that the CSM has an up-to-date knowledge of all the union agreements and current employment legislation; and also that they are sufficiently confident to be able quietly to advise a director who is in full flow that the rehearsal must end within the next five minutes in order to avoid overtime. CSMs may also be asked by the producer to supervise understudy rehearsals and any emergency cast rehearsals in the absence of the director or a resident director.

The box office will give the daily sales figures to the CSM once the show has gone up, and the CSM then relays these to the producer as part of a nightly 'show report'. As well as the sales figures for the day, the numbers in attendance and the income for the performance, the show report details the start and finish time of the performance, any understudies or crew substitutions, any technical errors or missed cues and any other untoward events. It will also often give a brief summary of how well received the show was by the audience. The show report is thus the producer's way of keeping in touch with the production and getting an idea of how it is going down with audiences, and a version of it, usually without the financial data, is also sent to the creative team so that they can respond to any artistic matters arising.

In the West End some CSMs stand in the foyer in smart attire and act as the producer's ambassador, looking after any VIP guests and providing a point of contact for the theatre's management. Others prefer to lock themselves away in an office backstage and focus on paperwork or actively to participate in the running of the show from the wings. Whatever their personal approach to the role, the best CSMs successfully walk a delicate line between being the producer's eyes and ears and being a trusted *confidante* for members of the performing company. The job requires supreme organisational skills, natural authority, a calm demeanour and a high level of tact and diplomacy, and is likely to be carried out by someone who has risen up through the ranks of stage management and knows a bit about the way the world works. On particularly big shows the technical and administrative elements of the job may be split between a Stage Manager and a Company Manager, in which case the Company Manager is the senior member of the team.

Assistant Stage Managers (ASMs) are the junior members of the stage management team, responsible for co-ordinating and setting props and furnishings. There can be some overlap with the responsibilities of the theatre crew here, although the crew are more likely to be involved with the shifting of heavy items of scenery. ASMs tend to fall into two categories; those who are vocational stage managers and those who are young actors who may well also have some understudy responsibilities. The ones who want to make a career in stage management are likely to be designated as 'book cover' (i.e. the 'understudy' for the DSM) whilst for young actors the role of ASM offers an excellent opportunity to get involved with the backstage hurly-burly of a production and learn something about stage techniques and discipline. Any young actor straight out of drama school who is happy to roll their sleeves up and be 'hands on' working as an ASM, rather than sitting at home waiting for their big break, gets my vote.

During rehearsals the stage management team will work very closely with the director, designer and other members of the creative team to deliver the production according to their vision. The DSM will send a daily 'rehearsal report' (the equivalent of the show report) detailing how rehearsals have gone and any matters arising. Through this report the stage management alerts the production manager, and ultimately the producer, to any matters arising that may have scheduling or budgetary implications. Ironically, although stage management are responsible for watching the clock on your behalf, the nature of their work (from preparing the rehearsal room before the actors arrive to completing the paperwork after they have left) means that they themselves tend to clock up more overtime than anyone else, and you'll ultimately be relying on your production manager to keep an eye on this. Senior stage managers may be open to a 'buy out' deal where they accept a weekly wage well above the minimum in return for not clock watching on their own accounts.

Stage management, like walking understudies, have a contractual get-out clause after a period of time in the event of being offered a better job; but if as a producer you can rely on a regular team to look after your work then the battle is already half won. In particular a diligent, calm and diplomatic stage management team can be the key to avoiding a feeling of 'them and us' developing between the producer's office and the performers and creatives. People with experience in stage management are particularly well equipped to become producers themselves, and producers should always take the time to ensure that they understand at least the basics of stage management.

If you are producing a musical then a significant portion of your payroll budget will be allocated to musicians. As with actors, the engagement of musicians in a West End show is governed by a collective agreement, in this case between SOLT and the Musicians' Union, and there is a pro forma contract which goes with it. The working life of a West End musician is divided into sessions of up to three hours, for both rehearsals and performances. You can schedule the standard eight shows over six days within the agreed minimum salary, but just about anything else incurs overtime. The minimum weekly rates for musicians do not vary according to the size of theatre and are higher than those paid to actors. They also get paid extra for playing more than one instrument ('doubling' or 'trebling') which means that a percussionist is on to a winner from the outset.

For a skilled musician, turning up in the same place and playing the same piece of music every night is not a particularly rewarding outlet for their talents, so it is fair enough that they get paid more than the actors and structure their contracts in a way that allows them to undertake other work. A system called 'deputising' enables a player to sub-contract their 'chair' in the pit to a deputy for a performance or a number of performances while they go off and do something else, such as themselves working as a deputy on another show. This can be a bit worrying the first time you come across it, but provided it is strictly controlled by the musical director (and 'band fixer' if there is one), and provided that the quality of the performance does not suffer as a result, it can actually be quite a good way of keeping things fresh. Some long-running shows effectively have alternate teams of players, although the actual contract for each 'chair' will only be in one player's name.

West End musicians tend to be comfortable with the anonymity of the orchestra pit, where it's often possible to settle down with a good book (or a Kindle) between numbers, and you'll have to pay extra to get them to sit on the set or wear a costume. Like actors, their contracts are governed in the first instance by industry-regulated conciliation procedures. Unlike actors, they can give you notice at any time. Generally speaking, West End musicians are happy enough to turn up, provide their unseen services, cash their pay cheque and go back to doing whatever it is they do the rest of the time. No news is good news where the band is concerned. And sometimes when you sneak in at the back of the auditorium and hear a brilliant score being brilliantly played it is frankly embarrassing as an employer that you probably can't name most of the people who are playing it.

In an ideal world your musical director will be responsible for engaging the band, but if you have a particularly grand musical director, or indeed a particularly inexperienced one, you may find that you need to engage the services of a 'band fixer'. Even if you use a fixer, the musicians' contracts will be with your company. As well as the usual 'family friendly', overtime and holiday clauses, and grievance and disciplinary procedures, much of the rest of the SOLT/Musicians' Union Agreement is taken up with clauses aimed at protecting the work of live musicians in a world where it is all too easy to replace them with electronic instruments and recordings. Provided all parties are reasonable it is usually possible to reach some sort of compromise between relatively costly live performers and relatively cost-effective electronically produced music. Musicals often make use of pre-recorded vocal tracks to supplement the performers' efforts, and it is also common practice for some instrumental sounds to be created on electronic keyboards. Producers and audiences aren't stupid, however, and of course appreciate that ultimately there can be no substitute for the thrilling dynamic created by a live band.

Some shows make a feature of the fact that the musical instruments are played by the actors, which is very different to simply locating your band so that they are visible to the audience. 'Actor musicians' are engaged on the SOLT/Equity contract but paid as per the SOLT/Musicians' Union Agreement (i.e. musicians' pay for actors' hours). Integrating the playing of instruments into the action of a musical is not without its difficulties, and requires a particular set of skills from your creative team.

Meanwhile, backstage, the majority of the technical staff and crew on the show will actually be engaged by the theatre and recharged to the producer on a weekly basis via the contra. These crew are divided between the theatre's 'resident staff' and additional 'show staff' which are brought in by the theatre according to the specific requirements of the show in question. On smaller plays the theatre's staff will operate the lighting (as cued by the DSM) and the DSM (who works for the producer) may operate the sound. For larger musicals the producer may have sound and lighting operators, automation operators and the like on their own payroll as well, but in any event the people who operate the flying system for the scenery are likely to be engaged by the theatre. The wardrobe and wigs departments will be staffed by the producer, whilst the box office staff, house management and casual front of house staff will be provided by the theatre. The producer and the theatre will also engage additional staff for the fit-up and the get-out.

This strange division between the producer's staff and the theatre's, and between the resident technical crew and show staff, makes it very difficult to budget correctly; not least because BECTU has somehow persuaded theatre owners to staff their buildings on the basis of a five-day week when performances occur on six days, leading to the costly necessity of ensuring that every role is 'covered' one day a week. Theatre owners of course know that they will ultimately be passing on the costs of their technical staff to the producer (handsomely 'marked up' in some cases), so have little interest in dealing with some of the archaic working practices that still prevail, not least that of retaining full-time resident technical crew when it would be much more efficient and cost-effective for the producer if the theatre retained simply sufficient staff to maintain the building infrastructure and the producer was able to bring their own team in for the actual show. In fairness, the theatres' own heads of department and their deputies, particularly electrics and stage, tend to be skilled practitioners who bring a high level of expertise to the party and are fully invested in what you are trying to achieve; but employment of casual staff on shows seems shockingly haphazard at times, and it is not unheard of to find a student in charge of the delivery of a key technical moment in a show or a follow-spot operator who can't even change a light bulb.

West End crewing is a highly unionised environment and things tend to operate a lot more smoothly if you give your production manager some budgetary flexibility to use his skill and judgement to 'oil the wheels' a bit. In particular, crew will want an extra payment for doing something that is even slightly out of the ordinary, such as operating a trap door or helping with the flying of a performer. And don't forget to take account of any additional staffing costs that might arise from PR activity, particularly any filming, taking place at the theatre. Of course, if you try to challenge backstage working practices in the West End then you encounter the very real problem that you are dealing with the people who know where the fuse box is and who carry the keys to the stage door; and whilst actors and musicians who go on strike may arguably to an extent be replaceable, it is very difficult to perform in the dark or if you can't get into the building. At time of writing negotiations for a new SOLT/BECTU Agreement have been running for almost as long as *The Mousetrap*, but frustrating though all of these backstage shenanigans may be, in the West End they are still fundamentally good-natured. On Broadway the situation is out of hand and, frankly, terrifying.

As a West End producer your weekly payroll encompasses an extraordinarily diverse range of individuals and talents, from highly paid headline artistes with a huge emotional investment in the success of the show to chorus dancers on Equity minimum, from the percussionist in the pit to the sound desk operator, from the rookie Assistant Stage Manager just out of drama school to your trusted Company Stage Manager. Some of them will be cherished creative fellow travellers and others will be bolshy trade unionists who want nothing more than to convince the rest of the world that you are ripping them off. Some of them will have health problems and some of them will have personal problems, many of which will add to your problems. Their engagement in your show is governed by at least three different union agreements, which are in a pretty well constant state of flux, and a plethora of constantly changing employment law that often seems better suited to safeguarding the interests of factory workers in Poland than those of a West End chorus line.

At the end of the day it's up to you to decide just how 'compassionate' and 'family friendly' you want to be as an employer; whether you want to grant someone a Saturday off to sing at a wedding, a Wednesday off to attend a funeral or two weeks' holiday on a particular date because their kids have broken up from school. Bear in mind that any absence from work that is agreed by you 'at point of contract', because you think it is worth it in order to secure the services of a particular artiste, obviously carries a different weight to requests that come out of the blue. Some production companies elect to take on the role of a branch of the welfare state whilst others operate on the basis that the first duty of a group of artists is to the work they are creating and its audience. Some think that it's fine for several performers in the same show to be on holiday and several more to be off sick all at the same time, and others don't. Some will unquestioningly accept that a performer has been ill for four consecutive Mondays and some will seek a second medical opinion. Some engage enough understudy and swing cover to allow for every possible combination of sick leave, compassionate leave and holiday amongst the performing company, and others appear to have a greater faith in the traditional concept that 'the show must go on'. The one certainty is that the number of cast absences from a West End show will expand to make full use of the understudy cover available.

Whatever your approach, the most important thing is that you are consistent and that you treat all of the people who are working for you on an equal basis and without bias or favouritism, so that everyone knows exactly where they stand and what to expect from you as an employer. One of the hardest lessons to learn is that, when it comes to the management of your business, it is more important to be respected than to be liked.

8. HOW TO MARKET
A WEST END SHOW

'It is a hopeless endeavour to attract people to a theatre
unless they can be first brought to believe that they will
never get in.'

– Charles Dickens, *Nicholas Nickleby*

One of the largest areas of expenditure for any West End
show is advertising and marketing, and there are plenty
of expert individuals and agencies happy to advise on
exactly how the money should be spent. The overall strategy for
reaching the target audience for a particular production is likely
to be supervised by a specialist theatre marketing agency. The
actual purchase of advertising in the media will be the remit of a
media buying agency and the design of the production's poster
image will be in the hands of a graphic design agency. In reality
you will probably end up engaging a single company that deals
with all of these areas, and that specialises in marketing, media
buying and graphic design specifically for theatre.

These companies are listed in *Contacts* and it is worth
shopping around before you decide on one. A big, flashy agency
with impressive premises, a massive staff and posters from
legendary hit shows on its walls is not necessarily what you need.
Remember that these are marketing agencies, and one of the
things they are best at is marketing themselves. The pitch will
always be hugely impressive and probably presented by one of
the senior figures in the company. You should seek assurances,
however, that your account handler (the person with whom you
will have day-to-day contact) will actually be the person who
presented the pitch and not some work experience student who
you haven't even been introduced to. At the pitch the agency
will present its concepts for marketing your show, along with

a timeframe for the campaign and a suggested budget. They
will often ask in advance what your marketing budget actually
is, but it is better to pretend that you don't know and to see
what they come up with. You should meet with at least three
agencies before deciding who to appoint, and take someone
along with you who knows a bit about the industry so that you
have an informed second opinion. What the agencies have to
offer will probably be fairly similar but there can be significant
differences in price. As well as the costs of the campaign itself
they may want to charge an up-front fee for strategising it and
a weekly retainer. In any event, remember that all the agencies
are hungry to establish relationships with new producers, so if
you play your cards right you should be able to negotiate some
sort of 'introductory discount'.

Like most things in theatre, the success of your relationship
with your marketing agency comes down to individuals in the
end, and whether you feel you can trust and work with the
people concerned. It is also important that you enjoy their
company, as you will be spending a lot of time together. There
is a relatively high staff turnover in marketing agencies, so it can
be worth checking 'off the record' that someone you have been
particularly impressed with at the pitch is still going to be there
in three months' time when the campaign actually starts. You
are unlikely to be shown much creative work tailored to your
own production at the pitch as the agency obviously does not
want to play too many of its cards in case you don't appoint
them. There will be plenty of examples of work on previous
similar shows, however, and one of the most important factors
in deciding whether you are on the same wavelength can be
seeing what they regard a 'similar' show to be. Don't be too
impressed if they happen to have designed the artwork for some
long-running hit musical; it is more than likely that the person
who actually designed it has since moved on from the company.
It is usually better to be a big client of a small agency than a

small client of a big agency; although the bigger agencies do tend to have more 'buying power' when it comes to purchasing advertising space in the media, and even the printing of posters and leaflets, because of volume discounts that are available to them. Appointing your advertising and marketing agency is one of the most significant decisions you will make. Don't rush into it. Ask as many questions as you want and make sure that you are happy with the Terms of Engagement that they will ask you to sign.

However happy and constructive your working relationship turns out to be it is very important that you personally stay in charge of the advertising and marketing strategy and don't just hand it over to the agency. Most things that you buy through an agency (such as advertising, printing and mailings) will make a profit margin for them, either because they 'mark up' the price before passing it on to you or because they receive an inside commission from the supplier. Or both. Their margin is usually around 15% and this is absolutely standard practice. The theory is that it should still be more cost-effective and efficient for you to buy through the agency, although this does create the problem that the people who are in charge of allocating your budget have a vested interest in you spending as much money as possible, and may also have a bias toward certain suppliers. Another potential conflict of interest arises because the majority of the advertising and marketing expenditure occurs before and immediately after a show has opened. It can be difficult to retain an agency's interest once the show is up and running because the weekly spend is a great deal less than the pre-production spend. A cynic might suggest that it is actually better for the agency if your show closes and makes way for another producer to come along with a big pre-opening advertising and marketing budget. On the other hand, it wouldn't impress potential new clients if all of the agency's previous West End productions had come to grief.

Deciding on the graphic design image (the 'artwork') for your show is a distracting and time-consuming process and can mean that you take your eye off far more important elements of the campaign. The three most successful theatre graphic design concepts of all time are arguably those for *Cats*, *Les Misérables* and *Phantom of The Opera*. They were created by the graphic designer Russ Eglin who at the time was working for the agency DeWynters. These three iconic images defined the musical theatre 'boom' of the 1980s and have often been imitated but never bettered. They have been subliminally implanted in our consciousness so that there is instant product recognition in the same way that there is for the McDonald's golden arches.

The most important rule to remember is that the graphic image is a selling tool rather than a work of art. This may seem obvious, but it is amazing how often it seems to be forgotten during the hurly-burly of the design process. Although the 'showcase' usage of the image is on the 'folio' poster for the show, it is increasingly important that it works in a variety of media. If the production is intended to be a long-runner that is not cast-specific then generic, logo-style artwork like the three images mentioned above is the way forward; a design that is broadly evocative of the show's content and that can be reproduced across any medium and in any culture.

Even if the show in question does not have ambitions of mass production and global conquest, a bold and simple graphic statement is always preferable. The 'title treatment' will also be a significant part of the design, and will usually be placed at the top of the page layout so that it is visible when leaflets are placed in distribution racks. Most of all, it is important not to fall into the trap of trying to tell the story of the show through the graphic design. The worst posters are the ones where you actually have to see the production in order to understand the design concept.

It may well be that the show's biggest selling point is the people who are in it, in which case the image is likely to consist of photographs of the principal actor or actors. As you will probably want to portray them 'in character' long before the wardrobe department has got to work it may be necessary to set up a photo shoot and hire in some costumes in order to achieve the photographic images that you need. If the star is in Hollywood you obviously won't be flying them over in advance of rehearsals just for a poster shoot, so it may be up to the wonders of computer technology to provide the appropriate costuming for them. Canny star actors will include photographic approval in their contracts, and whilst you should at all costs avoid giving any third parties approval over the actual poster image, it is reasonable to allow someone whose photograph is going to form a major part of the graphic design to have approval ('not to be unreasonably withheld') over the picture that is going to be used, particularly if it has been doctored in some way. You will increase the likelihood of obtaining that approval if the designer takes the opportunity to airbrush out any unsightly wrinkles. However skilled your graphic designer may be, though, do make sure that you haven't inadvertently turned your leading actor into Frankenstein's monster. Designers will often 'flip' a photograph in order to make it look like a person is facing in the other direction, but for the individual concerned it can be very disconcerting to see their hair parted on the wrong side. If you are going down the route of the photoshoot then make sure that a wide range of photos are taken of the actors in a variety of poses, and both in costume and in civvies. This will give maximum flexibility when designing the poster as well as meaning that you always have useable pictures to hand if requested by the media at short notice.

The problem with images that are based around the leading actors is what to do when the actors' contracts finish and they are replaced with other performers. There are still likely to be posters featuring the original cast on public display and you may therefore inadvertently be guilty of 'misleading advertising'. With any luck the actors who replace the original stars will also be sufficiently well known to merit the photographic treatment and the original poses can be re-created. If they are not then you may suddenly find yourself stuck for a graphic design and having to go back to the drawing board. In this case the only continuity you may have in the graphic image is the title treatment, which underlines the importance of a strong concept in this area of the design. Whatever you do, make sure that the rights in your poster and logo concept have been assigned to you by your marketing agency. If you fail to do this then you could run into trouble further down the line, for instance if you decide to remount your production or produce it overseas.

The design format on which most time and effort will be spent is the folio poster. This is the standard 'small' poster size which is pretty well unique to the West End. Many agonising hours will be spent getting the folio poster exactly right, as it is regarded as acting as the official 'marker' of the production. This means that as well as the image and title treatment it needs to incorporate all of the official 'billing' for the show, including the creative team and performers and, of course, the producer. You are more than likely at this point to regret some of the sizing agreements that you have entered into in relation to billing, particularly those that involve a percentage of the title size. Billing that is specifically 'above' or 'immediately below' title may well compromise the graphic design. On the other hand, if your star actor is your major selling point then the more prominently their name appears the better. Given all the time, effort and money that are devoted to developing the folio poster it is ironic that it is repeatedly proven to be one of the least effective forms of advertising. One of its main functions is as a momento of the production; whether as a first night gift to participants or as a historical record of your efforts gathering dust on a wall in a forgotten corner of the theatre bar.

The folio poster may be the official piece of print for the production, but the print requisition for the show will also include many other items. When deciding on print quantities it is obviously important to work backwards from the distribution strategy. There is no point in printing up loads of material if it is just going to sit around in boxes. Print distribution for the show will include the hourly-paid 'footsoldiers' who trudge around restaurants and shops trying to persuade their owners to display the folio posters. It is unusual for any incentive such as free tickets to be offered for displaying theatre posters, which means that they tend to appear in vast quantities in specific poster-friendly establishments, sometimes effectively forming part of the interior design.

Leaflets for West End shows are usually produced in the 1/3 A4 ('DL') format, either single sheet or folded once or twice (the latter effectively being a full sheet of A4). They will feature a variation of the folio graphic design along with billing and 'selling copy'; a description of the show designed to entice the potential audience. Although the office of Fair Trading may occasionally haul up an over-enthusiastic theatre producer for some particular flight of fancy there is a bit of scope for good old-fashioned showmanship in the selling copy; your production does, after all, have to sound more exciting than the forty other shows in town. The marketing agent will draft the copy for you, and will have a good idea of what you can get away with, but you should make sure that you personally sign it off. It's always much easier to edit someone else's copy than to write your own from scratch. If the production has had a previous life and has been reviewed before by the national critics then quotes and star ratings from these reviews should be included. It is probably best to avoid quoting the *Southend Echo* on print for a West End show, however glowing their review.

The quality of the paper on which the leaflets are printed is also important, budget allowing. Something that's printed on thick, glossy paper is always more likely to be picked up than something that looks cheap and flimsy. It's basic human nature.

There are numerous methods for the distribution of leaflets, one of the most effective of which is direct mail. The act of opening an envelope and looking at the contents creates a direct physical and visual contact with your potential customer in a way that no other medium does. Even if the leaflet is not viewed immediately (and provided it is not binned of course) it may be left on a coffee table or pinned on a notice board for later perusal. A piece of direct mail will usually be accompanied by some sort of time-sensitive special offer to push sales ('book by 21 May to get £5 off!'). This also helps the marketing people to monitor the effectiveness of the direct mail hit.

Direct mail can be quite precisely targeted in these days of computerised ticket sales. A great deal of personal data is collected at point of sale by the theatre box offices and ticket agencies and can be made available (with the customer's permission and subject to the provisions of the Data Protection Act) for the purpose of targeting direct mail campaigns. 'Profiling' is relatively easy and you can target anything from fans of a particular theatrical genre to people who have booked for a specific production or who live in a certain area. All of this comes at a price, of course. The lists are available for purchase (though you won't get direct access to the actual data) and then there is also the cost of putting the leaflets in the envelopes, not to mention the envelopes themselves and postage. There are various special low-cost postage rates which are available for mass mailings and you should be given the option to use these, although the items will take longer to reach their destinations. Your marketing agent should be able to organise all of this for you with the list brokers and the mailing houses so that all you have to do is choose from a wide menu of options (i.e. central

London theatregoers, comedy bookers, or whatever), choose the quantities involved and agree the overall price per unit. It is always important to make sure you know how long the whole process is going to take and exactly when the mailing will land on people's doormats, so that you can set the cut-off dates on special offers correctly and maybe even take out some advertising at the same time to reinforce your message.

As well as direct mail there are companies that will distribute your leaflets for you around leaflet racks that they control in various outlets. Again, you will be able to choose from an impressive sounding menu of options; from self-explanatory categories such as 'arts centres', 'fringe theatres' and 'bars' to intriguing lifestyle-profiled outlet lists such as 'ladies who lunch' and blanket coverage of certain geographical areas of London. You can choose one-off distributions or distributions that are topped up on a regular basis (the former being costed in your production budget and the latter in your weekly running budget). Again, your marketing agent will be happy to advise which distribution companies and circuits to choose and will make sure that the companies concerned are kept supplied with the correct quantity of leaflets. If the theatre you are in is part of a chain then they will be happy to distribute your leaflets throughout their West End venues.

'Outdoor' advertising may involve print of various shapes and sizes, such as on telephone boxes, taxi and bus sides, bus stops and London Underground platforms and escalators, as well as various one-off large-scale advertising sites. Hours will be spent agonising over which bus routes and underground stations offer the best value and the best exposure. As with all things you tend to get what you pay for, and five posters at Piccadilly Circus station are worth a great deal more than ten at Amersham. All of these outlets will be rented to you by the week or month, so their timing within your overall campaign strategy is crucial, as is the time of year when the campaign is

happening; are you aiming to appeal to tourists in the summer
or to the domestic Christmas market? Sometimes you will
benefit from the fact that they can't find another client to take
over your advertising space once your contract has finished,
so your posters may well stay up for a longer period than you
have actually paid for. This is obviously more likely to occur
in 'non-premium' sites, and you'll occasionally see a bus in an
outlying area of London adorned with a poster for a show that
closed several years ago. Flyposting onto deserted shop fronts
and hoardings around building sites is generally illegal and for
this reason tends not to be a feature of theatre campaigns. It
is more often used for one-off events where the promoters are
difficult to track down; if you have a long-running show in a
West End theatre then the authorities will know where to find
you. Travelling shows such as funfairs and circuses have special
dispensation for certain sorts of outdoor advertising which do
not necessarily apply to theatre, so make sure you know what is
permissible before you are tempted to emulate them.

Having made your selection from this veritable smorgasbord
of print distribution outlets you will be able to draw up your
print requisition. Remember that each outlet not only requires a
quantity of print over time but probably also a different format
of print, which will give rise to additional design costs as well as
printing set-up costs. And then there is the cost of delivery on
top of all of that. Your agency will be making a bit of money 'off
the top' on everything from graphic design 'adapts' to print and
distribution deals, direct mail and even delivery charges, but it
is well worth it because life is too short to be hands on with all
of this. After the show has opened, and if it looks like it is going
well, you may want to produce a second wave of print, mailings
and intensified distribution. The new print can now feature
photographs from the actual production along with quotes
and star ratings from the critics. The immediate post-opening
booster campaign should be included in the production budget;

the weekly advertising and marketing budget being simply a sum sufficient to keep things ticking over.

The best outdoor advertising site available to your show is the theatre's own 'front of house'. The front of the theatre is in effect a dedicated prime location advertising hoarding for the entire run of your production, and is of course included in the price that you pay to rent the theatre. From the canopy edge and top-sign to the below-canopy panels, it is all there to carry your advertising message. The front of house design will again be created in two waves; pre-opening and post-opening, the total cost of which will be included in the production budget. If your show immediately follows another then you may not be able to decorate the front of house until you actually take occupancy of the theatre (i.e. from the date of the get-in). If, however, the theatre is dark for a period of time prior to your arrival then it should cost you nothing extra to decorate the front of house from the earliest possible opportunity, and indeed the theatre owner will be delighted for you to do so as it does them no favours for their theatre to look deserted.

The initial front of house design will be based around the colour schemes, logos and title treatments of the graphic design used on the poster. It is essential to include somewhere a 'billing panel' which is usually a large-scale version of the folio poster, and which includes all of the agreed billing for the production including the names of all of the performers. This will enable you to say with your hand on your heart that everybody was billed correctly on the front of house. At this stage you will leave blank the panels designed to carry the production photographs (because you won't have any until the dress rehearsal) and the panels for the critics' reviews. It is generally thought best not to tempt fate by putting quotations from reviews for any previous incarnations of the production outside the theatre until after press night. Critics don't like to feel that you are attempting to influence their verdict in any way (particularly by quoting their own words back at them).

Production photographs usually go up on the front of the theatre at some point during previews, and certainly in time for the official opening night. It is polite to include all of the actors somewhere in the front of house production shots, although you will be wanting to feature close-ups of the star actors most prominently. After press night there is then much fun to be had selecting which critics to quote on the front of house display, post-opening advertising and post-opening print. Critics like to see their name in lights as much as anyone else, and it is only fair to credit the individual writer as well as the publication concerned. They may even give you a good line in the almost certain knowledge that it will be used to promote the show. But beware that the Critics' Circle has of late been clamping down on the practice of 'selective editing', particularly where it changes the actual meaning of what is being said. Although it is interesting to see how just about any review is quotable given sufficiently skilful editing, it is counter-productive to use the words of someone who clearly did not enjoy the production at all. Like anyone else critics do not like to be misquoted or for the meaning of what they have said to be twisted; and remember that the easiest way for them to get their revenge for this sort of sharp practice is to give a bad review to your next production. Exactly which of the front of house panels the review quotes and production photographs appear on is very important. Are they facing up or down the street? Will they be obscured by the theatre doors when they are opened to let the audience in? A detailed plan of the proposed layout will be made available to you, but this will probably not make much sense out of context and it is well worth going down to the theatre and seeing for yourself exactly where 'panel G' is before committing to what goes on it.

Decorating the front of house may well be delegated by your agency to a specialist theatre signage contractor (not just any old sign-writer), and will of course be subject to the usual mark-ups along the way. As ever, you pay extra for that little bit of extra knowledge, and in this case it is well worth paying for. Your front of house display is a significant and very public statement about your show, and if it goes wrong then the whole of the West End will be laughing at you. Some West End theatres are better located than others in terms of pavement footfall and passing trade, and some have a great deal more space available to cover with your advertising message than others. The more space you have to cover the more expensive it gets to cover it, and of course you don't want to leave any part of the front of house undesigned or it will look like your show has closed or not yet opened. In this respect, a theatre with a large frontage in a West End backwater can be less than ideal.

If you have previously worked in smaller-scale theatre then the time, effort and money spent on getting a West End theatre front of house display right can come as quite a surprise. But it is well worth all the effort and expenditure, and once all the pictures and critics' quotes are up it should be, in its own way, a thing of beauty. Watching the top-sign go up is a significant moment in the timeline of your West End production; this is the point where you have literally arrived. Pop the 'House Full' sign outside and get someone to take a photograph of the whole front of house display. And don't forget to make sure that your own name appears on it somewhere.

Media advertising will be the subject of much lively discussion between you and your advisors. Your agency probably won't be marking up advertising but they will most likely be getting the equivalent of a sales commission from the supplier, so once again they have a vested interest in you spending as much as possible. However, they will also have access to some extremely good discounts which would not be available to you directly so it is always worth buying your media advertising through them. Media advertising outlets include newspapers, magazines, television and radio. The prices tend to be fixed as a result of quite detailed analyses of the readership figures and demographic for particular sections of particular newspapers, and if the front section of the *Sunday Times* 'Culture' and the showbiz section of the *Daily Mail* appear to be particularly expensive then that is for a good reason. On the other hand, if you are of the opinion that having a presence in as many different titles as possible is the priority then there are usually good bargains to be had in some of the publications less widely read by West End theatregoers. In any event, you will need to come up with a pre-opening advertising strategy that involves buying at least some display advertisements in publications ranging from national newspapers to *Time Out* magazine. In each case you will have to balance cost with the size and positioning of the advertisement as well as the potential readership and each one will require the resizing and provision of artwork which is an additional cost that is sometimes overlooked. Some of the best bargains come at the last minute when publications have failed to fill the space available, so having the ability to adapt and provide artwork at short notice is an advantage.

Exactly the same principles apply to radio advertising, and both the cost and the actual value will depend on the station, the size and profile of the listenership and the timing of the slots that you are being offered. And once again, the cost of actually producing the advertisement should not be forgotten. The received wisdom is that television, even on a localised basis, does not represent good value as an advertising medium for West End theatre, as against other options vying for your advertising buck. If you think your show is going to be around for a while then it can be worth buying advertising in programmes for similar shows, although some theatre chains can be a bit restrictive when it comes to offering programme space to productions being hosted by their competitors.

'Classified' advertisements are the small-ads style paid-for listings that appear in a number of the national newspapers; not to be confused with the free listings offered by some weekly magazines. Classifieds do not represent particularly good value but unfortunately it's a case of 'if you're not in you're out', and although some producers have countered seemingly continuous price rises by reducing their lineage in the nationals to a bare minimum (you pay by the line and the type size), it would be a brave move not to advertise in them at all. This is theoretically a particularly good medium for getting across an immediate message, such as a cast change or 'final three performances', although the newspapers are notorious for their rather slapdash approach to adapting copy in the classifieds, and many a show has found themselves advertising as 'opens tonight' when they in fact opened three days previously.

SOLT publishes an excellent fortnightly guide to London theatre which is distributed in all theatre foyers and other key outlets. You have to pay to be listed in it, but like the newspaper classifieds this is an essential part of the advertising running budget. For additional payment it is possible to purchase display advertisements in the SOLT guide, or even the front cover. Whilst you are guaranteed a listings entry if you are presenting your show in a SOLT theatre there is often a waiting list for display advertising, which is in itself indicative of its perceived value as a publication amongst the theatre community. An edited-down version of the SOLT guide listings also appears in some newspapers that do not sell their own classified advertising, and these newspaper entries are included in the price that you pay to be in the printed version of the guide.

It is said that a picture paints a thousand words, and in no context is this truer than in selling a show. Your marketing agent will be able to recommend a choice of good production photographers and you should be able to assess their work by looking at their portfolio or browsing their website. The production shoot will usually take place at the dress rehearsal, as capturing what is effectively a live performance infuses the pictures with a dynamism that is absent from posed set-up shots. The wonders of digital technology mean that you will be presented with a vast selection of shots from which to choose. These are the pictures that will appear on the front of house display, and may be incorporated into post-opening display advertising or a post-opening 'quotes' leaflet. They may also be the ones used in a souvenir brochure. The press agent also makes them available to those publications which do not have their own photographers. Occasionally a star actor will have the right of approval ('not to be unreasonably withheld' of course) over any production photographs that feature themselves in the scene.

Your marketing team will also be responsible for coming up with creative promotional ideas to attract audiences 'outside the box' of paid-for advertising. Technically it is these ideas that earn them their weekly marketing retainer fee, as most of the other logistical work that they do, considerable though it is, involves them making money from commissions or mark-ups. One of the tried and tested promotional tools for theatre is competitions for free tickets in publications and on the radio, where you are effectively trading tickets for free 'advertorial' space or airtime. These competitions are often organised in conjunction with promotional partners such as restaurants, airlines and hotels, with whom your marketing people may also be able to create added value package deals for sale through ticket agencies. Ticket offers can also be extended via specific publications and retail outlets, either exclusively to their general readership or customers or via the various loyalty schemes that many of them operate. The one thing that most of these promotional opportunities have in common is that they involve the producer either discounting or giving away tickets. If you are happy to discount on a large scale then the sky is the limit in terms of the number of outlets available to you; from the proliferation of 'last minute' websites to the austere official SOLT half-price ticket booth located on the wrong side of Leicester Square and its more colourful and better-located competitors for the walk-up tourist dollar. Be warned, though; your theatre landlord has a vested interest in maximising sales through their own phone room, so they may attempt to impose restrictions on the proportion of the ticket inventory that is accessible via other outlets, and may even impose their own handling charges on sales that are made through them.

Sadly, the trend for discounted ticketing as a sales incentive is ultimately counter-productive and self-defeating. We will eventually reach a point where the face value of tickets is set on the basis of the fact that they will actually end up being sold at half price, and in the meantime the level of discounting that the market appears to be able to sustain simply indicates to the public that there is a huge built-in profit margin and that theatre tickets are overpriced. The fact of the matter is that the price of theatre tickets is a fair reflection of the costs of staging a show, and compares favourably with other forms of live entertainment such as pop concerts and sporting events. Theatre suffers, however, from being placed in an entertainment category with cinema in the public and journalistic perception, which overlooks the fact that it is vastly more economical to show a film on multiple screens than it is to present a performance of a play. The production costs of film may be a lot higher but the running costs are a lot lower; and it is the running costs in theatre that have to be covered in order to ensure survival.

Another side to the pricing debate is that the underlying economic structure of the commercial theatre industry means that producers are in a position to keep shows on and earn their management fees without actually ever recouping their investors' capital. It is thus all too easy to sacrifice the profit margin through discounting tickets when you yourself can stay in business without paying off someone else's investment.

The temptation will always therefore be artificially to boost the volume of sales in order to create a 'perceived hit' even if the side-effect is to reduce the actual value of those sales.

This isn't helped by the fact that the industry's Achilles heel is that the experience of theatre-going is qualitatively enhanced by sitting in a 'full house'. Actors will inevitably give a better performance to a bigger audience, and those present will be less inhibited and more vocal in their response if they are not sitting in a half-empty auditorium. Nobody wants to walk into an empty theatre any more than they want to walk into an empty restaurant. The customer's feeling of well-being is enhanced if they believe that they have made the 'right choice'; they will respond more openly and in the end experience a better performance and have a better time if they are surrounded by other people. All the advertising and marketing campaigns in the world cannot compete with 'word of mouth' as a sales tool for theatre and this makes producers particularly vulnerable to the argument 'wouldn't it be better to fill the seat at any price, or even give it away, rather than leave it empty?' The airline analogy is often used when it comes to ticket sales. If you don't sell a can of beans today then you can always sell it tomorrow. If you don't sell a ticket for the 8pm show or the 8pm flight on Wednesday then you can't sell it on Thursday. The difference, of course, is that people enjoy themselves more in a full house at the theatre but nobody likes a full flight.

George Bernard Shaw in his entertaining short story *The Theatre of the Future* predicts a scenario where theatre tickets are given away free and audiences decide what show to see based on which one is offering the best package of free restaurant meals and hotel rooms. And that was written in 1932! The holy grail of theatre marketing is to find a large-scale methodology for boosting sales that does not involve discounting, and in the meantime the theatre industry needs to educate the public to the fact that theatre tickets, even at full price, represent remarkably good value for money. The case for full-price ticketing isn't helped by regular mass discounting initiatives such as SOLT's 'Get Into London Theatre' scheme, and even less so by the fact that the West End has to compete with the heavily subsidised and sponsored National Theatre offering best seats for £12 just across the river. Interestingly, those producers who now offer 'premium' price seats, on the basis that there will always be someone who specifically wants the most expensive seat in the house, find that they tend to sell very well. It's a strange world.

The internet has undeniably become a significant marketing tool for theatre as well as its fastest-growing sales outlet, enabling your show's advertising message to reach millions of people within seconds at the touch of a button. The real bonus of internet ticket offers is that, as with airlines, prices can be altered very quickly according to supply and demand, although this does require some quite time-consuming monitoring of multiple sales outlets throughout the day. No show is now complete without its own website linked to the box office, Facebook page, promotional YouTube clips, and even printed posters that can communicate directly with your mobile phone. Most importantly, the internet has made the entire ticket-buying process (at least in theory) a great deal more user-friendly; the customer can now connect directly with the theatre 'box office' and purchase a ticket without the need to spend quality time on the phone with an unemployed actor. Bizarrely, though, it has somehow failed to reduce all the add-on charges for ticket sales levied by the theatre owners from both the producer and the public.

As someone who must appear on goodness knows how many internet mailing lists as having at one time or another expressed an interest in theatre, I have to say that I find internet marketing intrusive if not a little sinister; and when I receive a dozen exclusive offers for discounted tickets in the same day I am more likely to click on the exit icon than to reach for my credit card. On the other hand, when I receive the new season brochure for my local theatre in the post I will spend at least ten minutes looking through it over breakfast and then store it in the newspaper rack for future reference.

Similarly, if I was socially networked, which I have to confess I am not, and received a tweet, a twitter or even a chirp recommending a certain production then I would simply assume that the sender was in the pay of the producer. We are advised that this medium is a particularly good way to spread the word about theatre amongst young people, but it seems to me that whilst a Facebook message or a tweet may help to guide the X-box generation towards the latest video game it is unlikely to entice them into a theatre, unless of course you are offering 3-D projected scenery. What we do know is that it enables people who are working on a show to spread gossip about their colleagues and the production at an unprecedented speed, frequently compromising delicate contractual negotiations. And whilst a positive tweet about a production from one of its stars is undoubtebly a good thing, a thoughtless 'show was shit tonight' can equally do damage. You are probably supposed to have something called a 'social media policy' which deals with all this. Certain shows go out of their way to tell us that they've been marketed via social media, ironically by buying large newspaper advertisements and underground poster sites to boast about the success of their twitter campaigns. I'm sure that somebody will soon write a very good book about the application of the internet and social media to the marketing of theatre, but as you've probably gathered by now it won't be me. I look forward to downloading it to my Kindle.

For all our efforts as an industry to appeal to the younger end of the market, theatre politicos have developed an obsession with the fact that 'young people' tend not to want to go to the theatre very much; and indeed a whole industry has grown up (government funded, of course) to attempt to counteract this perceived trend. The theory is that if we theatre producers fail to get young people into the habit of theatre-going then the theatre audience will eventually become extinct (literally die of old age) and it will all be our fault. Cue a scheme whereby the government suddenly bought up theatre tickets for a derisory sum from theatres throughout the country and gave them away to over half a million people for no other reason than that they were 'young' (well, aged under 26 anyway); unhelpfully instilling in an entire generation the perception that theatre tickets have no financial value. This initiative thankfully bypassed the West End. The fact is that it has never been 'cool' to go to the theatre if you are a teenager and it probably never will be.

Despite this, the good news is that the theatre audience is not going to die out. It shows every sign of having its own age-related cycle of attendance (not dissimilar to Shakespeare's seven ages of man) and is a naturally renewable resource without the need for government-assisted genetic modification. Our first experience of theatre will usually be going to the pantomime with our parents. Our next experience will be being dragged reluctantly along to some Shakespeare play by our school, or happily along to a musical if you are lucky enough to have a particularly cool teacher. These youthful theatre visits can be life-enhancing experiences, but young people then tend to want to take a bit of time out from theatre-going because frankly sitting still in the dark and concentrating for three hours without being able to eat popcorn, use mobile phones or misbehave on the back row does not really suit the teenage lifestyle. And why spend money on theatre tickets that you could spend on a new pair of trainers? But this apathy regarding all things theatrical does not mean that we in the industry have to ring alarm bells and panic that we have been abandoned forever by a generation of theatregoers. These same teenagers will grow into young adults and will soon be queuing to buy their own children a sparkly sword at the local pantomime. A poster for something else that's on at the theatre (perhaps featuring a favourite television star) catches their eye, and they decide to treat themselves to a babysitter one night and give it a go. It turns out to be a great experience (not least due to the distinct lack of restless teenagers in the audience) and one that they vow to repeat more regularly once the children have flown the nest. And suddenly there they are; the archetypal middle aged to elderly member of the theatre-going public, despite the fact that theatre-going was not a major feature of their teenage years.

Of course I am generalising hugely in order to make a point. There are plenty of young people who love going to the theatre and plenty of older people who don't. As a producer it is wonderful to see a schools matinee packed with riotous teenagers experiencing the thrill of live performance, even if they (or rather their parents) have only paid 25% of the face value for their tickets. There are plenty of West End shows which appeal to young people, or at least to their parents or schools sufficiently for them to organise tickets; and well-directed marketing initiatives such as SOLT's West End 'Kids Week' scheme can be very successful in varying the regular attendance demographic, at least on a temporary basis. A major production such as *Matilda* will doubtless introduce a large number of young people to the theatre-going experience, but it has to be said that if theatre specifically targeted at young people is your thing (and good for you if it is) then the West End is not the most user-friendly arena in which to present your work. High production costs necessitate high ticket prices which are a deterrent to family audiences, and even short Christmas seasons are difficult to schedule because of the erratic nature of theatre availability. In any event, it would be good if the government could spend a bit less time giving away theatre tickets to young people and a bit more cutting away the growing tangle of red tape that makes organising school theatre visits such a thankless logistical challenge for teachers.

And for young people who for one reason or another are unable to go to the theatre, Mousetrap Theatre Projects very expertly redresses the balance, ensuring that those with limited resources, opportunities or support, or with disabilities, have the chance to experience live performance. The issue of anyone, young or old, finding it difficult to attend the theatre is entirely different to the issue of them being uninterested in doing so, and as a producer you will quite rightly be obliged to provide and pay for a number of access-friendly initiatives including sign language interpreted and audio-described performances of your shows. There is no point in doing this, though, unless you actually sell tickets for these assisted performances to audiences who will benefit from such provision, and SOLT will be able to give you expert guidance on targeting your marketing appropriately. When these events are properly planned and managed they can in fact enhance everyone's enjoyment of the performance, including that of the cast, and I will forever cherish the memory of a sign language interpreter good-humouredly grappling with a particularly notorious speech in Steven Berkoff's *East*, not to mention the one who turned up dressed as a Kit Kat girl to interpret *Cabaret*. Issues regarding the physical accessibility of the actual theatre are the responsibility of your landlord; quite a challenge when you are running a listed building designed in the nineteenth century, but nonetheless one that I know West End theatre owners take extremely seriously. The SOLT Guide indicates the West End theatres that offer wheelchair spaces (most of them do) and provides a list of scheduled assisted performances for the fortnight in question.

And let's not forget that it can actually be quite difficult for elderly people to attend the theatre. When I look out on the maelstrom that is Shaftesbury Avenue on a Saturday night I am full of admiration and gratitude for the fact that the oldies actually make the effort at all. And yet they do, and in large numbers. So if a significant proportion of our audience happens to be of pensionable age then let us celebrate that fact. They are one of our most consistent and reliable markets and it would be nice if as an industry we could reward their loyalty by allocating some resources to making the experience of theatre-going a little bit easier for them. In the meantime, true to form, our friends at the Arts Council recently allocated £1 million to 'improving and marketing family friendly arts experiences'. At least this time they put SOLT and other industry organisations in charge of managing the programme.

The truth is that there is no such thing as 'The West End audience'. The theatre buildings, with a couple of exceptions, do not themselves attract a regular clientele. We know a few basic facts such as that women buy more theatre tickets than men and that a proportion of the audience in London will always be tourists; exactly what proportion being dependent on the global economic and political climate at any given time. Ultimately, though, the West End audience demographic is as broad-based and eclectic as the menu of shows on offer. From *The Big Life* to *Mamma Mia!*, from *Bombay Dreams* to *Cat on a Hot Tin Roof*, from *Peppa Pig* to *The Pitmen Painters*, the West End offers an intoxicating mix of commercial producers' personal passions, and our country's theatrical landscape is all the richer for having this extraordinary, unregulated melting pot at its centre.

Because of this, once you have gathered all your highly qualified advertising and marketing consultants around you and listened to their advice, the best thing to do is to ignore them and trust your own instincts. When a show sells well it is inevitably due to a combination of positive press reports (both reviews and editorial) and word of mouth. Hearing about it from a trusted source, be it a friend or a media commentator, will always come top of any 'what made you buy a ticket?' survey (although in fairness it is worth noting that the results of one audience survey of legend conducted by the Royal Shakespeare Company during their residency at the Barbican indicated that 'the car park' was the single most significant factor in their audience's decision to attend). Everything else in the marketing mix (posters, leaflets, press and radio advertisements, tube escalator panels, special offers, mail-outs, emails, websites and so on) simply jogs the memory that the show is still on if you should happen to want to see it. The jury is still out on how much the genetically modified word of mouth created by tweeting and the like genuinely contributes to the underlying buzz about a hit show.

Of course, a good short cut to getting your show talked about is to cast a major star actor in it; although it has to be said that several of the biggest hits of recent decades have succeeded in capturing the public's imagination without star casting or have at least survived the departure of the stars who launched them. Legendary *Buddy* producer Paul Elliott tells the delightful story of a young producer in the 1960's whose play was failing to sell tickets at a regional touring venue. The producer asked the theatre manager what he should do to get sales moving and received the advice 'Place a one line advert in the local paper. It worked for the show last week. They sold out' 'What did they say in the ad?' enquired the young producer. 'Oh, not much,' replied the manager 'It just said "For one night only – The Beatles"'. This story reinforces the message that when it comes to producing theatre you are only as strong as your product. Of the much-touted 'Four Ps' of marketing (Product, Price, Place and Promotion) the only one that really matters is the first. And no marketing 'focus group' or audience survey is ever going to prove otherwise.

Ticket sales, whatever demographic they are targeted at, are the only income source of any real significance available to a West End show, although there is a small market for merchandise such as souvenir T-shirts and mugs, the creation and management of which will often be outsourced to a specialist merchandising company at their own risk. For long-running musicals the production company will usually produce a souvenir brochure, the content of which will be generic to the show rather than cast-specific, so that its shelf-life is not dictated by cast changes. Items such as these will be sold by the theatre's front of house staff in return for an 'off the top' commission which is usually quite punitive. It's worth doing a detailed analysis of the potential sales, based of course on the predicted longevity of the show, before investing too much time and energy on merchandise, and certainly before investing in large quantities of stock if you decide to tale the risk yourself. VAT and sales commission have to be deducted from the retail price and various creative participants, such as the author and a star actor whose image forms part of the artwork may also receive a cut of sales revenue. For a musical, particularly a new one, a cast album is generally considered a necessity. You may be able to get a deal with a record label if the writer is well-known or there are some big stars in the show so make sure that the writers' agreement gives you first option to produce one. Failing that, self-publishing is not out of the question. Production costs for recordings are relatively low these days, and the relevant union agreements fairly reasonable. As merchandise of all varieties (including recordings) is likely to be a separate cost centre to the actual production, and therefore separately financed, there may be third parties who have a call on net profits. However, it is good practice for a share of the profits to accrue to the production account as 'income to the production' which the show's investors may ultimately benefit from.

West End theatre programmes are published by the theatres themselves and producers have no share in the income from them or the advertising in them, which explains why the theatres charge such a high commission for selling the producer's own merchandise brochures. Although brochures and programmes are two entirely different things, the audience only has so much money to spend on this stuff, and the theatre wants to ensure that one way or another as much of it as possible ends up in their own tills.

The producer's office is responsible for providing and proofing the majority of the editorial content of the programme and ensuring that it conforms to contractual requirements. The programme cover will usually be generic to the theatre chain in which the production is appearing, but the inside title page, like the folio poster and the front of house billing panel, acts as an official log of all the billing, so all positionings and type sizes must be correct. The order in which leading artistes appear in the programme and the amount of space afforded to each of them is also likely to be contractual. All actors and members of the creative team will be entitled to a short biography outlining their careers (actors get a photograph as well), and there will also be a list of acknowledgements of people and organisations who have assisted the show in some way. It is up to you whether you standardise the format of the biographies or whether you allow people to thank their families and advertise their personal websites. In any event, everyone should personally get to proof their programme biography and photograph before it goes to press and it is extraordinary how long this process can sometimes take. Frustrating though it is when the second spear-carrier sends through the third set of corrections to his programme biography it is worth remembering that this is a significant advertisement for a performer that carries with it a level of importance that may be overlooked in a busy producer's office. And of course don't forget your own billing, biography and (if you have any) list of staff. As you are only the producer, your billing at the top of the inside title page will probably be the smallest, and your biography will probably be the last; but it's important to know your place in the great scheme of things. The 'setting the scene' articles that appear in West End programmes can be provided by the theatre's chosen programme publishing company or by the producer. The ones provided by the publisher tend to be of a poor standard and it is usually better for the producer to persuade the director or some other relevant authority on the subject matter of the production to put pen to paper.

It is fair enough that income from bars, ice creams and other refreshments should accrue to the theatre as the producer has no input into any of this, and even fair enough that the theatre should charge a commission for its staff to sell show-related merchandise and brochures. But given the time and effort put into preparing the programme material by the producer it is pretty shocking that the theatre does not share any of the programme income with them.

The person in charge of co-ordinating your show's relationship with the media is the press agent, or publicist. As with the marketing agent it is best to shop around a bit and set up initial meetings with a few potential candidates before deciding who to go with. Theatre publicists are a unique breed and, as with your marketing agency, you are looking for someone who specialises entirely in this field; do not be tempted to engage someone who simply includes theatre in a broader portfolio of media interests. This is another expert who you are going to have a very close working relationship with throughout the production process, so once again it is very important that it is someone who you feel you can get on with on a personal level. The most important thing about a press agent is how well connected they are. You will be relying on their personal relationships with writers, editors and presenters in the media in order to secure the widest possible coverage for your production. It is usually therefore the case that the longer they have been around the better. This may seem a bit harsh on younger press agents, but they will find plenty of work to cut their teeth on at the Edinburgh Fringe and in smaller London venues. It is essential that your press agent has previous experience of working on a West End show and, if you are engaging star actors, that they have relevant experience of working with high-profile performers. If you are presenting a musical, is this a genre that they are familiar with? Or if you are presenting a transfer from the subsidised sector have they got experience in this particular area? It is important that your West End production is not part of your press agent's 'learning curve', however energetic and enthusiastic they may be.

The press agent, like the marketing agent, will want to charge an up-front fee and a weekly retainer, although once a production is up and running and the initial media *furore* has died down it is questionable whether a press agent can justify a retainer. They will also charge expenses for sending out mailings and sometimes for entertaining key journalists. Press agents tend to employ only a very small staff and do not operate from large offices so their overheads are relatively low. However, they need to take on more than one client at a time to make ends meet, and it is important that they do not have too much else going on when they are supposed to be working for you. It is perfectly legitimate to ask what other projects they are working on and whether these will create too many demands on their time. It may also be the case that they are working on another similar project or for a rival production company which may in your view create a conflict of interest. On the other hand if the press agent is working on another project which is particularly 'hot' you know that the media will be in constant communication with them and opportunities may actually arise as a result of conversations they are having about that other project. If you are the only client they have then opening doors on your behalf may be less easy. They need to be busy but not too busy.

The press agent's work is divided into two main areas; securing editorial coverage and liaising with the critics. It is also their responsibility to ensure that free listings in newspapers and magazines are kept up to date. In the weeks leading up to opening the press agent will be responsible for securing as much media coverage as possible for the production, usually via the route of interviews with its stars and other key players. The first step is to send out a press release announcing the production, which will coincide with its 'on-sale' date at the box office; it may sound obvious but there is no point in announcing a project unless people can actually buy tickets for it. The best format for a press release is a single side of A4. It's good to have an eye-catching headline, along with the opening date, prominently at the top of the page, and the listings information (venue, times, etc.) at the bottom, along with the contact details of the press agent. The blurb in the middle should be limited to the facts and not be too hyperbolic, and should emphasise the areas that are likely to be 'newsworthy', in particular who is starring in the production. Although the press agent will write the press release it is essential that the producer approves it and signs it off, as it is an extremely public statement about the production and will often be quoted verbatim in the media. The press agent will send the press release to all their contacts (you won't actually get to see the list) and any resulting enquiries will then go direct to the agent. Channelling all media enquiries through the press agent in this way takes a huge pressure off the producer's office, and is an important part of the service that the agent offers. Media people themselves prefer to connect with the world of theatre via publicists, who they are likely to have an existing relationship with, rather than being bombarded with information and telephone calls by individual production companies. And if you manage to secure a particularly high-profile publicist, whose judgement and taste the media trust, then this in itself can appear to be a sort of endorsement.

If there is something exceptionally newsworthy about your production then the issuing of the press release may coincide with a press conference, or if your star actor is not available at that point then a press conference may take place on the first day of rehearsals when the company is gathered together for the first time. Theatrical press conferences tend to be a bit of a damp squib, however, because you are not imparting any information that journalists cannot pick up from a press release and they know that they will have plenty of opportunity to meet with and interview your stars throughout the rehearsal process; it's not like they are just in town for the day.

Some press agents try to appear to look busy by sending through impressive-sounding lists of people who they have made contact with or who they are waiting to hear back from. The only thing that matters with a press agent is results; when and where they have actually secured media coverage for your production. Quality is generally much more important than quantity, and a piece on the National News or an interview in the *Sunday Times* 'Culture' is vastly more useful than any number of 'me and my hobbies' or 'my favourite pet' columns featuring your stars. If your show or your star is a particularly hot property then some media may require exclusives, in which case you need to assess the value of the coverage you are getting as against the value of the coverage you are potentially ruling out.

If the press agent is particularly successful in securing media interviews for the star performers in the run-up to opening night this can conflict with the director's rehearsal schedule. The answer to any scheduling conflict is that the PR always wins, unless it is the technical or dress rehearsal. Actors are contractually obliged to give interviews promoting the production within their working hours without further payment, and even if it is outside of their hours it would be reasonable to expect a performer to whom you are paying a star salary to co-operate with media requests. Some actors may have objections to certain newspaper titles or to particular TV or radio interviewers based on bad past experiences. In this case it is usually best not to force the issue, although technically they are unlikely to have the contractual right to pick and choose and they should not really be in a position to decline any 'reasonable' request. The star performers are the media ambassadors for the production and every appearance increases their own public profile as well as the production's, so it should be a win-win situation.

The press agent will deal with all the logistics of interviews; liaising with the Company Manager and the actors' agents, organising cars where necessary (these should actually be provided and paid for by the media concerned) and making sure that the actors are properly briefed about the likely nature and content of the piece. Most actors are very good at interviews but a few can be oddly shy and awkward, sometimes even forgetting to deliver the key information such as the title of show, the venue and the opening date. If a press interview is likely to be particularly in-depth and personal an actor may ask for copy approval, which editors are reluctant to give and which reduces the chances of the interview going ahead. Most press and radio interviews can be done by phone ('down the line') though a major feature may involve meeting with a journalist or going into a studio.

An actor will be entitled to payment if they are invited onto a television programme where they are effectively providing the entertainment, for instance a celebrity cookery programme, rather than simply appearing as a guest interviewee. Any such payment is a matter to be negotiated between the actor's agent and the TV programme and you should not get involved in brokering this deal. Some producers of television entertainment programmes may invite your cast to present a number from the show in the TV studio. Whilst this is undoubtedly good publicity it is important that the performers' work is not exploited by the TV station. In this age where everyone seems to want to perform on TV for free, television producers can sometimes forget that the performers from a stage show are professionals and that this is how they make their living. In this context, always insist that the television station pays the performers for their appearance. There are set union rates for this, which the television company's contracts department will be well aware of.

A good press agent will carefully manipulate and build up a media frenzy surrounding your show. They won't just send out the press release and wait for the phone to ring, but will be in constant communication with their key contacts, suggesting and creating opportunities for the production to be featured in the media. It is a golden rule of theatre PR that if a production features ducks, one of the ducks will inevitably be kidnapped and held to ransom. Throughout the ensuing *furore*, said duck is usually to be found nesting quite happily under the press agent's desk.

As soon as the theatre contract is signed it is essential that the date for the production's press night is logged with the SOLT press office. SOLT keeps a press night clash diary and the system only works if everyone registers their press night in it. Although some fringe and Off-West End productions will also register, as well as some major regional theatres who may expect to attract national critics, it is really designed to avoid clashes between openings in major London theatres. If you find that the date you want is already booked by another producer then you must do your very best to find an alternative date. It is not good for you or for the other show to be competing for the critics' attention on the same night. It will put the critics in a bad mood for both productions and may result in them attending your show at performances other than press night or in your production being reviewed by second stringers. The press agent will log the press night with SOLT, but if you have not yet appointed one when the date is fixed then you should get on and do it yourself. Even though many West End productions are announced at relatively short notice, the National Theatre will block book dates for press nights throughout the year because of the complexity of its repertoire, and some non-West End theatres that the leading critics traditionally attend, like the Almeida, the Royal Court, the Royal Shakespeare Theatre in Stratford-upon-Avon and the Regent's Park Open Air Theatre also announce their schedules a long time in advance.

The leading national newspapers will insist that their reviews are accompanied by a photograph taken by their own photographer, or a freelance photographer working on their behalf. This involves the press agent setting up a photo call on stage at the theatre, to which the key theatre photographers are then invited. SOLT runs a clash diary for photo calls similar to the press night clash diary and if you want to ensure a good turnout then it is important that you register yours in it. Press photo calls should be scheduled at some point during previews and in any event in time for editors to select the pictures that will run with the reviews.

The shoot itself normally takes no more than half an hour and the photographers do not like to be kept waiting. Four set-up shots should be sufficient and each one should feature the actors that are most likely to be the focus of the accompanying reviews. Spear-carriers can be a bit put out that they are not invited to attend, but they would only be wasting their time if they did. Bear in mind that the shots that make it into print are likely to be close-ups, so set-ups featuring key actors standing on opposite sides of the stage are unlikely to be of much use. The set-ups should be chosen by the press agent and directed by the director, who needs to mediate in a good natured and relatively informal way between the actors' instincts as to what makes a good picture ('make sure they get my good side') and the photographers' ('just lean forward a bit more...'). The official lighting design is dispensed with for the purpose of these photographs, and the lighting operator will usually be asked simply to shed as much light as possible on proceedings.

It's worth checking the suggested shot list yourself to make sure that everyone is working to the same agenda, and when you are happy with it the list should be sent to the Company Manager. They will then work with the stage management team to ensure that the set-ups are presented in an order (not necessarily chronological in terms of the action of the play) that makes the best use of time in terms of any necessary scene and costume changes.

There is no right of approval over these pictures; you won't even see the selection that is presented by the photographers to their editors. Given the circumstances under which they are taken it is a credit to the skills of the photographers concerned that excellent results can often be achieved. It mustn't be forgotten that, however quickly they appear to work, they instinctively know what to focus on and what makes a good theatre picture. Don't make the mistake of inviting paparazzi to the photo call; they are a different breed, and paparazzi and theatre photographers do not mix well together.

The News Access Agreements with the unions allow for short extracts from the actual production to be filmed and broadcast by certain specified television news programmes without payment to the performers or technicians. Such extracts should not trigger payment to the author, director or designers either, and this will have been made clear in their contracts. The filming of these extracts will often be undertaken by the television news teams during the same call as the press photo call, immediately after the photographers have departed. This should not be confused with the filming of an EPK (Electronic Press Kit) or an archive video.

Each production is allowed by the unions to film one performance of the show as an 'archive recording', which cannot be copied or distributed in any way. This is done from a fixed camera position, effectively ensuring that it is not of commercial quality. It is used as a point of reference by the creative team, particularly when rehearsing replacement performers into the show.

If your production is intended as a long runner then it is probably worth producing an electronic press kit (EPK) the costs of which should be included in the pre-opening marketing budget. This is a short video containing extracts from the show, interviews with key players and other snippets of interest, which can be used to promote it in various media. There are special arrangements in place with the entertainment unions to enable these essential marketing tools to be created and exploited at minimal cost. They still cost a fair amount to film and edit, though, so you should be confident of your production's longevity before committing to making one.

The first few performances in the West End theatre will be designated as previews. This gives the creative team a chance to make last-minute adjustments and the actors the opportunity to fine-tune their performances. It is traditional to offer the public reduced price tickets during previews on the basis that the show may not yet be quite ready in a number of respects. As always, however, work expands to fill the time available and a show can sometimes suffer from too much artistic 'tinkering' during previews. It is perfectly possible for a production to get overcooked and actually become worse rather than better if the preview period is too long. Previews can also be quite expensive, because not only are the tickets cheaper but the key technical staff such as lighting programmers and production sound engineers, all of whom are being paid by the day, have to be on call to incorporate any adjustments required by the creative team. Six previews for a play and ten for a musical (maybe fourteen for a new musical) should be about right. If the creative team ask for more than this then you should start asking some serious questions. Of course, the number of previews, like the date of the press night, has to be settled before the show goes on sale to the public, which means that at the point when you decide on the schedule you have very little sense of exactly what creative issues the production is likely to be facing during the preview period.

Although proper critics will leave you alone during previews the dreaded internet chat will start as soon as the curtain goes up for the first time. Because you are likely to be papering the previews (giving away seats in order to fill the houses) tickets tend to fall into the hands of all sorts of self-appointed experts who will start 'reviewing' the production on their blogs and Facebook pages. Unfortunately a lot of these people seem to have some sort of axe to grind (I imagine them mostly as having in some way failed to make a career for themselves in the theatre) and will pour scorn and negativity over virtually any theatrical enterprise. It often comes as quite a relief to get the official verdicts from the professional critics. I have seen shows which have been the subject of relentless internet barracking during their previews go on to garner unanimous critical praise and multiple industry awards.

The best night for a press night, when your production will finally face the critics, is a Tuesday or a Wednesday. This gives the actors the chance to get back into gear after the weekend and it also means that there is some chance of reviews being published in that week's Sunday newspapers. It is still traditional to schedule the press night performance for an early start (typically 7pm) in deference to the critics who have to file their copy in time to reach the morning editions. In reality, email now makes it much easier to achieve this and in any case several papers won't bother to run a review until a day or so later. The 7pm start does, however, mean that everyone can get to the first night party earlier.

On Broadway the critics attend the production in the latter part of the preview period and their reviews are then embargoed until the morning after the official opening night. The opening night itself is then attended by friends and guests, meaning that it is usually quite a relaxed and celebratory affair. It does mean, however, that the critics are not necessarily reviewing the same performance as each other and that they may be seeing a production that is not entirely ready. In the West End, the frenzied, high-pressure *frisson* of the official opening night, attended both by guests and all of the leading critics, is almost unbearable. The actors take on the role of gladiators, marching out into the arena to find out if they will get the 'thumbs up' or the 'thumbs down'. The adrenalin levels are off the scale, and are frankly probably unhealthy, and the audience tends to be even more nervous than the actors; not knowing whether they should cheer and clap in support of their friends on stage or keep quiet and not make it look like they are trying too hard to win round the critics. This collective tension, both on the stage and in the audience, means that press night performances are, ironically, rarely the best. But at least the critics are all sharing in and assessing the same experience, and because most of their theatre-going will be on press nights they will usually be comparing like with like as far as different productions are concerned.

We are fortunate in the UK in that we have a variety of respected theatre critics working for a variety of newspapers, so in terms of the actual reviews it is the overall trend that is important rather than one particular opinion. All of the reviews will eventually be collated by a wonderful publication called *Theatre Record*, which catalogues the entire critical response to every production reviewed in the national press, and as such is an invaluable point of reference for producers. Leafing through *Theatre Record* affirms the wide-ranging tastes and views of our theatre critics. By contrast on Broadway the fortunes of a show all hinge on one review; that of *The New York Times*. At around midnight a hush descends over the opening night party as the press agent hands the lead producer an envelope containing a print-out of the first internet edition of *The New York Times* review. The producer and co-producers then retire to a side room to read and assess it. Tradition has it that if the review is a rave the producer will stand on a table and read it to the partygoers. If it is a bad review the partygoers suddenly notice that the producers have made a discreet exit, and a sense of gloom descends over the room. Few Broadway shows survive a bad review from *The New York Times*, and it is not for nothing that its legendary critic Frank Rich was known as 'the Butcher of Broadway'.

The press agent is responsible for rounding up the critics for press night, and provided that it is not clashing with another major opening they usually turn out in force for a new West End show. Invitations will be sent out well in advance so that the critics can organise their extremely busy diaries, and they will only respond once an invitation has been received. The SOLT clash diary is not a notification of the event to the critics, it is simply a point of internal reference amongst producers. If the lead critic is unable to attend (and like anyone else they have the right to be ill or on holiday) then the editor may send along a second stringer. A second stringer may be out to prove themselves by writing a particularly opinionated review, or they may be a 'soft touch' compared with the lead critic they are standing in for. In any event, every review is a personal response and it is important to make the reviewer's visit to the theatre as pleasant and trouble-free as possible.

Being a critic can sound like a bit of a cushy number, but in fact the professional critics work extremely hard, with a very busy schedule of theatre-going and writing, and are not particularly well paid for their efforts. The best ones are extremely knowledgeable about theatre and are great enthusiasts for it, but if you get them at the end of a bad day or the end of a long week it can work against you. This is another reason why scheduling a press night for relatively early in the week is a good policy. A good press agent will have developed a personal relationship with all of the critics, including the second stringers, and will know their seating preferences and preferred interval drinks. Critics don't like to be caught up in the crush in the foyer on opening night, and it's important that there is a dedicated and clearly marked desk for them to collect their tickets from and somewhere for them to get away from the crowds to enjoy some refreshment pre-show and during the interval. Providing a free drink, a sandwich and a programme for the critics is basic politeness and is not looked upon as bribery.

Traditionally critics will be put in aisle seats, allowing them to make a quick exit at the end. The departure of the critics while the actors are still taking their bows can be a bit disconcerting the first time you see it and is usually explained by the fact that they have to rush off and file their copy, or that they don't want the audience's inevitably rapturous first night response to influence their reviews in any way. It is more likely that in reality they are trying to avoid the crush as the audience leaves and get home for their dinner. Critics are not invited to the first night party as it would be awkward for them to socialise with people whose performances they are assessing, and in any case they should be busy writing their reviews at this point in the evening. The problem with sitting in an aisle seat is that it generally does not offer the best view of the stage, unless of course there is a centre aisle in the auditorium. Some producers make a point of introducing a centre aisle during previews for the sole purpose of seating critics on press night, although the cost of removing that number of seats (and reinstating them so that they can be sold thereafter) can be quite surprisingly high. It is important that you have personally sat in every seat that will be occupied by a major critic on press night, not only to make sure that they have a clear view of the stage, the set and the action of the piece, but also to check that the seat isn't annoyingly squeaky or dysfunctional in some other way (and it is amazing just how many West End theatre seats are). Your press agent will advise you on such details as which critics prefer to sit on a particular side of the aisle because they have a bad leg or whatever; and although you should always give them the option of bringing a guest many of them will attend alone, either because they regard it as a working engagement or more likely because their friends and family are fed up of being dragged along to the theatre with them. Once you have identified the best seats for the critics (usually about a third of the way back in the stalls) it is important that you don't then surround them with distracting celebrities or put a particularly tall guest in the seat in front of them. Finally, etiquette dictates that critics' seats are always in the stalls (even though the view can sometimes be better from the circle), that you don't sit the critic from the *Dog Owner's Gazette* in a better seat than the critic for *The Times* and that you avoid the subject of the show they are actually reviewing when chatting to them in the interval.

Because of the proliferation of internet sites and smaller publications that now run 'professional' theatre reviews, not to be confused with the amateur blogging community, it can be worth inviting them to attend a 'second press night' rather than the official one. This means that it is more likely that there are good seats available for them and that the national critics are not competing with them for interval refreshments. It also keeps the actors on their toes for the second official performance, which can otherwise be a bit of a damp squib. Some marketing agencies will also recommend a special 'media night', where movers and shakers in the media such as producers, editors, presenters and other commentators are invited to attend the show and perhaps meet the cast over a drink in the bar afterwards. This event can of course be combined with the press night, but the limited availability of good seats and the need to focus one's attention on the critics means that it is usually advisable to schedule it on another date. If the media night takes place in the week following the first and second press nights then those present will be in a position to either add their weight to or argue against the reviews that have been published. Several of the national critics have become tweeters and bloggers themselves, so you may get a tantalising taster of some of their reviews, transmitted to the virtual universe from their mobile phones on the way home.

Having invited the critics, and taken particular care that their evening is as enjoyable as it can be for them, it is important to give some attention to the composition of the rest of the audience on press night. First night audiences can be notoriously nervy and it is generally acknowledged that they either over-react or under-react, thus not giving the critics a true picture of how the theatre-going public will respond to the piece. Although there are a large number of guests to accommodate it is always a good policy to have some 'real' people in on press night, and keeping as many rows as you can at the front of the stalls on sale to the general public will make the audience response more genuine. There is then the matter of making sure your investors have decent seats as well as the guests of the cast, writer and creative team (usually a pair each unless there is a particular contractual requirement for more for certain key players). Some producers like to sprinkle the audience with random celebrities in the hope that their attendance will merit a press photograph or a few column inches the next day. Others feel that this cheapens the occasion, unless a celebrity happens to have a particular connection with the production (such as being the partner of someone who is in it). Guest tickets should be handed out on the night from a collection point in the foyer rather than the box office (and separate again from the press ticket collection point). This enables you to monitor any 'no shows' and make any last-minute adjustments to the seating plan to avoid embarrassing gaps in the audience.

Despite the logistics of handing out so many tickets and getting so many people to their seats there is no reason why a carefully planned press night should not start on time. There is no point in holding the curtain for guests; delaying the show for a late arrival in any case only causes embarrassment to the guest concerned and resentment amongst those who have been kept waiting. Latecomers on press night should be escorted to the balcony to avoid them tripping over the critics in the stalls, or preferably taken out and shot. If the critic from a major national newspaper hasn't turned up, however, then that is another matter entirely and it is an important judgement call on your part as to just how long you should wait; bearing in mind that the critics who have arrived on time won't want to be inconvenienced just because one of their colleagues hasn't made it.

The opening/press performance is the most important few hours in the life of your production. It is often said that you never enjoy your own party, and never is this truer than for a producer at the opening of their West End show. As well as the myriad of logistical issues, from checking that the critics have been allocated the correct seats to ensuring that everyone involved has received an appropriate first night gift, the producer has to be on show for the entire evening; charming the critics, greeting the guests and generally being seen to lead the whole enterprise from the front. The last thing that you want to do in the middle of all this is to take your seat in the stalls and watch the actual production yet again; but much though it may be tempting to retreat to the bar during this part of the proceedings the producer, of all people, has to be seen to be there. As the curtain goes up the feeling of helplessness is almost overwhelming. At this point there is absolutely nothing further that you can do to influence the outcome. With luck, all of your notes will have been taken on board by the creative team during the preview period but, for all the meticulous planning, the only way to stay sane is to take the view that from this point onwards the votes have effectively been cast and are now simply being counted.

It is amazing to think just how much rides on the press night and its critical outcome and I am always full of admiration that the actors make it as far as the stage let alone the curtain call. Careers can be made or broken on the basis of this one performance – not just the careers of the performers but those of the writer, the creative team and indeed the producer. For a few nerve-wracking hours the entire future of your production very publicly hangs in the balance. And it's all in the hands of a team of adrenalin-fuelled actors and stage managers and a lighting desk operator with a nervous twitch.

When the morning editions finally arrive and the verdict is out the marketing people immediately set to work cherry-picking the best quotes from the critics for use on the front of house display and post-opening advertising and print. Some actors and creatives don't read reviews, or at least pretend not to, but to me this smacks of arrogance. We put on theatre for the benefit of the audience, and in this country at least the reviews are likely to be indicative of the wide range of opinion that the average audience represents. If a reviewer picks up on something that you yourself don't like about the production then this could be your opportunity to get it fixed, even belatedly. An actor or a director may resist a producer's note throughout the rehearsal process but it is amazing how quickly they take it on board when they see it in the form of a printed critique. Even if there are individual criticisms, or indeed entire reviews, that you object to or disagree with, the fact is that the overall verdict is likely to be the correct one. For all the love and care lavished on the production by the entire team it may be that the result is a turkey, in which case the sooner you wake up and smell the coffee the better. With a following wind, however, the critics will come down on side, and critical endorsement is one of the best possible selling points for a West End show.

The few hours between the end of the press night performance and the first reviews appearing are some of the most stressful of the producer's working life, and yet at this precise moment they are expected to turn into the perfect party host; meeting and greeting, smiling and handshaking, offering words of reassurance and support to investors, writers, directors, designers and actors. Most of the guests will be invited to the after-show party, which should be at a venue within walking distance of the theatre. The actors tend to arrive later than the guests at these events, because they are getting changed and meeting friends and relatives in their dressing rooms after the show, so it is important that an area is allocated for them and plenty of food and drink kept by. Actors can feel a bit swamped and neglected due to the sheer number of guests but this is easily avoided with a bit of advance planning and sensitivity.

Everyone is 'off duty' at the party and should get the chance to relax and unwind after the extreme high pressure of the press night show, so it is very important that journalists and photographers, particularly paparazzi, are not invited to mingle with the actors and guests. The press agent will organise for photographers to stand outside or in the lobby so that pictures can be taken of people arriving and a room may be set aside for brief 'on the spot' interviews about how it all went. If the party access policy is made clear to the media by the press agent then they will usually respect your guidelines. It is a mistake to think that allowing the media in to the actual party will result in wonderful coverage the following day. You are more likely to end up with a front-page picture of a celebrity guest throwing up into a plant pot.

Inevitably the press night performance will not be as good as the previous night's preview. If you survive making small talk with the critics in the interval, telling the cast member who 'dried' spectacularly that no one would have noticed and apologising to your biggest investor for the fact that he was seated behind a very tall lady with a beehive hairdo, not to mention reading the 'mixed' reviews in the early editions of the morning papers, then you might just make it home to bed in one piece. Provided that the first batch of reviews are not so damning that you are attempting to ignore the distinctive sound of the fat lady tuning up, there then follow a few days of unaccustomed calm in the life of the producer. After the relentless hurly-burly of the build-up to opening night, the morning after the night before is inevitably crashingly anti-climactic. It's a sort of 'phoney war' while the stragglers from the daily press publish their reviews and you wait for the verdict of the Sunday newspapers and the ensuing flurry of activity as the box office response is analysed and the post-opening marketing campaign is strategised and activated. You may actually find yourself with a bit of quality time on your hands. Enjoy it. Reacquaint yourself with your long-suffering nearest and dearest. Dine out a bit in town. Put in an appearance at the Ivy Club. Live the life. You'll be back at your desk on Monday.

9. HOW TO CUT YOUR LOSSES ON A WEST END SHOW

'It's not the despair. I can take the despair. It's the hope I can't stand.'

– John Cleese as Brian Stimpson in *Clockwise*

The bad news is that, for all your efforts, it is statistically unlikely that the West End Show you have so lovingly nurtured into life will actually become a West End hit. Unless you happen to have stumbled across the next *Blood Brothers* or *The Woman in Black* your primary concern is now most likely to be preventing your show's box office revenue from falling below the break figure and thereby making you vulnerable to eviction by your landlord. You will know pretty well as soon as the ink is dry on the reviews whether or not your show has 'legs', and closely monitoring sales patterns in the weeks immediately following press night is critical to formulating the correct onward strategy. If your assessment is that you can at least play to the weekly break and meet your running costs for a period of time then you might as well give it a go, particularly if you are taking enough at the box office every week to bank a regular management fee.

By keeping the show running for a while you may even create a 'perceived' hit, though this can sometimes be a bit confusing for the investors when they don't see any money coming in. And don't forget that in staying on for longer you may well qualify for overseas rights and for residual income from amateur and repertory companies, which can be worth a few bob over time for a show that has benefited from the profile afforded by a 'respectable' West End run. Most importantly, your production is likely to have gained sufficient credibility to undertake a post-

West End tour, so make sure you that you have at the very least secured a licence option for this. Such tours can be quite lucrative in their own right, though the production itself is likely to be completely remounted, with a new cast replacing the West End team, and possibly with an associate director at the helm. It's a sound business philosophy that you should never do anything for only one reason, and keeping a West End show running is no exception. As well as securing valuable future rights you may well be cementing valuable relationships with the writer, stars and creative team. If a play lasts for at least sixteen weeks in the West End, or a musical for a year, then few people will remember how long it was originally supposed to be booking for. You'll just have to ignore certain ghoulish websites which take a particular pleasure in pointing out premature theatrical closures.

Sticking around for a while may even qualify you for an award or two. Broadway producers notoriously attempt to schedule the opening of their shows in a manner that allows the shortest possible lead time for them to be judged for the Tony Awards. They may then close quickly if they don't receive a nomination or if, having received a nomination, they don't receive an actual award. In London, SOLT organises the annual Olivier Awards, presented in April and covering productions that have opened in the previous calendar year in its member theatres. The continuing struggle to secure and retain television coverage for the event, and to make it as newsworthy as possible, has resulted in a number of format changes over the years. But the real problem is not so much the issue of media coverage as the fact that the efforts of commercial West End producers are pitched directly against the major building-based subsidised companies such as the National Theatre and the Royal Court. The latter invariably (and deservedly) sweep the board; but if they didn't then questions would be asked. With state of the art facilities, long rehearsal periods and an extensive repertoire of work including the pick of new writing, it would be a scandal if the subsidised sector didn't come out on top in any qualitative assessment of London theatre. As a result, it's often slim pickings for commercial play producers, though the commercial sector tends to pick up the musical theatre gongs. We just have to hope the RSC doesn't start making a habit of staging new musicals for West End presentation. Another consequence of rewarding the efforts of the subsidised theatres is that many of the awards go to productions that are no longer in repertoire; so with the best will in the world it is difficult to get as excited about the outcome as our Broadway colleagues do at Tony time. Until recently members of SOLT were only allowed to vote for the nominations, and the Olivier Awards themselves were in the gift of a panel comprising 'industry experts' and members of the public. However, the membership is now allowed to vote alongside the Panel on the final outcome, and there is a chance that this will give proceedings a slightly more commercial edge. There is a brief window of opportunity between the announcement of the nominations and the awards ceremony itself in which to make the most of any nominations you may have received for publicity purposes. Then, come April, it's usually a case of spending the evening sitting in an expensive seat in a dinner jacket and watching the National Theatre triumph yet again. In the end, though, an annual dish of sour grapes is a small price to pay for being able to work in an industry that benefits from the existence of a thriving subsidised sector.

If you don't scoop an Olivier then there are always the Evening Standard Awards and Critics' Circle Awards; but our subsidised friends tend to dominate these as well. The theatre website Whatsonstage.com does something to redress the balance with its increasingly high-profile Theatregoers' Choice Awards. These are voted on by the public via the internet and feature numerous categories; and it is often instructive to see how the 'people' vote as opposed to the specialist panels and 'industry' voters fielded by the other awards. For all the momentary hype surrounding the various ceremonies, however, and even if their timing is helpful to you, you are unlikely in reality to achieve any high-profile wins that will actually assist you at the box office. And unless you happen to qualify in a category with very few potential candidates then you are unlikely in any case to be garnering nominations for a production that has not caught the imagination of audiences and critics.

If things aren't sparking at the box office then the temptation is to spend some of your reserve funds on additional advertising and marketing, and for obvious reasons this is the solution that your advertising and marketing agency will recommend. In reality, however, it is unlikely that this strategy is going to assist very much. If people don't want to come to a show then they won't, however many times and however many ways you suggest to them that they might like to. As Oscar Hammerstein II once remarked, 'The number of people who will not go to a show they don't want to see is unlimited.'

Once the critics have given their verdict, there is also little point in attempting to 'fix' a show that isn't working. It is an expensive and time-consuming process and rarely pays dividends. I have seen productions gloriously transformed through painstaking and costly work over a number of weeks, but even if the critics can be persuaded back to reassess your efforts there is no escaping the fact that the damage has already been done.

It may well suit your agenda to keep your show running for a while even if it looks as if it may fail to cover its weekly running costs. In this case there are potentially plenty of deals to be done to bring those costs down. Faced with the prospect of you giving notice, your landlord may well offer to reduce or waive the theatre rent, and even some of the contra, while they search around for a new tenant. They will want to avoid going dark for even a short period of time, and a small amount of income is better for them than none at all. Even if you are not already operating a royalty pool, the royalty holders may well be amenable to waiving or reducing their royalties along the lines of a pool system. After all, their job is done, and having a West End show running with their name on it is a prestigious showcase for their work, whether or not they are actually earning from it. And, let's face it, nobody wants to be seen to be associated with a flop. If waivers or reductions are agreed then this is usually on the understanding that the revised terms are proportionately the same for each royalty holder (i.e. favoured nations). Other suppliers such as the technical hire companies may rally round and reduce their rates and anyone on a retainer, such as your marketing agent, should do their bit as well. Your accountant and production manager are likely to be the notable exceptions to this, as you will be relying on their skills more than ever in adversity. The one thing you can't do is to ask those responsible for delivering the show on a daily basis to reduce their salaries, even if they are being paid well above the required minimum rates. The actors, musicians, stage management and backstage staff must in any event get paid at their contracted rate; but that is fair enough, as in this scenario they are all likely to be unemployed in a few weeks' time.

Striking deals to keep the show running for a bit will usually involve divulging quite a large amount of financial data to those concerned about just how bad things are; so whilst the public won't realise that there is anything wrong do bear in mind that bad news travels fast within the industry, and the vultures will quickly smell blood. It won't be long before your landlord gets a better offer, so make sure you spend the intervening time putting your affairs in order for a well-executed crash landing.

Closing a West End show is in some ways more difficult than opening it. Many conflicting emotions, pressures and loyalties will come into play; but whether your run has been for ten weeks or ten years (and unless you happen to produce *The Mousetrap*), the point will eventually arrive when you can no longer postpone the inevitable. When the time does come to close, it is all over very quickly, and with any luck relatively painlessly. Having first agreed a closing date with your landlord and advised your investors and creative team of the situation, a notice is placed on the company notice board announcing your show's demise and thanking everyone for their participation. If you have managed the situation correctly and with appropriate sensitivity (maybe you will have held a company meeting the week before to prepare everyone for the likelihood of closure), then it should not come as a surprise to anyone. The posting of the closure notice is not the moment for grand pronouncements; everyone just wants to know the date on which they will be out of work.

If your show's booking period extends beyond the date of its closure then the box office will contact customers with bookings beyond that date and encourage them to exchange their tickets for the remaining scheduled performances, failing which they will be offered a refund. Most customers will exchange their tickets under these circumstances, so the final weeks of the run are likely to be quite busy and this can be a timely morale booster for everyone involved. Of course, if you were only due to run for a limited season then you may well have made it through to the end of that season and to the scheduled closure date of the show, albeit with some assistance along the way.

It is always critically important to keep your investors informed about what is going on, and never more so than when the show is in jeopardy. They must be made aware of the ongoing financial position as well as of your tactics and reasoning, and must feel fully involved in the strategy either to extend the run or to close. This is particularly important as it is more than likely that your show will appear to have completed a successful season whilst at the same time losing them all of their money. But as you will have made it clear to them from the outset that this is the most likely financial outcome, they can at least only be impressed by your honesty. And you will of course have ensured that they have found the overall experience of financing your show an enriching one despite the loss of their investment.

If your production really is on its last legs then it is particularly important to ensure that you are surviving on *bona fide* reserve funds rather than cashflow. The intricacies of theatre accounting mean that it is very easy suddenly to find yourself in a position where you are trading whilst insolvent, and it is deeply humiliating to have to apply to The Theatre Council to release your salary bonds; though even this is preferable to having to liquidate your company. In either of these unfortunate events then you will live to fight another day provided that you conduct yourself with honour, openness and integrity.

There is a big difference between taking responsibility for your actions and beating yourself up over your mistakes. If you have a hit then there will be plenty of people queuing up to take the credit for it (there are no awards at all for producers, by the way) but if your show flops then you can suddenly feel very isolated at the helm of the sinking ship. A good rule of thumb at this point, and indeed throughout the whole production process, is to ask 'what's the worst that can happen'? Theatre practitioners have the ability to enrich people's lives, but our work is not changing the world. We are privileged to be in a position where we can create our art and it's important that we learn how to face up to failure. If your show has flopped spectacularly then learn from your mistakes and next time it will be easier. As a producer you will become very good at dealing with disappointment; but in developing this ability do not forget the importance of striving for and enjoying success. And if for any reason you do need cheering up then I thoroughly recommend Nichola McAuliffe's novel *A Fanny Full of Soap*; a side-splitting insight into how *not* to produce a West End show.

The good news is that, whether you are winning or losing, it is actually remarkably calm at the centre of the theatrical storm. I found working as an actor and a director far more stressful than I find working as a producer, even though on paper I should have much more to keep me awake at night. The following passage from Evelyn Waugh's *Decline and Fall* goes some way towards describing this. I am not trying to say that everything in theatre revolves around the producer, just that the role gives you a perspective that in many ways makes the whole thing less scary:

> Shall I tell you about life? Well, it's like the big wheel at Luna Park. You pay five francs and go into a room with tiers of seats all round, and in the centre the floor is a great disc of polished wood that revolves quickly. At first you sit down and watch the others. They are all trying to sit in the wheel, and they keep getting flung off, and that makes them laugh, and you laugh too. It's great fun. It is very much like life. You see, the nearer you can get to the hub of the wheel the slower it is moving and the easier it is to stay on. … Of course at the very centre there's a point completely at rest, if one could only find it… Lots of people just enjoy scrambling on and being whisked off and scrambling on again. How they all shriek and giggle! Then there are others who sit as far out as they can and hold on for dear life and enjoy that. But the whole point about the wheel is that you needn't get on it at all, if you don't want to. People get hold of ideas about life, and that makes them think they've got to join in the game, even if they don't enjoy it. It doesn't suit every one.

So you've given everyone two weeks' notice and your show has closed. And this is where you learn the most important lesson of all for a producer. It wasn't actually the show you just closed that was the most important one. Although a single project demanded your focus and energy over a long period, the real skill of producing is to have another one (or more) waiting in the wings to replace it if necessary. It is often said that performers are only as good as their last show, but for a producer you are only really ever as good as your *next* show. So you should be embarking on the process that has been described in this book simultaneously for at least half a dozen different projects. Your plate spinning, juggling and tightrope walking acts really should be part of a three-ring rather than a single-ring circus. Developing multiple projects simultaneously ensures that you always have something ready to bring to the boil, and helps to keep the relative importance of each individual project in perspective. Many of these ideas will of course fall by the wayside, often because they prove impossible to cast, to raise the finance for or to find a theatre for; but that's not to say that it isn't worth starting the process in each case and seeing how far it leads. It is also important to give your investors something new to get their teeth into or they may lose interest or, worse still, start supporting one of your competitors. Two or more projects that you are developing may of course reach fruition at the same time, in which case the fun really does begin. Above all, it is important that you support your West End operation with a portfolio of work in less risky areas, such as the UK and overseas touring markets; a prudent strategy which forms an essential part of the business model for most succesful West End production companies.

I do hope that I haven't put you off producing a show in the West End. It is an extraordinarily challenging and rewarding experience and one that I would thoroughly recommend. Several years ago an amazing lady called Marla Rubin walked into my office with a proposal for a show adapted from a Danish film called *Festen*. She didn't have an office of her own, but she had a mobile phone, a copy of *Contacts* and an idea that she was passionate about. She was earning a living working in a bookshop and had persuaded some investors to put up some seed money. She'd commissioned an adaptation from a writer called David Eldridge and lined up a creative team headed by a director called Rufus Norris. I hadn't heard of any of these people, and didn't really fancy the production, but helped her to draft a budget and wished her the best of luck with it. Some years later *Festen* re-emerged as a co-production between Marla and the Off-West End Almeida Theatre, where it was an overnight sensation. I introduced Marla to the prolific West End producer Bill Kenwright, a man of infinite good taste and wisdom, who was able to propel *Festen* on to a (twice extended) West End season, an expedition to Broadway and a major national tour produced out of Birmingham Repertory Theatre and funded by the Arts Council. Throughout this process Marla retained her position as originating co-producer of the project. The adaptation which she commissioned has gone on to be performed throughout the world and she has since embarked on other highly successful producing ventures including the Olivier-Award-winning *The Mountaintop*. David Eldridge is now firmly established as one of our leading playwrights, and I hear that Rufus Norris has also done quite well for himself. The story of *Festen* pretty well sums up the entire process I have been describing in this book. But most importantly it demonstrates that it is all possible.

If your show defies the odds and turns out to be a *bona fide* hit, then huge congratulations to you. Once your investors have been repaid you have every right to enjoy your extremely hard-earned 40% of profits. The bad news is that you are now likely to find yourself under enormous pressure to risk all of the money that you and your investors have made by presenting your show on Broadway.

But that's another story…